SOUTHERN EUROPEAN WELFARE STATES

Between Crisis and Reform

Edited by

Martin Rhodes

FRANK CASS

LONDON • PORTLAND, OR

First published in 1997 in Great Britain by
FRANK CASS & CO. LTD
900 Eastern Avenue
London IG2 7HH

and in the United States of America by
FRANK CASS
c/o ISBS
5804 N.E. Hassalo Street
Portland, Oregon 97213-3644

British Library Cataloguing in Publication Data

Southern European welfare states : between crisis and reform
1. Public welfare – Europe, Southern 2. Europe, Southern –
Social policy
I. Rhodes, Martin
361.6'8'094

ISBN 0714647888 (cloth)
ISBN 0714643440 (paper)

Library of Congress Cataloging in Publication Data

A catalog record for this book
is available from The Library of Congress

This group of studies first appeared in a Special Issue on
'Southern European Welfare States: Between Crisis and Reform' in
South European Society & Politics 1/3 (Winter 1996)
published by Frank Cass & Co. Ltd.

Printed in Great Britain by
Antony Rowe Ltd., Chippenham, Wilts.

Contents

Acknowledgements

Earlier versions of all but two of the papers in this volume were presented at the conference on 'Comparing Welfare Systems in Southern Europe' held at the European University Institute (EUI) in February 1996 and sponsored by the Robert Schuman Centre at the EUI and by MIRE (Mission, Recherche, Experimentation), Ministère du Travail et des Affaires Sociales, Paris. The editor and the authors would like to thank the Robert Schuman Centre and MIRE for their support.

Southern European Welfare States: Identity, Problems and Prospects for Reform

MARTIN RHODES

This introduction considers the debate on the existence of a southern European welfare state 'model', and stresses the distinctive developmental context and institutional structures of welfare provision in the region. While they may embody similar principles of social policy organization to their northern European counterparts, understanding the particularity of the southern European welfare states requires that their specific political-institutional characteristics are taken seriously. Similarly, while there may be some convergence in terms of spending and policy-orientation across western Europe, and while they share many challenges in common with their northern neighbours, the problems confronting their welfare states and societies, as well as their responses, reveal the persistence of a 'southern syndrome' in European social policy.

This volume is the first in English to be devoted entirely to the analysis of social policy developments in southern Europe. It comes at an opportune moment, for not only are the southern European welfare states – in common with their northern counterparts – under stress, but they have also only recently become the object of in-depth studies, exploring for the first time the particularities of the southern 'type' or 'model' of welfare. The aim of this collection is to contribute to this growing literature on two levels. The first is to provide a series of both comparative and specific country analyses, furnishing new empirical detail and more general reflections on the character of social policy and welfare in Greece, Italy, Portugal and Spain. The second, related, objective is to buttress the argument that, although welfare states in the region share many of the features of other European welfare states, the existence of specific features, levels of development and institutional forms provide them, collectively, with what Ferrera (1996) calls a 'hugely different socio-political etiquette' which makes them worthy of analysis in their own right.

Although at first glance quite disparate, all of the articles in this special issue seek to relate their comparative or country analyses to a central theme – the specificity of a southern 'type' of welfare state – in addition to their focus on particular issues: institutional structures, the role of the family, territorial disparities, the nature of poverty, policy innovation (or inertia), the character of reform and so on. The aim of this introduction is to stress the importance of that central theme, to point to the special difficulties facing southern European welfare states, and to consider their potential for reform. While encountering similar problems to other western European countries – in terms both of domestic challenges and external constraints – the responses to those problems are conditioned by the particular nature of the southern welfare 'syndrome'.

IS THERE A SOUTHERN MODEL?

Southern European welfare states have only recently become the specific subject of academic interest. In the past, they have either been excluded from comparative studies of social policy, or subsumed within broader 'families' or 'worlds' of welfare capitalism, and viewed as under-developed systems on the same trajectories of institutional development as their more advanced counterparts to the north. The main example of the latter approach is Esping-Andersen (1990) who, while not explicitly including Spain, Portugal or Greece, made Italy a member of his 'conservative-continental' world of welfare capitalism, distinctive for its 'status differentiating' welfare programmes and systems of income maintenance and health care strongly related to employment and family status. To some extent, this tendency to include southern welfare states in broader groupings alongside more economically advanced nations has paralleled the trend in analyses of broader political development to deny the existence of a specific 'southern' model and place southern countries firmly in the mainstream of comparative analysis (e.g. Lijphart *et al.* 1988). In many ways this has been a useful corrective to the traditional assumption that these countries were still under-developed, both politically and economically, and outside the mainstream of western democratic societies, even though Italy had been a solid member of that camp since the late 1940s, and Portugal, Spain and Greece had all made transitions to democracy – and experienced rapid economic development – since the early 1970s. Yet, in the process, something valuable – namely, the specific character of the southern countries, in terms of institutions, class structure, the clash between 'tradition' and 'modernity' – was marginalized or lost. Comparative studies that did focus on a 'southern type' either did so in terms of a model of democratic transition or a particular type of political economy – placing these countries, for example, on 'the periphery of the core' and analysing the consequences of this location for international linkages and domestic development. But while useful, those studies typically failed to extend their analyses to the particular form of welfare state that emerged in those circumstances (for exceptions, see Santos 1994; Petmesidou and Tsoulouvis 1994).

More recently, there has been a proliferation of comparative and single-country studies of southern European social policy. These include attempts both to re-affirm the commonalities between southern European welfare states and their better developed northern counterparts and to 'reclaim' the specificity of southern Europe. An example of the first is Castles (1995) who, while deploring the neglect of southern Europe in comparative analysis, seeks once again to correct the impression that these countries still represent the underdeveloped welfare 'rearguard'. Focusing on social security and welfare transfers, Castles argues that the countries of southern Europe must be seen as quite typical members of the conservative family of nations, which simply happen to spend less than others in the grouping only because they are poor and have relatively youthful populations.

In the same vein, although focusing mainly on Greece, Katrougalos (1996) denies the utility of focusing on the southern type as a fourth, rudimentary 'Latin Rim' model – as suggested, notably, by Leibfried (1993). Katrougalos argues that neither Greece, Spain nor Portugal are part of a distinctive group, and that their undeniable lag in terms of social spending has little to do with any 'specific institutional and organizational feature' but rather 'reflects the delay in the construction of the welfare state, and more generally, the relative economic underdevelopment of the Mediterranean South' (1996: 43). Studying specific institutional and organizational features would therefore delineate the topography of these welfare states but would have little explanatory purpose. In other words, the essence of these welfare states lie in the principles on which they were founded (that is, the organization of social insurance, entitlements related to the employment and contribution record, etc.), rather than the institutions or organizations that have been constructed over the years as the embodiment of those principles in the domestic setting.

However, Katrougalos reveals the weakness of this argument in his own conclusions concerning the crisis or under-development of the Greek system, which, he states, is attributable to:

> the inheritance of the distortions of past (...), as an overblown and

often parasitic public employment apparatus still represents the main substitute for the residuality of social protection. What is required to resolve the crisis are deep, structural changes of the political system and the whole of the public sector and, above all, the abandonment of clientelistic policies and political patronage.

But if these are not 'specific institutional and organizational features', then what are they? Can one simultaneously argue that they bear responsibility for the crisis of the Greek welfare state but have nothing to do with its 'undeniable lag in terms of social spending' or the 'delay in its construction'? Katrougalos is, in fact, arguing that this institutional tradition is separable from the form and functioning of the southern welfare states which, if abstracted from their particular institutional environment, do bear a formal resemblance to their more developed northern neighbours in the continental 'state corporate model' (Germany, France, the Benelux countries). Petmesidou (1991: 35–6), by contrast, argues convincingly that although Greece follows the 'continental pattern' in its reliance on social security spending by independent public organizations, functioning on the basis of contributory schemes, such a comparison is limited because of the large amount of money distributed in the form of transfer payments through direct or indirect state intervention (and frequently according to a party political logic). Moreover, as Haris Symeonidou and Dimitrios Veneiris demonstrate in this volume, the original Bismarckian design of the Greek welfare system has been systematically distorted throughout its history precisely by the factors Katrougalas finally concedes are responsible for its crisis. Both argue that existing disparities in social protection between Greece and other countries of the EU clearly reflect key institutional, structural, as well as economic differences. Neither, unfortunately, believes that the Greek system has the capacity to resolve its crisis and embark on an effective process of welfare reform, making it very much the 'sick man' of the southern welfare states.

Taking Institutions Seriously

Attempting to separate the institutional topography of these systems from their organizational principles or original design would appear to be of limited value. It certainly prevents an understanding of Greece's extreme example of the problems confronting the southern welfare systems. Several contributors to this volume point to other ways in which subsuming the southern countries within a broader 'continental' model diminishes our understanding of their basic form, functioning and distributive consequences. In his study of Portugal, José Pereirinha indicates two limits to the application of Esping-Andersen's regime approach to southern Europe: by focusing on the decommodification of the rights of workers in the formal labour market, the informal labour markets which play such an important role in the south are excluded from analysis; and by failing explicitly to incorporate the solidaristic mechanisms of southern civil society, the informal institutions on which these systems rely so heavily to combat poverty and social exclusion are similarly neglected. Pereirinha therefore favours a conceptualization of welfare states in terms not just of the relationship between the state and the market, but one which fully embraces the role of civil society, differentiated into the household and the voluntary sector. Claude Martin makes the same point by focusing more specifically on the continuing centrality of the family, arguing that the key issue may be less the family's contribution to the protection of individuals, but the kind of specific arrangement that exists between welfare society (neighbours, families and relatives) and the welfare state and between the welfare state and the market. For Martin, the specificity of southern welfare is possibly to be found in the fact that the family was engaging in a process of change linked to the transformation of the labour market, and the extension of a number of values relating to the domestic sphere, at precisely the point when the development of formal welfare institutions was jeopardized by economic recession.

The analyses in this volume broadly confirm the value of focusing on the particular institutional character of southern welfare states. Indeed, as Ferrera (1996) argues, the 'socio-political etiquette' which inspires the functioning of all of the southern European welfare states is so different from that of the other corporatist and Catholic countries to their north, that it effectively creates a distinctive type of welfare system – one in which there are actually 'unparalleled peaks of generosity' for certain categories of the population (particularly the 'core' work force) and which, regardless of a process of 'catch-up' in terms of social spending, is highly resistant to institutional convergence. For, while the differences between the southern and continental systems can be ascribed in part to under-development, the socio-political organization of these societies has ensured that when and where development has occurred it has been seriously distorted in favour of certain privileged groups, creating a specifically southern welfare 'syndrome'. Ferrera specifies the principle characteristics of this syndrome as:

- a highly fragmented and 'corporatist' income maintenance system characterized by dualism and polarization in terms of income maintenance and pensions (which includes a particularly skewed distribution of both housing resources – i.e. ownership – and welfare transfers in favour of privileged sections of the elderly) (Castles and Ferrera 1996);

• a departure from corporatist traditions (typical of the 'conservative', continental model) in health care and the establishment of national health services;

• a low degree of state penetration of the welfare sphere (reflected in still low levels of welfare spending in these countries, apart from Italy);

• a distinctive welfare mix (state/family/church/charity); and

• extensive clientelism and 'patronage machines' which distribute cash subsidies to political client groups.

As already suggested above, these features can be explained in both institutional and developmental terms. The politico-institutional factors – referred to by Ferrera as the 'power games' resulting from the specific structures of south European politics – are:

• the weakness of state institutions and the failure to endow these countries with a 'rational-Weberian' civil service prior to the mass expansion of welfare programmes;

• the prominence of parties as the main aggregators of social interests; and

• ideological polarization (and, in particular, the presence of a radical-maximalist *and* divided Left) in southern party systems. Thus, Ferrera attributes the internal imbalances in the Spanish and Italian income maintenance systems partly to party competition both within the Left (socialist parties that sought to dismantle occupational 'separatism' in social insurance and introduce a Scandinavian style universal pension were opposed by the communist parties in both countries) and between the Left and conservative, patronage-oriented parties (Ferrera 1996: 30–1).

If we make institutions our focus in this way, there are wider implications for the conventional division of Europe into several, more or less self-contained, 'worlds of welfare capitalism'. Symeonidou considers Greece to be a mix of the 'liberal' and 'conservative-corporatist' types, for example, while Ferrera (1996; 1997a) notes that the southern welfare states are distinctively 'mixed systems' which, while universal in health care, are occupational in social security. In her contribution to this volume, Valeria Fargeon refers to a territorial cleavage which links southern Italy with Portugal and certain southern regions of Spain, in terms of social needs (high dependency ratios and insufficient wage income for a substantial number of families), while the central and northern regions of Italy (and, by implication, Spain) appear closer to continental and northern Europe in terms of population ageing, female labour force participation and changes in family structure – not to mention their political-institutional capacity for reform (see below). There may also be a case, as Bonoli and Palier argue in their contribution, for identifying the 'southern' characteristics in the French system, including the strong degree of occupational fragmentation of the social insurance system, the non-state apparatus dimension of social insurance organizations and the centrality in the current debate over welfare reform of notions such as 'polarization of protection', 'particularistic welfare' or 'low degree of state penetration within the welfare sphere'. None of this is to deny the insights or continuing utility of Esping-Andersen's 'three worlds' approach; but such nuances simply reinforce the point that other tools of analysis may be necessary to understand the special character of the southern countries.

Developmental Factors

Understanding the special character of the southern welfare states requires that particular attention is paid to developmental aspects. In this respect, regardless of certain similarities, the French system is set apart from the southern countries, since it clearly bears the imprint of a much older form of industrial development, in which company-based social insurance schemes developed in the earlier part of this century were gradually centralized and endowed with legitimacy and quasi-public status by the state (Hatzfeld 1971). The social commonalities which span the southern countries, by contrast, derive to a significant extent from their relatively recent, rapid and spatially-restricted phase of economic growth and development which, being quite distinctive from the process of development in northern Europe, has also created a specific context for the development of social policy and the welfare state, the legacy of which is only slowly being eroded by economic 'catch-up'. The pattern of socio-political development is clearly also critical, for a late and territorially unequal form of modernization has produced a much more heterogeneous social structure than exists in northern Europe, marked by a large petty-bourgeoisie which, having always been an important social force, has gained in significance as small traders and the self-employed in personal services have constituted a growing proportion of the population. At the same time, the emergence of a new middle class has had important consequences for the evolution of some of the southern systems (notably Greece) by exerting considerable influence on the distribution of welfare resources (see Petmesidou 1991; Symeonidou, this volume).

Disparities of income, labour market and educational opportunities and life chances are often acute in these countries, as reflected, for example, in the distribution of employment and unemployment between the Italian Mezzogiorno and the regions of the centre and north and between Objective 1 regions and other regions in Spain. Although economic development has helped attenuate these disparities in Spain (recent research shows that inter-provincial per capita income inequalities have decreased significantly as incomes have grown across the country as a whole) (Villaverde 1996), in Italy the extent of poverty, and its concentration in certain southern regions, has increased (Niero 1996), while in Portugal a population shift from inland regions to centres on the Atlantic coast has exacerbated rural stagnation and decline. But perhaps more important than economic disparities as such are the quite different political, cultural and class disparities that persist in these countries of uneven growth, which to some extent also coincide with contrasts between pre-industrial and increasingly post-industrial areas and populations. As Pereirinha argues, these disparities lie behind a particular southern type of poverty, linked to lower average incomes, higher income inequality, a higher poverty rate and a greater reliance of households on social protection transfers which, nonetheless, tend to be less effective in alleviating poverty than in northern Europe.

The development of social policies of various types – ranging from social security and health care to employment promotion – has occurred against this background of social heterogeneity, territorial disparities and in the context of resource constraints and inadequately institutionalized state structures which have been based in many instances on clientelistic rather than 'rational-bureaucratic' forms of administration. While social heterogeneity and the existence of extensive informal, or parallel, economies militate against universalism and the establishment of forms of solidarity based on more than particularistic group structures, the institutional factors discussed above – that is, the absence of a strong state technocracy, the prominence of political parties as aggregators of social interests, alongside the weakness of civil society, and the persistence of clientelism – have also undermined the effectiveness of policy and helped fuel undisciplined spending (Petmesidou and Tsoulouvis 1994; Sarasa and Moreno 1995; Ferrera 1996). The uneven spatial application of social policies and social policy reform has been a particular characteristic of the less centralized countries, Italy and Spain.

As Fargeon points out in the case of Italy, the decentralization of social policy since the 1970s may have exacerbated inequalities, with regional policies on social assistance remaining backward and fragmented in the south, and minimum income programmes non-existent precisely where they are most needed. While in Spain, the introduction of minimum incomes programmes has been similarly differentiated by region – helping correct intra-regional inequalities but exacerbating wider cross-national ones (Ayala 1994; Laparra and Aguilar). In the more centralized polities such as Portugal (see Pereirinha), there is concern that the new trend for central government to decentralize responsibility for provision to lower levels of administration may be tantamount to *shedding* responsibility for social problems at a time of growing resource constraints.

Periods of authoritarian rule have contributed a final and essential ingredient to the southern recipe, although with different effects, disrupting considerably the modernization process in Greece and Portugal, while helping usher in a more orderly process of economic development in Spain (Malefakis 1995). But in all cases, non-democratic interludes and structurally flawed democracy have left an important legacy, in terms of:

• the weakness – and radicalization – of a Left excluded from government for significant periods in all of these countries;

• the resilience of institutional traditions established under authoritarian rule – corporatism in the cases of Greece and Spain; the persistence of an essentially state-dominated system (the exclusion of organized interests, and a 'state-charity' view of welfare) in Portugal (see Santos 1994; Guibentif); and

• reactions *against* the policies of the authoritarian period, which, for example, in the Spanish case has contributed to the *absence* of a strong family policy, precisely because of the pro-natalist, anti-feminist family policies of the Franco regime (Valiente 1996).

Democratic transition in the 1970s has also produced a particular type of social democracy in Greece, Portugal and Spain which has been much less well entrenched as a social force than in northern Europe. Its contribution to the construction of the welfare state has been restricted, primarily by the fact that the economic crisis of the 1970s coincided with the emergence of these parties from opposition, and their attempts to make their imprint on the paternalist welfare arrangements they inherited. But they were also constrained by the fact that, unlike their northern counterparts, they have had to compete with well-organized communist parties which have been much better rooted in the working class movement, parts of which have retained a 'maximalist' orientation and remained rigid defenders of the entitlements of their core work force clienteles. As a result, the socialist parties quickly assumed a quite different character from those in the north, becoming the vehicles for the ascendance of a modernizing (and sometimes self-promoting and corrupt) bourgeoisie and quite open to the appeals of the neo-liberal ideas which, as Rico points out, became a new international policy paradigm at a critical moment in the ideological development of these parties and in southern welfare state construction. In all four southern countries, the full implementation of reform programmes and the expansion of provision was interrupted by the onset of economic recession, the emergence of public sector deficits and a shift to austerity policies in a context of new obligations linked to EU membership. This is particularly marked in the case of their health systems, for all were latecomers to the adoption of a national health service model which, even as they embraced it, was coming under fire – especially in Britain, its country of origin.

Partly as a result of this form of uneven, interrupted and incomplete welfare state development, traditional 'pre-industrial' forms of welfare – provided by the family and charitable institutions – remain much more important than elsewhere, as already indicated, and are essential for filling certain important welfare protection gaps: for example, there is no income maintenance for first job-seekers in Spain, Portugal and Greece and very low minimum benefits in the case of old age and invalidity (Gough 1996), although Portugal has recently introduced a national minimum income scheme (Pereirinha), while local and regional authorities step in to fill the gap in Italy and Spain (Fargeon; Laparra and Aguilar). The nature of the family and kinship networks in southern Europe is explored in this volume by Teresa Jurado and Manuela Naldini who argue persuasively for the existence of a specific southern family model which, like the other socio-political components of southern welfare, is proving highly resistant to pressures for change or convergence with northern European patterns. Basing their analyses on the Spanish case, Guillén (1996) and Laparra and Aguilar also demonstrate how critical the southern family remains as a provider of social services and the linch pin of social solidarity, preventing widespread social precariousness from spilling over into social exclusion and social problems, producing much lower crime rates, for example, than in France and Britain. Santos (1994) describes how the Portuguese hospitals rely on family networks to provide a free, informal and rather high quality equivalent of professional social workers in northern welfare states. Of course, relying on the family as a functional substitute for a comprehensive welfare system has its limits: there are those without families who fall through the safety net of social solidarity, while the social and personal costs, especially for women and the young, can be high. Moreover, if the nature of the southern family *is* changing, then social solidarity will be seriously undermined. We return to this point below.

PROGRESS, PROBLEMS AND THE PROSPECTS FOR REFORM

Before considering the particular problems faced by the southern welfare states, either in coping with the legacy of uneven institutional and economic development, or in responding to new challenges, it is worth pointing out that the quality of life and life chances have improved greatly in these countries over the last thirty years and that the progress of welfare state programmes has played an important role in enhancing individual and collective well-being. The introduction of new social shock absorbers also played an important function in underpinning both the transition to democracy and its consolidation. This is not to deny, of course, considerable shortfalls in provision and development in these systems. The creation of national health services and extensive reforms to health care systems were highly ambitious and inevitably fell short of expectations, more so in some of the southern countries (Portugal and Greece) than in others. In Portugal, infant mortality is the highest in the OECD and diseases eradicated elsewhere in Europe (tuberculosis, for example) are still prevalent, due both to poor living conditions and inadequate health services, whereas Spain and Italy are well above the OECD average in terms of all the broad indicators of health status (infant and prenatal mortality, life expectancy, etc.). In Greece, rural health services are so poorly developed that travel to major centres for much treatment is required. In both Portugal and Greece, health care is fragmented and under-funded and retains a dual public–private structure, despite the formal creation of national health systems. The rate of catch-up in other areas has also been slow: the education system in Portugal is still under-developed (responsible for one of the highest illiteracy rates in Europe), and suffers from declining investment in Greece (where recent improvements, especially in vocational education, have been entirely dependent on EU Community Support Framework funding). In Italy, the ratio of spending on education between northern and southern regions was 3:1 in the late 1980s, and, as elsewhere in southern Europe, rates of participation in compulsory and post-compulsory education (especially vocational courses) continue to be low relative to other European countries (Rhodes 1995).

But in some of the southern countries, and in some areas of welfare, the quality and extent of provision have reached the levels of programmes in some northern welfare states, especially as the latter are now being pared back or allowed to erode (a recent survey on British pensioners who have retired to Spain showed that they are happier with the quality of health care there than at home). In all of them, however, the chances of a successful 'reform of the reforms' made necessary by the rapidity and often imbalanced growth in welfare provision were severely reduced by the onset of recession in the mid-1970s and the shift from expansionary to austerity economic policies, to which none of the western welfare states has been immune: indeed, Rico argues in her article that the implementation of institutional change may have as much to do with external factors – a change in the dominant international policy paradigm to one based on market principles, and the evolution of the economic cycle – as with domestic politico-institutional structures. In this respect, some countries are luckier than others. In the Spanish case, a successful expansion of the public network of health care centres occurred in the 1960s and 1970s *before* the onset of recession and, while a policy paradigm favouring the expansion of state institutions was still extant, apparently explaining why there is much less user dissatisfaction with the Spanish system and less of a legacy of impediments to further reform than elsewhere in the south, and why there is much less impetus in Spain towards private-sector solutions. It is clear, therefore, that reforming these systems in the contemporary period must deal both with the problems inherited from the past as well as with the new challenges confronting all welfare systems.

Old Legacies, New Challenges

While southern European welfare states do bear many similarities to their northern counterparts, and advances in social security cover and health in all countries of the region have narrowed the gap between them, they remain strongly marked by particular institutional traditions and trajectories. It is therefore unsurprising that while they face challenges common to other welfare systems, these take on a special character in the south. As in all welfare states, there is a perception in the south that welfare spending has reached its limits, even if in Greece and Portugal, social policy spending is still well short of, and in Italy and Spain is just below, the EU (12) average. For given the scale of public sector deficits in the region (which are especially acute in Italy and Greece), not to mention growing anti-tax mobilization (apparent especially in Spain and Italy), this reflects a genuine concern rather than just anti-welfare rhetoric. As elsewhere, demographic changes (ageing) are forcing a restructuring of pension systems (again, Spain and Italy face particular problems in this respect); and new family and labour market patterns are transforming the nature of 'needs' and altering the gender/family/work nexus in which welfare states have traditionally been based. The costs of health care have increased, as they have in other countries, due to the same 'demand-side' factors (ageing, higher incomes and increased insurance coverage) and 'supply' effects, including a growth in medical personnel and facilities and increases in real health care prices (Oxley and Macfarlan 1995), compounding the costs generated by inefficient organization. Meanwhile, low economic growth and high rates of unemployment (especially in Greece, Italy and Spain), have led to higher spending on income support and the search for new ways of creating new jobs, while the spread of new and 'precarious' forms of work (which has been extensive in the Spanish case) has created new risks and added a new layer of working poor to more traditional forms of poverty. Policy choices meanwhile are being constrained by external factors, primarily globalization (and concern over competitiveness in more open and rapidly changing world markets) and movement towards European Monetary Union, with all that implies for inflation (leading to income restraint) and the reduction of public deficits and debts (Rhodes 1996).

At the same time, the mix of policy responses is also similar to those in northern Europe, and includes modifying funding arrangements (seeking to widen the basis of funding); tightening regulations and qualifying conditions (to reduce costs, welfare dependency and the incidence of 'moral hazard'); the search for more effective 'active' labour market policies to replace 'passive' schemes of income support; and privatization and 'marketization', abandoning a 'public integrating' model in favour of a 'public contract' model of welfare, most notably in the health sector (Rhodes 1997a). Consequently, some of the consequences are the same, including the adverse impact of such reforms on the poor and disadvantaged – the result, for example, of more regressive health-care systems (as complementary payments become more common) and increasing disentitlement, produced by explicit policy (excluding certain categories of the population form cover) or neglect (by failing to respond to new needs). In reforming their systems, and in creating or failing to avoid these pitfalls, the southern welfare systems face the same dilemma as their northern counterparts in maintaining the balance between the three goals of welfare: insurance against risk, the welfare safety net and income redistribution (Sigg *et al.* 1996). Failure to achieve that balance results in a loss of social solidarity and/or a legitimacy deficit, as public support ebbs away.

Yet to these challenges and problems must be added the particular contradictions and, in certain countries, the 'systemic' flaws, of the 'southern syndrome'. Striking a balance between insurance, the safety net and redistribution is a somewhat different task in most southern countries, given that these incomplete and unevenly institutionalized welfare states have barely managed or failed to strike that balance in the past: the insurance systems are marked by peaks of generosity, defended by unions who are wedded to the principles of corporatist social protection; the safety net has large gaps in all of these countries; and the distribution of costs and benefits has often been dictated by the influence of pressure groups and political lobbies rather than principles of equality or equity. Equity deficits are quite apparent in southern health and social security systems, and the promise of universal national health systems has been far from fulfilled in terms of equality of access, efficiency in production or quality, as discussed in the Italian case by Granaglia. Disparities in the labour market are particularly acute, and employment promotion has been restricted both by an incapacity to build effective administrative structures and by the legacy of privileged protection. As Dell'Aringa and Lodovici argue, the development of an efficient administration aimed at removing the causes of labour market exclusion has been prevented in Italy and elsewhere in southern Europe by the prevalence of an 'insider–outsider' problem, for 'the fragmentation and disparities in the income support system for the unemployed, with extreme differences and gaps in the level of social protection given to core and marginal workers, are the result of a complex system guaranteeing full-time, stable jobs for core workers (traditionally males in middle-age groups) through employment protection measures, income support to laid off workers and a public monopoly in job placement'.

These entrenched inequalities and the skewed or incomplete distribution of welfare resources in the south creates serious strains at the micro-level which are absorbed by the family. For, as shown by Jurado and Naldini, not only does the family has a welfare function in terms of direct support, but it is also a mechanism for the redistribution of resources, either earned or received as benefits. But whether the family can retain its function as a social shock absorber is a moot point. While Castles and Ferrera (1996) argue that the highly integrated southern family is under threat (due to a vicious circle of inadequate external support and opportunities which lower fertility rates and block family formation and expansion), Jurado and Naldini suggest quite the opposite – that the persistence of the southern family is likely, despite changing social norms (divorce, co-habitation, births outside wedlock) and economic pressures; and that this is precisely because it deals so well with the consequences of lasting employment shortage and the scarce availability of social services for families. Nevertheless, low fertility rates and the nature of the family are the subject of debate in all of these countries, and as the strains absorbed by the family increase, the costs borne by women and the young must also grow, especially in areas of high and persistent unemployment or where the working poor or those in precarious jobs are widespread.

The Problems and Potential of Reform

Not only are there already major distortions or inadequacies in these countries' social insurance systems, safety nets and policies of redistribution; but reforming those systems, either to deal with their original defects or accommodate new challenges, is heavily constrained by the features of the 'southern syndrome': the strength of vested interests, clientelistic collusion, an absence of political consensus and the weakness and fragmentation of administrative structures. The relevance of these factors clearly varies from one country to the next, or, as in Italy and Spain, may vary by region; the dysfunctional nature of the 'southern syndrome' appears to be at its most intense in Greece and southern Italy, where both Symeonidou and Fargeon, respectively, identify vicious circles of pre-political particularism, an instrumental approach to politics, an absence of collective action, widespread distrust and negative expectations. Yet they represent important impediments to reform across all of southern Europe, undermining public management and steering capacity and contributing to user dissatisfaction, a high attitudinal potential for a tax-welfare backlash and voter disillusionment with universalism. Ferrera (1997b) attributes the crisis of the entire Italian welfare state to the prevalence of these factors, while Ayala (1994) argues that even in Spain (where, as Rico points out, the construction of the welfare state has had many achievements), new challenges, particularly de-industrialization and high unemployment, are simply adding to unresolved problems, such as the limited universalization of some benefits and services, the lack of an adequate safety net, and inequalities created by territorial and functional decentralization. The issue then becomes whether external pressures – especially EU membership – will help 'modernize' and consolidate these welfare systems, by galvanizing political and social forces behind a process of consensual reform, or whether they will simply compound their contradictions and generate social and political conflict.

The impact of external pressure will clearly depend on how chronic the 'southern syndrome' is in each of these countries and on their existing and potential capacity for reform. Although one of the principle features of southern welfare states referred to by Ferrera (1996) is their poor capacity for reform compared with other European countries – including France where, as Bonoli and Palier illustrate, a process of quite radical reform is now under way – several contributions to this volume point to the innovative capacity of certain southern welfare states, or at least of their sub-national governments. Rico, for example, argues that in Spain the standardization of the rules and organization of health care institutions and the expansion of tax-based financing reflects considerable reform capacity, while Fargeon and Aguilar and Laparra document the commitment – and some success – of regional authorities in Italy and Spain to improving and expanding public welfare services (in health care, social services and minimum income programmes), at a time when national policies have been re-oriented towards retrenchment. However, from another viewpoint, this uneven distribution of reform capacity is itself an intrinsic feature of the 'southern syndrome', and rather than a solution is actually part of the problem. For as Fargeon also points out, because both Spain and Italy have engaged in a substantial transfer of functions to regions and local authorities, in the present climate of austerity they are presented with an additional problem to those they share with their neighbouring countries – inter-regional tensions over the different levels of benefits and services available within their national boundaries.

A brief survey of recent reforms and their success or failure provides some idea of where, in which areas of policy, and in which particular direction, change and adjustment are likely to proceed. One important trend in these countries has been the search for greater effectiveness and steering capacity, by reforming the administrative and political-institutional context of decision making. This is being achieved in two ways.

The first is bureaucratic reform. In response to manifest administrative inefficiencies, made all the more glaring by the need to implement EU directives, and the need to make public sector economies, all of the southern countries have engaged in rationalization and re-organization, with important consequences for welfare. Such policies range from the attempted rationalization of social security funds (Greece), the restructuring of ministries and changes to the territorial distribution of responsibilities (Portugal), and the progressive decentralization of social services, education and health to the Autonomous Communities (Spain). Policies to make revenue raising more effective (by clamping down on evasion) and spending less wasteful can also be considered a part of institutional reform, since more efficient tax inspectorates and monitoring services are the key pre-requisites for their success. But making administrative and fiscal reform work is far from easy. As Cananea (1997) remarks in a discussion of Italian public sector reform (although this applies to all of southern Europe), the key obstacles are the vested interests which view public posts as sinecures and the fact that, while the inefficiency of public services has adverse consequences for most people, it does have advantages for those who provide those services, and whose utility would be reduced if the administration were able to function efficiently. Territorial redistribution may add to this problem. In Spain, where decentralization is credited with the reduction in inequality of provision (Almeda and Sarasa 1996), Rico points out that in 1992, by when around 60 per cent of the Spanish population was served by special region health bureaucracies, the number of health care bureaucrats in Madrid (about 6,000) remained the same as in 1982. Fiscal reform also faces enormous obstacles, and notably in the Italian and Greek cases, the line of least resistance is often taken, by increasing the tax burden of the honest or those (taxed at source) unable so easily to evade. Progress in these areas is therefore slow and problematic, and far less straightforward than reforming public finances where, for the time being at least, external constraints – primarily EMU convergence criteria – can be mobilized to bolster the credibility of government policies and tarnish opponents with accusations of irresponsibility.

This is why the second solution to defective steering capacity is proving to be effective: that is, involving interest groups (primarily employers associations and trade unions) in reforms of those areas of the welfare state that intersect with domains of vested employer/union interests and issues of labour market regulation – namely social security funding, pensions and employment creation. Recent years have proven that there is greater potential for this type of reform in Italy and Portugal than elsewhere in southern Europe via so-called 'social pacts'. For while interest associations and relations between government, unions and employers have developed least in Greece during democratization (Schmitter 1995: 313–14), in Spain ideological divisions and organizational weaknesses have limited an effective recourse to consensus-based policy making, despite the importance of pacts underpinning the transition to democracy, although this may be changing (Rhodes 1997b). In Italy and Portugal, the 1990s have seen significant reform in pensions and social security matters as a result of 'competitive corporatism' – i.e. pacts designed to adjust the labour market and welfare state to external constraints (Rhodes 1997c). In both countries, important changes to pensions, benefits and tax regimes have resulted. As for Spain, the years since 1993 have seen an agreement on the re-organization of national vocational training and industrial relations reform, and in March 1995 a broad agreement (including the parties of both government and opposition) on the future of welfare – the Toledo Pact. However, although this focused on a wide range of changes to pension, as yet it has led to little in the way of concrete policy. Indeed, it may delay a revision of the social security system for several years, despite problems accumulating in the pensions system due to the rapid ageing of the population.

By contrast, in Portugal and Italy – where the problems of reform were arguably more pressing – social pacts have allowed significant changes to occur, tackling the problems of pension funding, removing peaks of generosity, repairing gaps in the safety net and removing fiscal inequities. In Portugal (where the exclusion of organized interests from policy making described by Guibentif has been reversed), there have been five such agreements since 1987, the last of which in 1996 links employment promotion measures with numerous social security and fiscal reforms, including minimum incomes and favourable tax treatment of health and education benefits and old age pensions. A major reform of the Portuguese pension system in 1993–95 and of the social security scheme for self-employed workers in 1994, raised contributions and contribution periods, but also improved coverage, while the privileges of public sector workers were removed. Despite tight budgetary constraints, the government agreed that social spending in 1996 would rise by over 8 per cent and social welfare by 14 per cent. In Italy, a renewed national tripartism that originally focused on the reform of wage indexation and collective bargaining, extended to pensions in 1995 and initiated a major reform, even if the employers abstained from the final agreement. As a result, the entire basis of the pension system was shifted from one related to earnings to one directly linked to contributions paid, and the existing 'particularist-clientelist' retirement funds (of which there were over fifty) were harmonized by the creation of a single scheme (Reynaud and Hege 1996; Regini and Regalia 1997). The reform still faces many problems of implementation, but it nonetheless represent a milestone in the direction of a viable and more equitable pension system.

Italy has also seen a relatively successful 'reform of the reform' in the post-1992 restructuring of the national health service which removes local health authorities from political control and transforms them into independent enterprises, with responsibility for financial balances, while greater scope for private care is allowed, through private rooms in public hospitals and the likely adoption of internal market rules within agreements with GPs, designed to turn them into fundholders. As

Granaglia notes, however, the impact on expenditure may be marginal and there has been as little thought given to the nature of incentives in the new reforms as in the original establishment of the NHS. Universalism in health care is likely to be jeopardized, as in other countries where 'marketization' is occurring (Niero 1996). But while the direction of reform may be disputed, efforts to rectify existing defects are being made (Ferrera 1997b).

In Greece, by contrast, successful reform faces many more obstacles. But while both Symeonidou and Veneiris despair at the future of the Greek welfare system, some innovations have occurred. Despite their clear limitations (see Venieris), reforms in 1990–92 attempted to remove many anomalies from the Greek pensions system (civil servants paid no premiums while public utility workers and employees in state-controlled banks paid only nominal contributions) while the pension age was raised in 1993 to 65 for men and women (from 60 and 58) and pensions and sickness contributions were increased to allow the generation of income surpluses which can be used to pay of the pensions funds debt. As elsewhere, privileges are being reduced: since 1990, public sector workers have been treated the same as private sector workers for pension purposes. In the health system, by contrast, which remains over-bureaucratic, fragmented in terms of funding and decision-making, and highly inefficient, pressuring many to use the private sector instead, reform has been blocked. Thus, a 1995 bill to unify the health funds and increase efficiency by introducing competition among providers, while also encouraging health care purchasers to focus on the effectiveness of the care they provide, failed – both because of the opposition of vested interests (the more 'privileged' social insurance organizations) and budgetary and fiscal constraints (Papadopoulou 1997).

CONCLUSION

The coming years will be critical ones for the southern European countries, as they adjust their economies, administrative cultures and welfare states to pressures from beyond their borders – including the consolidation of the single market, EMU convergence and greater competition in more open world markets. To some extent these pressures will lead to greater conformity, in terms of budgetary discipline, the rationalization of bureaucracies, the reduction of clientelism and attacks on anomalies in taxation and benefits. In the process, the skewed nature of welfare provision and the peaks of generosity that are still characteristic of these systems should gradually be corrected, depending of course, on a political determination to tackle entrenched inequalities and take on the vested interests which defend them. There is likely to be continued convergence on a 'public contract' model of welfare in the health sector, and the spread of market principles of organization and an expansion of the private sector, especially in those countries with extensive user-dissatisfaction with the present system (Greece and Italy). There will also be some convergence in the dynamics of policy change, for agreements on change involving the social partners in areas ranging from labour market regulation to social security funding and pensions will remain indispensable in Italy, Spain and Portugal. As revealed by recent policy developments in Portugal, improvements in welfare coverage in Spain, and the successful removal of anomalies in the Italian and Greek pensions system, there is cause for measured optimism concerning the capacity of these systems for reform.

None of this means that the basic features of the 'southern syndrome' will disappear overnight. Administrative structures will remain fragmented and colonized by vested interests, high rates of poverty and unemployment will persist in many regions of the south and the reform of health systems, social security and pensions will be slow, falling well behind expectations in most cases. Tax evasion and benefit fraud will remain a major problem, and one dependent as much on a reform of social attitudes as on an essential reform of state administrations. Clientelism is ingrained in the politics of these countries and is difficult to eradicate, especially when the agents of change – the political parties – remain dependent on client groups for support. At the same time the developmental divide between the poorer and the more prosperous regions (northern Italy and Spain, the Atlantic coast of Portugal and major urban centres in Greece) may well widen, creating new disparities in welfare provision, especially where responsibility for funding and organization is decentralized, a trend which is now appearing in Portugal and, although beset by political opposition, in Greece as well. Nevertheless, and despite the context of economic turbulence, the direction of change in all countries of the region has been positive in recent years, even considering a rather uncritical acceptance of the virtues of market rules and competition in health service reform. Some of the major systemic flaws of the southern 'syndrome' are being tackled for the first time, especially in Italy and Greece, although still far from successfully in the latter. New instruments – such as minimum income programmes – are helping repair the weak and fraying safety nets of these countries. Social security and pension inequities are slowly being removed. However, the continued reform and consolidation of these welfare states is highly dependent on external variables, most importantly the 'shield and the threat' provided for governments of the region by the Maastricht Treaty and the policy requirements flowing from it. If that external constraint were to be relaxed, so, one fears, would the impetus behind reform.

REFERENCES

Almeda, E. and S. Sarasa (1996): 'Spain: Growth to Diversity', in V. George and P. Taylor-Gooby (eds), *European Welfare Policy: Squaring the Welfare Circle*, London: Macmillan, pp.155–76.
Ayala, L. (1994): 'Social Needs, Inequality and the Welfare State in Spain: Trends and Prospects', *Journal of European Social Policy* 4/3, pp.159–79.
Cananea, G. della (1997): 'The Reform of Finance and Administration in Italy: Contrasting Achievements', *West European Politics* 20/1, pp.194–209. Also in M. Bull and M. Rhodes (eds), *Crisis and Transition in Italian Politics*, London: Frank Cass.
Castles, F.C. (1995): 'Welfare State Development in Southern Europe', *West European Politics* 18/2, pp.291–313.
Castles, F.C. and M. Ferrera (1996): 'Home Ownership and the Welfare State: Is Southern Europe Different?', *South European Society & Politics* 1/2 (Autumn) pp.163–85.
Esping-Andersen, G. (1990): *The Three Worlds of Welfare Capitalism*, Cambridge: Polity.
Ferrera, M. (1996): 'The "Southern Model" of Welfare in Social Europe', *Journal of European Social Policy* 6/1, pp.17–37.
Ferrera, M. (1997a): 'The Four Social Europe's: Between Universalism and Selectivity', in Y. Mény and M. Rhodes (eds), *A New Social Contract? Charting the Future of European Welfare*, London: Macmillan.
Fererra, M. (1997b): 'The Uncertain Future of the Italian Welfare State', *West European Politics* 20/1, pp.231–49. Also in M. Bull and M. Rhodes (eds), *Crisis and Transition in Italian Politics*, London: Frank Cass.
Gough, I. (1996): 'Social Assistance in Southern Europe', *South European Society & Politics* 1/1 (Summer) pp.1–23.
Guillén, A. (1996): 'Citizenship and Social Policy in Democratic Spain: The Reformulation of the Francoist Welfare State', *South European Society & Politics* 1/2 (Autumn) pp.253–72.
Hatzfeld, H. (1971): *Du paupérisme à la sécurité sociale: essai sur les origines de la sécurité sociale en France, 1850 à 1940*, Paris: Armand Colin.
Katrougalos, G.S. (1996): 'The South European Welfare Model: The Greek Welfare State in Search of an Identity', *Journal of European Social Policy* 6/1, pp.39–60.
Leibfried, S. (1993): 'Towards a European Welfare State? On Integrating Poverty Regimes into the European Community', in C. Jones (ed.), *New Perspectives on the Welfare State in Europe*, London: Routledge.
Lijphart, A., T.C. Bruneau, P. Nikiforos Diamandourous and R. Gunther (1988): 'A Mediterranean Model of Democracy? The Southern European Democracies in Comparative Perspective', *West European Politics* 11/1 (Jan.) pp.7–25.
Malefakis, E. (1995): 'The Political and Socioeconomic Contours of Southern European History', in R. Gunther, P. Nikiforos Diamandouros and H-J. Puhle (eds), *The Politics of Democratic Consolidation: Southern Europe in Comparative Perspective*, Baltimore and London: The Johns Hopkins University Press, pp.33–76.
Niero, M. (1996): 'Italy: Right Turn for the Welfare State?', in V. George and P. Taylor-Gooby (eds), *European Welfare Policy: Squaring the Welfare Circle*, London: Macmillan, pp.117–35.
Oxley, H. and M. Macfarlan (1995): 'Health Care Reform: Controlling Spending and Increasing Efficiency', *OECD Economic Studies* 24/1, pp.7–55.
Papadopoulou, I. (1997): 'The Organization and Financing of Health Care Services in

Greece', mimeo, Department of Politics, University of Athens.

Petmesidou, M. (1991): 'Statism, Social Policy and the Middle Classes in Greece', *Journal of European Social Policy* 1/1, pp.31–48.

Petmesidou, M. and L. Tsoulouvis (1994): 'Aspects of the Changing Political Economy of Europe: Welfare State, Class Segmentation and Planning in the Postmodern Era', *Sociology* 28/2, pp.499–519.

Regini, M. and I. Regalia (1997): 'Employers, Unions and the State: The Resurgence of Concertation in Italy?', *West European Politics* 20/1, pp.210–30. Also in M. Bull and M. Rhodes (eds), *Crisis and Transition in Italian Politics*, London: Frank Cass.

Reynaud, E. and A. Hege (1996): 'Italy: a Fundamental Transformation of the Pension System', *International Social Security Review* 49/3, pp.65–74.

Rhodes, M. (1995): 'Regional Development and Employment in Europe's Southern and Western Peripheries', in M. Rhodes (ed.), *The Regions and the New Europe: Patterns in Core and Periphery Development*, Manchester: MUP, pp.273–328.

Rhodes, M. (1996): 'Globalization and West European Welfare States: A Critical Review of Recent Debates', *Journal of European Social Policy* 6/4, pp.305–27.

Rhodes, M. (1997a): 'The Welfare State: Internal Challenges, External Constraints', in M. Rhodes, P. Heywood and V. Wright (eds), *Developments in West European Politics*, London: Macmillan, pp.57–74.

Rhodes, M. (1997b): 'Spain', in H. Compston (ed.), *The New Politics of Unemployment: Radical Policy Initiatives in Western Europe*, London: Routledge, pp.103–22.

Rhodes, M. (1997c): 'Globalization, Labour Markets and Welfare States: A Future of "Competitive Corporatism"', paper presented to the ECPR workshop, *The State and the Globalization Process*, Bern, 27 Feb.–4 March.

Santos, B. (1994): 'Etats, rapports salariaux et protection sociale à la semi-périphérie – cas du Portugal', *Peuples Méditerranéens* 66, pp.23–66.

Sarasa, S. and L. Moreno (eds) (1995): *El estado del bienestar el la Europa del sur*, Madrid: Consejo Superior de Investigaciones Cientficas, Instituto de Estudios Sociales Avanzados.

Schmitter, P. (1995): 'Organized Interests and Democratic Consolidation in Southern Europe', in R. Gunther, P. Nikiforos Diamandouros and H-J. Puhle (eds.), *The Politics of Democratic Consolidation: Southern Europe in Comparative Perspective*, Baltimore and London: The Johns Hopkins University Press, pp.284–314.

Sigg, R., I. Zeitzer, X. Scheil-Adlung, C. Kuptsch and M. Tracy (1996): 'Developments and Trends in Social Security, 1993–1995', *International Social Security Review* 49/2, pp.5–126.

Valiente, C. (1996): 'The Rejection of Authoritarian Policy Legacies: Family Policy in Spain (1975–1995)', *South European Society & Politics* 1/1 (Summer) pp.95–114.

Villaverde, J. (1996): 'Interprovincial Inequalities in Spain, 1955–1991', *European Urban and Regional Studies* 3.4, pp.339–46.

Social Welfare and the Family in Southern Europe

CLAUDE MARTIN

After a critical analysis of the main typologies of welfare states in Europe, emphasizing the way they appear to neglect the southern countries, the author presents some of the arguments that might support the definition of a 'southern' profile of social welfare, pointing to socio-demographic characteristics, dominant values about private life and the way in which laws are produced in southern Europe. The author emphasizes the particular role played by the family and forms of primary solidarity and argues for the development of more genetic approaches, assigning a more central role to the 'family question' in these countries.

TYPOLOGIZING WELFARE SYSTEMS: THE EXCLUSION OF THE SOUTH

Most comparative work on welfare systems is carried out by Anglo-Saxon researchers[1] and the typologies they propose pay little attention to southern Europe. Is this because these systems are little known or are they deliberately sidelined? Or, as so often seems to be the case, is it because researchers imagine that social welfare measures adopted in southern Europe correspond approximately to those already found in northern and western Europe, but are simply less advanced in terms of implementation and therefore do not justify the identification of a southern European type?

Comparative work on the welfare state and social welfare systems principally relies on a comparison of statistical, socio-demographic, economic and financial indicators and on the production of typologies. The variables most frequently employed include economic factors (the development and restructuring of the market, re-organization of production and the level of social transfers), institutional dimensions (the role of the bureaucracy and the state apparatus) and political practices (in particular, the construction of political accords between the various segments or classes of developed societies). There is often disagreement between those who focus on the role of the state and its bureaucratic apparatus (the top-down model) (e.g. Evans, Rueschmeyer and Skocpol 1985) and those who believe that social welfare measures are somehow won by workers or by segments of civil society (the bottom-up model). According to some writers, the 'classist' dimension, or the question of alliances between the working class and the middle class, is of primary importance (Korpi 1978; Baldwin 1990). This approach is also evident in France: for example, Hatzfeld's seminal work (1971) sees the setting up of social security in that country as the result of a decline in the influence of certain socio-professional groups (farmers and the self-employed) opposed to the idea of collective, compulsory protection.

Within this largely dominant perspective, which gives the 'welfare state' a role in organizing and managing the economy, one of the most important reference points in recent years has been the work of Esping-Andersen (1990). Using a genetic approach to constructing the social role of the state in different countries and the power relations operating therein (Kemeny 1995), Esping-Andersen identifies three main models of welfare state regimes: the social democrat/universalist, conservative-Catholic/corporatist and liberal/residual. These do not include all countries, nor do they explain how different systems evolved: rather they are ideal-types. However, they have been criticized precisely because of their 'ideal' or static nature. The first type corresponds to northern European countries, and Sweden in particular. But it is quite clear that Esping-Andersen cannot characterize all these countries in this way: Finland, in particular, is difficult to assimilate into this model (Leira 1992; Kangas 1994). The second type includes not just Germany, but also Austria, Belgium, Italy and France, while the third incorporates the United States, Canada and Australia as well as the United Kingdom 'after Thatcher'.

While this approach significantly improves on the customary polarization between the Bismarkian and Beveridgian models, it nonetheless lacks nuance. Thus, strictly speaking, it is difficult to classify France within the German model.[2] If we consider France too narrowly on the basis of its (compulsory) corporatist range of insurance measures, we ignore the importance of the public assistance precursors of the provision of French welfare in various 'risk' sectors such as old age and the role of the Republican model of collective protection under the Third Republic (Dumons and Pollet 1994; Renard 1995). Social security 'French-style' is marked by the fact it did not choose between the major models, Bismark and Beveridge, that were available after World War II. For this reason, it is usual to present the French model as a compromise – a mixed, intermediate type that has been influenced by both Bismark and Beveridge, and has tried to enjoy the benefits of both approaches.[3]

The Bismarkian model was very influential until the late 1980s. But since then, the Beveridgian trend has gathered strength, with a growing role for the state and Parliament, the aim being to use taxation to fund certain risks (such as 'family risk' and the 'dependence risk') and to expand universal cover. Nor should we forget the growing role of private, optional insurance schemes (Join-Lambert 1994; Palier and Bonoli 1995).

But criticisms of Esping-Andersen are ill-founded if they simply reproach him for over-generality, for this is the cost to be paid by an ideal-typical approach. A more searching critique comes from those who point to the excessive attention paid by Esping-Andersen to the issue of the 'decommodification' of services – which refers to the varying degrees of an individual's dependence on the market, his possible 'free choice' over whether or not to remain in the labour market and the power games between the various social groups – and his underestimation of a critical element in the production and organization of collective protection: 'gender'[4] and, more generally, the issue of the family and the organization of private life (see particularly Lewis 1992 and 1995; Leibfried 1993; Taylor-Gooby 1991; Daly 1994; Sainsbury 1994; Del Re 1994; Siaroff 1994 ; and Scheiwe 1994).

Jane Lewis (1992) emphasizes that the notions of 'dependence' and 'decommodification', which are essential in Esping-Andersen's view, are 'gendered'. By adopting a problematic that is not macroeconomic but centred on relations between private life and public intervention and on the question of the sexual division of unsalaried work, Lewis provides the foundation for a quite different model. She contrasts:

- countries where the 'male breadwinner model' prevails (such as Ireland and the United Kingdom[5]), in which women's social rights are almost exclusively 'derived rights' (that is to say her husband's rights) or 'second-class' benefits (assistance rather than so-called 'first-class' insurance benefits), and where the state fails to facilitate (or even obstructs) the presence of women in the labour market, reinforcing the principles of obligation within the household;

- countries such as France which by concentrating more on the child than on women in their social policies – or at least by recognizing women both as parents and as workers – have developed a 'parental model';[6]

- and countries such as Sweden which, by acknowledging a formal equality between men and women, have promoted a 'two bread-winner family'.

At the heart of this critique and theoretical alternative lies the issue of the family contribution, and particularly that of women, to welfare and protection that takes the form of unpaid and unrecognized caring.[7] From this perspective, the 'family question' is no longer a sectoral one, as in the analysis of family policies or what the state and the social partners devise in order to sustain and protect families. It is a question of fundamental importance: that of the distribution of private and state forms of protection, and of the respective roles that the state, the market and the family play in the protection of individuals and their careers. This is surely where justification can be found for the importance of an analysis that incorporates 'Latin' social welfare systems.

Stephan Leibfried was the first, I believe, to have taken this need seriously in proposing that a fourth 'Latin Rim regime' be added to Esping-Andersen's 'three worlds'.[8] His analysis had a very specific objective, which was to understand the most likely effects of European integration on social policies and, more particularly, anti-poverty policies.[9] This was therefore more in the nature of a 'social policy regime' rather than a 'welfare state regime', in Esping-Andersen's use of the term. In addition to the (modern) Scandinavian, the (institutional) Bismarkian and the (residual) Anglo-Saxon models, Leibfried's paper also identifies a (rudimentary) Latin model in which he places Greece, Spain, southern Italy, Portugal and France. In some ways, he thought that, with the probable exceptions of France and Italy, these countries are close to the Anglo-Saxon countries in the sense that they emphasize entry into the labour market and the implementation of residual protection measures. However, these countries have something else in common: extremely large social security and pensions programmes, particularly old age pensions. Other common characteristics include the decisive influence of the Catholic Church; employment structures in which agriculture has long been, and may well still be, important; and traditional family structures (which have experienced upheavals of late, and give grounds for anxiety, particularly with regard to a sharp drop in the birth rate), with a major role for primary solidarities and mutual obligations. Moreover, in many cases, these countries have also undergone a delayed transition from an authoritarian political regime to a democratic regime, and have given a constitutional undertaking to construct a social welfare scheme. However, in this respect the welfare state may be more in the nature of a declaration or a promise than a fully implemented scheme (Leibfried 1993). Indeed, two important characteristics of the 'Latin fringe' are the delay in constructing social systems and the difficulties of implementation at a time of economic recession.[10]

THE IMPORTANCE OF THE FAMILY FOR UNDERSTANDING SOUTHERN EUROPE

There is no question that certain stereotypes are to be found in Greece, Italy, Spain and Portugal: they include the importance not only of religion and the Catholic Church, but also of the institution of the family and mutual obligations associated with bonds of kinship and marriage, and of recent transitions from authoritarian political regimes. However, are these specificities enough to establish a 'societal model' common to all of these different countries? Is France closer to these models or to the German model, as far as the construction of collective protection measures is concerned?

Practices and Values: Convergence or the Persistence of Specificities?

Roussel has recently commented on the concept of a 'Europe of families' (Roussel 1992; 1995). The diagnosis is based on two fundamental ideas. First, forms of family behaviour are still sharply contrasted and vary substantially between northern and southern European countries, with most of them in a kind of intermediate situation. Second, these contrasts are receding as a result of a slow process of convergence. Roussel presents the evolution of the main socio-demographic indicators relating to family life over the past 30 years, and identifies three major types of country: north European (Sweden, Denmark and Norway), with relatively high fertility rates and a high incidence of divorce, cohabitation and births out of wedlock; west European (Belgium, Luxembourg, the Netherlands, Germany, the United Kingdom and France), with a low fertility rate, an average-to-high incidence of divorce and a relatively low incidence of cohabitation and births out of wedlock; and south European (Spain, Greece, Italy and Portugal), with low fertility and divorce rates, and few instances of cohabitation or births out of wedlock. However, the most striking differences, which were reinforced during the period 1965–1975 (when there were rapid demographic changes in northern and then western Europe, and stability in the south), are now diminishing with the general shift of transformations within families moving from north to south, reflecting a decline in fertility rates, and an upward trend in the incidence of divorce, cohabitation and births outside wedlock. The impetus behind this change, according to Roussel, was the status and life situation of women – control over fertility and the achievement of independence through work. Other factors included the possibility or 'practicability' of these new forms of women's behaviour: on the one hand, a decline in institutional norms as well as in the role of religion (Catholicism in particular) and in the traditional values that it incorporates; and, on the other, the development of public support services for families, enabling women to shed some of the tasks that were traditionally devolved to them. From these changes there emerges a family model founded on the contract, the conjugal pact and affective relations: the 'individualist and relational family' (de Singly 1994), or the 'uncertain' family (Roussel 1989).

More recently, however, Roussel has claimed that the process of convergence is far from complete, with a difference opening up on marriage and as a function of the influence not of geography but of religious norms, bringing the countries of southern Europe and, for example, Ireland closer together.[11] Another specificity is the existing gap in the south between practice and opinion. For instance, on issues such as sexual freedom, abortion and the fact that a woman can want to have a child but refuse to live with the father, southern European countries are sometimes more radical than the rest. The tendency towards the liberalizing of opinions is therefore a phenomenon affecting the whole of Europe, with opinions apparently in advance of practice. This tendency towards the promotion of change and the move towards the modern family could well accelerate as young people are more open to change than adults and the elderly, and the process is gathering pace from one generation to the next. It is worth noting that the decline of religion is most marked among the young.

Galland and Lemel (1995) also reject the hypothesis of European convergence, demonstrating that the differences are still substantial. They contrast the 'Nordic group' and the 'Mediterraneo-Germanic group'. In addition to the 'modernity–tradition' contrast, Galland and Lemel propose a second analytical axis, which contrasts 'Europeans who are more prosperous and more supportive of a "civic culture" and Europeans whose level of satisfaction is lower and who feel less well integrated into their national societies' (1995: 125). Although these two typologies are very crude, they support the view that the transformation of forms of family behaviour is not in fact only an effect of values. Also involved are the conditions for the economic potential of these changes, with particular reference to the possibility of providing women with autonomy in domestic and family life.[12] This is where we rediscover the link between the economic model (and the welfare model) and the model of the family or the division of gender roles. Of course, such comparisons have their limitations, particularly when they operate on the basis of national averages and ignore local disparities,[13] but they do present interesting groupings of countries and indicate the possible direction of future change.

The north–south opposition is also at the heart of other approaches, including the work of Barrère-Maurisson and Marchand (1990) on links between family structures and labour markets. These two writers do not so much defend the hypothesis of a simple time-lag to explain differences, as that of 'societal models'; the latter include the effect of historical, institutional and political variables, which they mention but do not fully develop. In the south, where the trend for women to enter the labour market is poorly developed, there are more traditional family structures with a clear sexual division of roles and of distribution of domestic tasks – a kind of 'male breadwinner model'. By contrast, the north has a high incidence of female employment, often part time, and a larger number of single-person households; it is also characterized by a strongly de-institutionalized family structure. Here is another case where this opposition could be summarized in terms of tradition and modernity, with a number of west European countries (Belgium, France, the Netherlands and, to a certain extent, the United Kingdom) situated between the two extremes. This model also proposes another oppositional axis, based on dominant sectors of employment: the industrial East (Germany and Japan) and the tertiary West (the United States and the United Kingdom). In this model, France stands in some ways at the 'cross-roads of societies', Latin in one way and northern in another.

This review of elements of European comparison in terms of forms of family behaviour and values argues in favour of the hypothesis of irreducible specificities, which are removed as all countries in the European Union move closer together. At its heart lies not only the question of the place of women and the division of gender roles, but also the issue of economic development and the role that the state plays in supporting families.

Norms and Ways of Producing Laws: Basic Nuances, including Nuances between Latin Countries

There is no question here of trying to adopt an approach based on comparative law. But it is worth referring to a few recent works (Meulders-Klein 1993; Assier-Andrieu and Commaille 1995) that will help us assess whether the hypothesis of southern European specificity is sustainable in terms of norms and laws.

As far as relations between individuals, the family and the state are concerned, 'civil law' countries are frequently contrasted with 'common law' countries. The latter find their inspiration in an individualist philosophy, and refuse to allow the state to involve itself in private matters. There is hardly a single legal provision covering family relations.

The exceptions relate to the dissolution of marriage and problems over the transfer of estates. By contrast, civil law countries have always sought to guarantee a principle of mutual solidarity and legal obligations between family members (Lefaucheur and Martin 1995b). In this sense, to quote Portalis, 'the family is the source and basis of the civil society'.

Changes in family behaviour in civil law countries in the second half of the twentieth century have largely overturned the legal order instituted in the early nineteenth century. Some writers see this as a process of 'dejuridification' (Glendon 1989), or a gradual withdrawal of the law, which increasingly gives actors responsibility for inter-family relations – a kind of family self-determination. Others argue that this apparent withdrawal of civil law has been replaced by a considerable development in *social* law, and often compensates for the effects of this more liberal, individual behaviour (Schultheis 1992; Martin 1996a). Meulders-Klein acknowledges a general tendency towards neutrality in the law, but actually she supports the opposite hypothesis: this involves an extended juridification of the family in contemporary terms such as cohabitation and births out of wedlock. However, this tendency to update the law has not affected all civil law countries to the same extent; for example, it takes the form of very disparate legislation on divorce and a varying legal understanding of situations involving cohabitation. On the other hand, some tendencies seem to be relatively general: examples include the recognition, even the promotion, of parental co-responsibility for children and the promotion of the rights of individuals, particularly women and children, within the family.

Numerous differences are also to be found in the area of constitutional law. Most European countries make explicit references to the family in their constitutions, although with varying emphasis. Countries such as Ireland, Italy, Greece and Luxembourg are the most explicit; others, like Belgium, the Netherlands and Denmark, are not at all explicit. However, differences are most evident at the level of defining social legislation and setting up welfare states. Some countries, such as France and Belgium, have an explicit family policy; others, such as the United Kingdom and Portugal, have social measures that impact on the family. However, even where family policies are explicit, that is not to say that they necessarily have homogeneous objectives. For example, French family policies are characterized by an overlap and multiplicity of objectives: a birth rate objective, a 'familialist' objective, the distributive objective of providing horizontal compensation for the cost of running households with children, and the redistributive objective of providing vertical compensation for inequalities. These numerous approaches are the outcome of philosophical traditions aggregating and clashing with one another. Meanwhile, the neutrality of state intervention is sometimes guaranteed by the fact that these various objectives are pursued simultaneously and use a wide range of increasingly complex measures (Commaille 1994; Lhuillier and Martin 1995).

In spite of this diversity, a convergent tendency for the whole of Europe is emerging as a result of the overlapping crisis in the institution of the family and social welfare systems. Under pressure from what we might call the threat of exclusion, 'new poverty' or precariousness, the family seems to be more vulnerable when job insecurity and instability of relations coincide. However, the family is also seen as an irreplaceable source of protection, a kind of screen against the difficulties that exist in the world today, and sometimes as a substitute for the limitations of state intervention. To summarize, with the crisis that now faces measures of collective protection, the family has returned to the forefront of political preoccupations – whether in terms of expressing concern about, or criticizing, the spread of vulnerability and dependence (for example, single-parent families), or to urge the development of forms of solidarity of which it is the epicentre (Martin 1994; 1996b). I have proposed that we talk of the 'family question' in order to bring out the political debate on the family and its role as protector (Martin 1996a).

In fact, a fierce debate is now raging between those who defend the family unit and those who support the individuals who make it up, for example women and children; between those who are afraid that the opening up of individual rights will weaken the institution of the family still further, and those who believe that the family can be defended only at the expense of women, in particular, by awarding derived rights; and between those who would like more state intervention and those who think that responsibility for protection should be handed to the private sector. The tendency to make forms of private solidarity into a major political issue is now widespread, but the scenarios adopted in various European countries are sometimes very varied.

In this regard, the collection of essays edited by Assier-Andrieu and Commaille (1995) is illuminating. In their analysis of the process of constructing laws relating to family relations in five countries (Belgium, Spain, France, Italy and Portugal), they demonstrate the importance of:

- socio-political contexts;

- ruptures that legislation sometimes tries to mark;

- ideological debates and controversies;

- relational networks and public policy networks;

6881

- the confrontation of values ('freedom', the 'sacred' and 'progress');

- the Catholic Church's role in influencing the state to a greater or lesser extent;

- and genealogical effects, which explain how reform is carried out primarily in reference to what has gone before.

This comparison shows how essential a genetic approach is to any comparative project. Assier-Andrieu and Commaille are particularly insistent that the relationship between lawyers and politicians varies substantially from country to country.

Three models of regulation emerge from this comparison. First, there is 'dogmatic regulation', which is characterized by the fact that legal lawmakers prevail over political lawmakers (for example, the French law of 1972 on filiation). Second, there is 'active regulation', which is expressed in a complementary relationship between legal action and political action (for example, the laws of March 1988 in Spain and those of November 1977 in Portugal). These first two models both presume stable, legal reference-points on the family or, to put it in another way, secure social representations concerning the position of the family and the individual in relation to the state. In the third, 'passive regulation' model, however, the authors see the law losing ground to politics (for example, the French laws of July 1987 and of January 1993), and that is a good reason for using this model as the outline for future regulation, although it is a step that the authors are not totally prepared to make.

Given the views expressed in these various works, it is quite unsatisfactory to see southern Europe as a collection of countries experiencing delays in their processes of economic and social construction. Specificities exist, that much is certain. However, these specificities – or 'societal configurations' – are not necessarily shared by all the countries of southern Europe. Each country has its own configuration. Clearly, Spain and Portugal have several characteristics in common, such as a recent democratic transition, delayed economic development and commitments linked to this relatively abrupt political transition. However, the differences are just as great if we look at such issues as unemployment rates and female participation rates. Can the two countries effectively be brought closer together? It follows that it is sometimes more useful to talk about models of regulation that are common to various countries during certain periods, and about discrepancies that can occur at other times. Typologies have less to do with geographical discrepancies than with temporal discrepancies.

THE SOUTHERN MODEL OF WELFARE

Ferrera (1996) has attempted to search for a southern Europe model among the elements that are common to the social welfare systems of Italy, Greece, Spain and Portugal. He discovered that each of these countries has implemented a two-fold system: first, a transfer model based on occupational status, influenced by Bismarkian principles, and characterized by major institutional fragmentation; and second, a national health system aiming at universal cover. However, the most specific characteristic appears to be the dualist or non-egalitarian character of these systems. Briefly, they give (sometimes very) generous protection to people who are occupationally well integrated (with some of the best retirement pension levels in Europe), making them 'hyper-protected', yet they give very poor protection to those who belong to vulnerable, or informal, sectors of the economy, and no protection at all to people who lack money and status (there is no social security safety net or minimum wage system for individuals and families without enough money). This is why a lot of people are excluded from entitlement to social welfare – those who are neither old nor invalids, those with neither a job nor an income, and those with no rights from previous contributions.[14]

This dualism is equally identifiable at the level of health services. In fact, despite the existence of national health systems in Italy, Portugal and Spain, it is clearly a case of a policy of advertised claims, which in turn is frequently the result of promises made during the period of democratic transition (for example in Portugal). In fact, funding for this type of health service comes not out of taxation but from a contributory scheme; at the same time, there continue to be major territorial inequalities in terms of access to care, and the private sector plays a leading role. Ferrera even sees this collusion between the public and private sectors – with its clientelist dimension and a tendency to involve 'business' and corruption – as another specificity of these countries; access to social welfare even comes close to being a unit of monetary exchange in relations between political and social groups, including trade unions, and particularly at a local level. The clientelist dimension is also observable in the way the bureaucracy functions. The absence of a tradition of public service and of an administrative culture ensures that access to rights is not universal or egalitarian, but functions on the basis of personal connections, selection and 'patronage'.

De Sousa Santos (1987) confirms this analysis in his account of the way the welfare state was constructed in Portugal following the 'Carnation Revolution' of 1974.[15] He also emphasizes the extent to which the apparent analogy between what happened in Portugal and the construction of welfare states in western European countries has masked quite different political processes. For example, the revolutionary period promoted a series of social rights that were very substantial but were not founded on any social accord or long-standing social struggle. According to de Sousa Santos, this in turn explains why these rights were not internalized by the administration; there was even a vague feeling that they were undeserved and could well disappear. Revolution appeared to produce a kind of 'hyper-socialization' of the working class, and covered up an older tradition of atomized interests, clan individualism and 'social and political incompetence'. As far as the crisis is concerned, de Sousa Santos argues that it is important to avoid confusing the financial crises in all the social welfare systems. 'It is one thing to find ways of breaking or renewing a politico-social pact that goes back many years; it is another – and an absurd idea it is, too – to try to change a pact that has never existed' (de Sousa Santos 1987: 69).

A number of important common characteristics emerge from the above: long periods of authoritarianism abruptly followed by a kind of atrophy of civil society, with an especially influential role for left-wing parties, including radical parties; the powerful role of the Catholic Church, particularly in respect to moral family policy; sectoral and territorial dualism within the system; the strength of corporatist traditions; and the weakness of state institutions and administrative culture. Other common characteristics are of an economic nature: the issue of bureaucratic rationalization under pressure from European integration; control of public deficits and public debts; relatively low labour costs accompanied by low productivity and, therefore, low competitiveness; a high risk of social exclusion, particularly in certain regions; and a weakening of the family.

Once again, however, we find the 'family question' occupying centre stage. In this case, it makes its presence felt through the critical role played by the family in terms of protection. Much work on Portugal puts forward the same hypothesis of the existence of a real 'welfare society' whose protection provision is based on personal connections, affective links, networks of exchange and sociability, bartering and a non-cash economy (de Sousa Santos 1987, 1994; Hespanha 1995; Arriscado Nunes 1995). These writers stress that the strength of primary linkages may be less a sign of strong social links in southern Europe than the result of inadequacies in social welfare. In a way, the family fills the gaps of the welfare state, which in Portugal is very inadequately developed and non-egalitarian. Furthermore, these primary solidarities need to be supported by social exchanges and relations, but that is scarcely facilitated by the process of industrialization and geographical mobility. Portugal appears to be a society whose normative referential is strongly marked by a rural tradition, although it has experienced rapid and profound transformation, hence the major shifts in socio-demographic indicators between town and countryside, and between the north, south and centre of the country (Nunes de Almeida et al. 1995; Ferreira de Almeida et al. 1994; Rocha Pinto 1994).

These solidarities also have another characteristic: they are selective because they are essentially based on the identification of close family members and others (Arriscado Nunes 1995). In this way, they have a potential both for humanization and emancipation and for inequalities and exclusion. However, what makes the biggest impression on these writers is the re-encoding that these solidarities undergo: either they are coded as archaisms, a hangover from a traditional rural society that is sometimes thought to be disappearing, or they are coded as the foundation of the social and civic bond at the present time when only these private forms of solidarity seem to be able to compensate for the state's withdrawal. They are therefore seen either as a substitute for public intervention or as complementary to it. In a comparative analysis of the role that families play in dealing with the dependence of the elderly, I too have identified this permanent work of coding and re-coding the family question (Lesemann and Martin 1993; Martin 1995a; 1995b).

To summarize, in the above example of Portugal, we can see that the key issue may not be to seize on the importance of the family's contribution to the protection of individuals, but rather to understand the kind of specific arrangement that exists between the welfare society (neighbours, families and relatives) and the welfare state, and also between the welfare state and the market. This 'state/family/market' link ensures that the crisis in the system of social welfare inevitably produces a new linkage between other elements in the triad. The weakening of the welfare state may also bring about a similar process in 'welfare society'. This may be where a south European specificity is to be found: the fact that the development of social welfare systems took place in a period of economic recession, thereby jeopardizing complete development, while the family was engaging in a process of change linked to the transformation of the labour market and the extension of a number of values relating to the domestic sphere.

Such an interpretation might come close to the proposals put forward by Lautier (1995: 488) when he writes of the state and social matters: 'What we refer to as "social matters" springs not from one of the three orders (economic, political and domestic) but from the connection between them'.

SOME AVENUES OF ENQUIRY IN THE ABSENCE OF A CONCLUSION

We do not believe that a comparison of social welfare systems is possible without a genealogical or genetic approach. It may be that the key issue is not to bring the systems closer together on the basis of convergent indicators, but to identify a process and pinpoint elements of discussion that lie at the heart of decisions and measures that have been implemented. It follows that comparison cannot only be made at the level of an *a posteriori* assessment of measures and their effects, but must also incorporate an 'upstream' phase, so to speak, that focuses on foundations. Why is this or that measure adopted at a given moment, as a function of which arguments and controversies? As Merrien (1993: 89) suggests, 'the main feature of this kind of comparative analysis of public policies is an attempt to determine why an action is legitimate here, and not there, and why certain problems appear on the public agenda in some countries, and not at all, or more slowly or in a different way in others'. Accordingly, it is just as important to take account of what has gone before – 'the political heritage' (Heclo 1974); this means that, in order to be understood, a new public policy often has to be related to the policy that preceded it, and whose negative or 'perverse' effects it seeks to change.

We have used this approach in comparing European family policies. In an analysis of France, Italy, Portugal and the United Kingdom, we have tried to show how systems deal with the issue: 'Who provides for the child whose father is absent?' (Lefaucheur and Martin 1995a). This issue it translated differently, depending on the human group, and the place and time, into norms of relations between the sexes, the establishment of bonds and the allocation of responsibility for bringing up children. In turn, different solutions have been adopted and experimented with at different times and in different places. Different paradigms have appeared and continue to be operated, and the passage from one to the next triggers confrontations and controversies over the aims pursued, and the adoption of not only political positions, but also scientific and expert views. Merrien's (1993) concept of a 'societal paradigm' is useful in understanding these differences, but is less effective for contrasting countries than periods of history. For example, during the 1990s, France and the United Kingdom appeared to be clearly opposed in their choice of policies in this area, whereas their political choices or orientations during the 1970s were much more convergent (the policy of providing a single-parent benefit in France and the Finer Report proposals in the United Kingdom). If the comparison had stopped at the period 1970–75, one might have concluded that policies relating to the situation of single-parent families in the United Kingdom and France were similar. Fifteen years on, a striking gap had opened up between the two (Martin 1995c; 1996c). Depending on the historical period being analysed, an identical type of political choice and protection system in two countries can lead to a substantial difference in another period. The usefulness of comparing social welfare systems may lie in comprehending first the evolutions, the break-ups and the confrontations of philosophies that form the basis of these evolutions, and second, the paradigms that go beyond national specificities and geographical differences between systems, but that are continuously fashioning and re-fashioning them.

Many complementary approaches have to be developed for comparison, including classifications or typologies (*a priori* or *a posteriori*) on the basis of socio-economic and socio-political indicators; and genetic or genealogical approaches giving greater importance to the historical process of social policy development, and acknowledging that diversity is not necessarily a handicap but also a source of richness. It is essential, particularly with regard to the possible specificity of southern European countries, to look at processes reconstructing the question of social welfare, seen as a combination of private protection (family, close relatives and even individual insurance-based protection) and collective protection. The family question is therefore an inescapable component of any consideration of the welfare state.

NOTES

1. Although work in this field is also expanding rapidly in Italy and Spain. On France, see Meny and Thoenig (1989), Jobert (1994), Théret (1996) and Bonoli and Palier (this volume).
2. This applies even more to Italy where there is a manifest need to distinguish the principle of social rights from their effective implementation and consider the considerable regional disparities (see Fargeon, this volume, Bagnasco 1990 and Saraceno 1992).
3. 'The objectives of Beveridge using the methods of Bismark' (Palier and Bonoli 1995).
4. 'Key shortcomings are identified when the criteria underlying this typology are examined from a gender perspective. The family–State nexus has not been rigorously integrated into the analysis and the utility of the de-commodification concept for differentiating welfare states is thrown into question' (Daly 1994: 101).
5. This also applies to Germany (Scheiwe 1994).
6. This also applies to Belgium (Scheiwe 1994).
7. This schema may be further complicated if, as Lefaucheur (1992) proposes – with support from Brackman, Erie and Rein (1988) – account is taken of the fact that the provision of services to families to guarantee reproduction has been overtaken by a highly feminized labour market. In a way, women are 'wedded to the Welfare State', as these American writers put it, in the sense that they are both recipients and providers of reproduction services. The different welfare state regimes proposed by Esping-Andersen may now be seen in this light as offering women more or less opportunity to achieve autonomy from the marriage bond, and also more or less protection against

the risks of impoverishment that are linked to this autonomy (see Lefaucheur 1992).
8. Ferrera (1996) has made a more in-depth analysis which we consider below.
9. Leibfried contrasts two possible models of European integration of social policies: a Europeanization (bureaucratization) (top-down) model and an Americanization (or Balkanization) model of social policies. In Leibfried's view, the bottom-up model is still-born; he also considers that the Balkanization model is the more likely.
10. This proposal is much more convincing than the one put forward by F.G. Castles, which is based on a comparison of levels of social transfers, and makes south European countries into a sub-type of the conservative model – the 'weak conservative family of nations' (Castles 1995).
11. 'Today we have two Europes: one where marriage continues to be the threshold of family life, and another where this has ceased to be the case, or at least where it has ceased to be essential' (Roussel 1995: 56).
12. Roussel supports this diagnosis as follows: 'Economic stagnation among Mediterranean countries, and particularly aggravation of economic disparities with the north, could delay convergence between models of poorer and better-off countries. There will be convergence between matrimonial models only when it becomes economically possible' (1995: 60).
13. Work on Italy (Barbagli 1995), Portugal (Nunes de Almeida et al. 1995) and also the United Kingdom (Duncan 1995) point to very significant regional and local disparities. See also Fargeon, Rico and Laparra and Aguilar (this volume).
14. This was the situation at the beginning of the 1990s. Some important current changes are taking place with the implementation of minimum safety nets in Spain and Portugal.
15. An analysis of the specificities of the Portuguese welfare state is also contained in Mozzicafreddo (1992). In particular, this describes the rapid passage from a welfare state (which emerged from the revolution of 1974–1976 and stressed the promotion of social rights and the emancipation of the working class) to the definition of a system focusing more on economic development and employment support than on social protection for individuals and families. To a certain extent, this decidedly liberal policy, which was implemented from the beginning of the 1980s, is close to the British system in operation during the same period.

REFERENCES

Arriscado Nunes, J. (1995): 'As Solidariedades primarias e os Limites da Sociedade-Providencia', *Revista Critica de Ciencias Sociais* 42, pp.5–25.
Assier-Andrieu, L. and J. Commaille (eds) (1995): *Politique des lois en Europe*, Paris: LGDJ.
Bagnasco, A. (1990): 'Trois Italies', in D. Schnapper and H. Mendras (eds), *Six manières d'être européen*, Paris: Gallimard NRF, pp.173–96.
Baldwin, P. (1990): *The Politics of Social Solidarity. Class Bases of the European Welfare State 1875–1975*, Cambridge: CUP.
Barbagli, M. (1995): 'Diversités italiennes', in M. Gullestadt and M. Segalen (eds), *La famille en Europe. Parenté et perpétuation familiale*, Paris: La Découverte, pp.45–61.
Barrère-Maurisson, M.-A. and O. Marchand (1990): 'Structures familiales et marché du travail dans les pays développés', *Economie et Statistique* 235, pp.19–30.
Brackman H., S.P. Erie and M. Rein (1988): 'Wedded to the Welfare-State', in J. Jenson, E. Hagen and C. Reddy (eds), *Feminization of the Labour Force: Paradoxes and Promises*, Cambridge and Oxford: Polity Press and Basic Blackwell.
Castles, F.G. (1995): 'Welfare State Development in Southern Europe', *West European Politics* 18/2, pp.291–313.
Commaille, J. (1994): *L'esprit sociologique des lois*, Paris: Puf.
Daly, M. (1994): 'Comparing Welfare States: Towards a Gender Friendly Approach', in D.

Sainsbury (ed.), *Gendering Welfare States*, London: Sage, pp.101–17.

Del Re, A. (1994): *Les femmes et l'Etat-providence*. *Les politiques sociales en France dans les années trente*, Paris: l'Harmattan.

Dumons, B. and G. Pollet (1994): *L'Etat et les retraites. Génèse d'une politique*, Paris: Belin.

Duncan, S. (1995): 'Theorizing European Gender Systems', *Journal of European Social Policy* 5/4, pp.263–84.

Esping-Andersen, G. (1990): *The Three Worlds of Welfare Capitalism*, Cambridge: Polity Press.

Evans, P., T. Rueschmeyer and T. Skocpol (eds) (1985): *Bringing the State Back in*, Cambridge: CUP.

Fargeon, V. (1996): 'Social Assistance and the North–South Cleavage in Italy', *South European Society & Politics* 1/3 (Winter) pp.135–54.

Ferrera, M. (1996): 'The Southern Model of Welfare in Social Europe', *Journal of European Social Policy* 6/1, pp.17–37.

Ferreira de Almeida, J., A. Firmino da Costa and F. Luis Machado (1994): 'A recomposiçao socioprofessional e novos protagonismos', in A. Réis (ed.), *Portugal. Vinte Anos de Democracia*, Lisboa: Circulo dos Leitores, pp.307–30.

Galland, O. and Y. Lemel (1995): 'La permanence des différences', *Futuribles* 200, pp.113–30.

Glendon, M.-A. (1989), *The Transformation of the Family Law. State, Law and Family in the United Sates and Western Europe*, Chicago: U. of Chicago Press.

Hatzfeld, H. (1971): *Du paupérisme à la sécurité sociale. Essai sur les origines de la sécurité sociale en France, 1850–1940*, Paris: Armand Colin.

Heclo, H. (1974): *Modern Social Policy in Britain and Sweden*, Yale UP.

Hespanha, P. (1995): 'Vers une société providence simultanément pré et post-moderne'. L'état des solidarités intergénérationnelles au Portugal', in C. Attias-Donfut (ed.), *Les solidarités entre générations. Vieillesse, familles, Etat*, Paris: Nathan, pp.209–21.

Jobert, B. (ed.) (1994): *Le tournant néo-libéral en Europe*, Paris: l'Harmattan.

Join-Lambert, M-T. (ed.) (1994): *Politiques sociales*, Paris: Dalloz, Presses de la FNSP.

Kangas, O. (1994): 'The Merging of Welfare State Models? Past and Present Trends in Finnish and Swedish Social Policy', *Journal of European Social Policy* 4/2, pp.79–94.

Kemeny, J. (1995): 'Theories of Power in the Three Worlds of Welfare Capitalism', *Journal of European Social Policy* 5/2, pp.87–96.

Korpi, W. (1978): *The Working Class in Welfare Capitalism: Work, Unions and Politics in Sweden*, London: Routledge & Kegan Paul.

Lautier, B. (1995): 'L'Etat et le social', in B. Théret (ed.), *L'Etat, la finance et le social*, Paris: La Découverte, pp.483–508.

Lefaucheur, N. (1992): 'Maternité, famille, Etat', in F. Thébaud (ed.), *Histoire des femmes. Le XXe siècle*, Paris: Plon, pp.411–30.

Lefaucheur, N. and C. Martin (eds) (1995a): *Qui doit nourrir l'enfant dont le père est absent? Recherche sur les fondements des politiques familiales européennes (Angleterre, France, Italie, Portugal)*, Paris: Rapport pour la Caisse nationale des allocations familiales.

Lefaucheur, N. and C. Martin (1995b): 'Defining Family Obligations in France', in J. Millar and A. Warman (eds), *Defining Family Obligations in Europe*, Bath: Bath Social Policy Papers 23, University of Bath, pp.87–106.

Leibfried, S. (1993): 'Towards a European Welfare State?', in C. Jones (ed.), *New Perspectives on the Welfare State in Europe*, London: Routledge, pp.133–56.

Leira, A. (1992): *Welfare States and Working Mothers. The Scandinavian Experience*, Cambridge: CUP.

Lesemann, F. and C. Martin (eds) (1993): *Home based Care. The Elderly, the Family and the Welfare-State. An International Comparison*, Ottawa: U. of Ottawa Press.

Lewis, J. (1992): 'Gender and the Development of Welfare Regimes', *Journal of European Social Policy* 2/3, pp.159–73.

Lewis, J. (1995): 'Egalité, différence et rapports sociaux de sexes dans les Etats-providence du XXe siècle', in Ephesia (ed.), *La place des femmes*, Paris: La Découverte, pp.407–22.

Lhuillier, J.-M. and Martin, C. (1995): 'The Obscure Objective of Family Policies in France', *Social Policy and Administration* 29/4, pp.371–6.

Martin, C. (1994): 'Entre Etat et famille-providence', in J.-L. Laville (ed.), *L'économie solidaire, une perspective internationale*, Paris: Desclee de Brouwer, pp.223–51.

Martin, C. (1995a): 'Vieillissement, dépendance et solidarités en Europe. Redécouverte des solidarités informelles et enjeux normatifs', in C. Attias-Donfut (ed.), *Les solidarités entre générations. Vieillesse, familles, Etat*, Paris: Nathan, pp.223–44.

Martin, C. (1995b): 'Os Limites da Protecçao da Familia. Introduçao a uma discussao sobre as novas solidariedades na relaçao Familia-Estado', *Revista Critica de Ciencias Sociais* 42, pp.53–76.

Martin, C. (1995c): 'Father, Mother and the Welfare-State: Family and Social Transfers after Marital Breakdown', *Journal of European Social Policy* 5/1, pp.43–63.

Martin, C. (1996a): 'Le renouveau de la question familiale. Protection privée, protection publique', in D. Le Gall and C. Martin (eds), *Familles et politiques sociales. Dix questions sur le lien familial contemporain*, Paris: L'Harmattan, pp.247–72.

Martin, C. (1996b): 'Solidarités familiales: débat scientifique, enjeu politique', in J.-C. Kaufmann (ed.), *Faire ou faire-faire. Familles et services*, Rennes: Presses universitaires de Rennes, pp.55–73.

Martin, C. (1996c): 'La charge de l'enfant après la désunion: Logiques d'action publique en France et au Royaume-Uni', in R. Dandurand, C. Le Bourdais and R. Hurtubise (eds), *Enfances*, Québec: Presses de l'Université Laval, pp.59–80.

Meny, Y. and J.-C. Thoenig (1989): *Politiques publiques*, Paris: Puf.

Merrien, F.-X. (1993): 'Les politiques publiques, entre paradigmes et controverses', in CRESAL (ed.), *Les raisons de l'action publique, entre expertise et débat*, Paris: l'Harmattan, pp.87–100.

Meulders-Klein, M.-T. (1993): 'Individualisme et communautarisme: l'individu, la famille et l'Etat en Europe occidentale', *Droit et société* 23/24, pp.163–97.

Mozzicafreddo, J. (1992): 'O Estado-Providencia em Portugal', *Sociologia – Problemas e Praticas* 12, pp.57–89.

Nunes de Almeida, A., C. Ferreira, F. Ferrao and I. Margarida André (1995): *Os Padroes Recentes da Fecundidade em Portugal*, Lisboa: Cadernos Condiçao Feminina, Ministerio do Emprego e da Segurança Social.

Palier, B. and G. Bonoli (1995): 'Entre Bismarck et Beveridge. Crises de la sécurité sociale et politique(s)', *Revue française de sciences politiques* 45/4, pp.668–98.

Renard, D. (1995): 'Intervention de l'Etat et génèse de la protection sociale en France', *Lien social et Politiques* 33, pp.13–26.

Rocha Pinto, M.L. (1994): 'As Tendências Demograficas', in A. Réis (ed.), *Portugal. Vinte Anos de Democracia*, Lisboa: Circulo dos Leitores, pp.296–306.

Roussel, L. (1989): *La famille incertaine*, Paris: Odile Jacob.

Roussel, L. (1992): 'La famille en Europe occidentale: différences et convergence', in A. Nunes de Almeida *et al.* (eds), *Familles et contextes sociaux. Les espaces et les temps de la diversité*, Lisbon: CIES, pp.115–32.

Roussel, L. (1995): 'Vers une Europe des familles?', *Futuribles* 200, pp.47–62.

Sainsbury, D. (ed.) (1994): *Gendering Welfare States*, London: Sage.

Saraceno, C. (1992): *Italy*, Consolidated Report for the Observatory on National Policies to Combat Social Exclusion, Brussels: European Commission.

Scheiwe, K. (1994): 'Labour Market, Welfare State and Family Institutions: the Links to Mothers' Poverty Risks', *Journal of European Social Policy* 4/3.

Schultheis, F. (1992): 'L'avenir de la famille au centre des antinomies de la modernité', in Haut Conseil de la population et de la famille (ed), *Du politique et du social dans l'avenir de la famille*, Paris: La Documentation Française, pp.49–56.

Siaroff, A. (1994): 'Work, Welfare and Gender Equality: a new Typology', in D. Sainsbury (ed.), *Gendering Welfare States*, London: Sage, pp.82–100.

de Singly, F. (1994): *Sociologie de la famille contemporaine*, Paris: Nathan.

de Sousa Santos, B. (1987): 'O Estado, a Sociedade e as Politicas Sociais. O Caso das

politicas de Saude', *Revista Critica de Ciencias Sociais* 23, pp.13–74.
de Sousa Santos, B. (1994): *Pela Mao de Alice. O Social e o Politico na post-modernidade,* Porto: Afrontamento.
Taylor-Gooby, P. (1991): 'Welfare State Regimes and Welfare Citizenship', *Journal of European Social Policy* 1/2, pp.93–105.
Théret, B. (1996): 'De la comparabilité des systèmes nationaux de protection sociale dans les sociétés salariales. Essai d'analyse structurelle', in MIRE (ed.), *Comparer les systèmes de protection sociale, Rencontres de Berlin,* 2, Paris: Ministère des Affaires Sociales. pp.439–503.

Is the South so Different?
Italian and Spanish Families in
Comparative Perspective

TERESA JURADO GUERRERO
and MANUELA NALDINI

This article analyses family changes in Italy and Spain from 1960
to 1990 and contrasts them with four central/northern European
countries. Italy and Spain show extremely rapid family changes,
which nevertheless do not lead to a convergence between
southern and central/northern families. The particularities of the
southern family model are a high degree of cross-generational
cohabitation, a high frequency of social contacts and help within
kinship, a strong institutionalization of marriage, a low female
employment rate in the formal labour market, a low fertility rate
and widespread family and child-oriented attitudes. In addition,
relations between generations are seen more in terms of
obligations than in terms of individual choice. We conclude that
the specific economic situation, the particularities of social
policies and the family culture in Italy and Spain are important
barriers to a further individualization of family relations in these
societies.

The socio-economic crisis that has affected all European countries since
the mid-1970s has gradually produced a collective loss of faith in the
possibility of uninterrupted economic growth and disillusion concerning
the programmes and promises of the welfare society. As a result of the
crisis, the institutional framework began to change and the social
division of responsibilities among the various institutional spheres, state,
market and family, had to (and still has to) be renegotiated (Flora 1985).
In the new social and economic context, interest in the family in the
analysis of western welfare society has become greater.

From a cross-national perspective it is often assumed that southern
welfare states have a different division of labour between state, market
and family than other northern/central European societies (Ferrera

We would like to thank Peter Flora for proposing the idea of this article and for his useful
comments during the writing process.

1994). Studies show that, despite the development of the welfare state, the family and the 'serving work' carried out by women in southern welfare societies (Balbo 1983) are still indispensable for the satisfaction of many basic needs. The changing age structure of the population, the decreasing fertility rate and emerging female employment patterns in Italy and Spain may affect the southern division of labour in important ways. While analysts are now emphasizing the importance of the family for the satisfaction of basic needs in this period of welfare state crisis, the most 'family-oriented'[1] countries may be moving towards greater individualism. Is this a contradiction? First of all, we need to determine how far the family is changing in the south.

A SOUTHERN EUROPEAN FAMILY MODEL?

Since 1965, a reduction in the fertility rate and an increase in the divorce rate has taken place in most European countries, with varying intensity and timing. This new family behaviour has been related to the gradual diffusion of cohabitation and to the increase in births out of wedlock. Relations between the sexes and generations have changed most profoundly. Equal opportunities became an important issue in public life (Roussel 1992), and changes in family roles also occurred. More women have entered the labour market, in a wider range of occupations and for a longer period, than at any other time since the Industrial Revolution (Rapoport 1989). During the 1970s, these family changes were far-reaching in Scandinavia and widespread in central Europe, but they remained weak in southern Europe.

Roussel (1992, 1994) has classified European countries, on the basis of demographic indicators, into three homogeneous groups regarding the family: the Scandinavian countries (Sweden, Norway, Finland, Denmark and Iceland), which were at the forefront of family changes, given increasing numbers of cohabitees and births out of wedlock; central Europe (Germany, France, Belgium, Luxembourg and Switzerland) which soon followed Scandinavia; and the Mediterranean countries (Spain, Italy, Greece and Portugal) and Ireland which have only recently adopted elements of the 'new' family model. But how can we explain the persistence of differences in family structures and behaviour across countries? Are they due to differences in timing or in pattern?

An overview of Italian and Spanish families reveals several demographic similarities. First, since the 1980s, Italy and Spain have both experienced a rapid decrease in fertility rates. Second, unmarried young people remain at home longer and kin and solidarity networks are more intense than elsewhere in Europe, with single-person households remaining the exception. Third, in Italy and Spain the number of divorces, cohabiting couples and births out of wedlock are still quite low (Flaquer 1994). In other words, the degree of institutionalization of marriage as a central family institution seems to be higher, and family solidarity more important, than in central/northern European countries.[2]

These characteristics could be ascribed to late modernization. But while this interpretation is partly correct, it does not explain everything. First, Italy and Spain both display indicators of modernity (the rapid decline in fertility) and traditionality (marriage as an institution is still very important). Second, the modernization process has not produced the same results in each country, because traditions and cultural contexts have been incorporated differently during industrialization. For example, the economic importance of small enterprises in some areas of Italy shows how a specific family tradition (the extended family) can produce a special kind of modernization. Modernization does not affect all parts of society to the same degree. A more detailed investigation is required.

ITALY AND SPAIN: AN OVERVIEW OF SOCIO-POLITICAL CHANGES

Modernization has been very rapid in both Italy and Spain. In Italy, it took place later than in other European countries, between the end of the 1950s and the beginning of the 1960s. In Spain, it began later and was even more rapid than in Italy, as shown in Figure 1. This period was also characterized by structural employment shortages and profound geographical disparities within the two countries, prompting large-scale internal and external migrations from the 1960s to the mid-1970s.

The process of family change in Italian and Spanish societies was related to changes both in social stratification and economic development and was accelerated by an intensive and rapid development of the welfare state (cf. Figure 1). Indicators of discontinuity in family values and attitudes – first in behaviour and then in legislation – started to appear in Italy in the mid-1950s and accelerated in the second half of the 1960s. In Spain, families began to transform at the end of the 1960s, but because of the relatively high number of members in Spanish families, the low number of publicly financed places for child care and the low level of consumer goods to facilitate housework, traditional ideas about the family division of labour and the authoritarian political system made further changes difficult before democratization. In Spain, the imitation of western European behaviour was important: as a result of tourism, emigration and the mass media, new ideas began to penetrate Spanish society (Conde 1982).

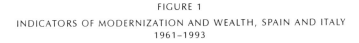

FIGURE 1
INDICATORS OF MODERNIZATION AND WEALTH, SPAIN AND ITALY
1961–1993

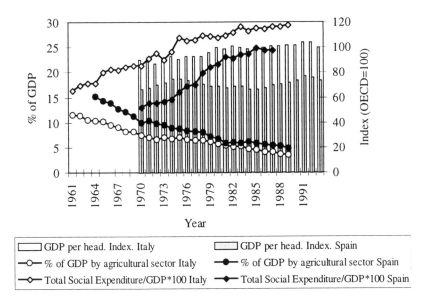

GDP per head. Index. Italy	GDP per head. Index. Spain
—○— % of GDP by agricultural sector Italy	—●— % of GDP by agricultural sector Spain
—◇— Total Social Expenditure/GDP*100 Italy	—◆— Total Social Expenditure/GDP*100 Spain

Sources: For per cent of GDP per sector: OECD 1980; 1989; 1991; MZES 1994. IC 1. For total social expenditure: Alcaide Inchausti 1988: Tab.24, 25; Ferrera 1984: Tab.4. For GDP per head: OECD 1995: 148

The Italian welfare state developed during the 1970s and early 1980s, and soon reached average European levels (Ascoli 1984). In the 1970s there was also a major expansion of social and caring services (kindergartens, day care for children under three, home help for elderly, etc.). In Spain, the welfare state expanded about ten years later, during the 1980s. The different social security systems were enlarged, health and old-age pension benefits were universalized and new assistance schemes were introduced (Guillén 1992).

As a result of the specific political-ideological configurations of the two countries, the process of legal change began only in the 1970s in Italy, and in the 1980s in Spain. Italy changed its institutional-political framework after fascism and World War II, but family relations were strongly influenced by the traditional values and norms defined by the Catholic Church and codified during Fascism (i.e. the *codice Rocco* in 1942). For more than forty years, the Christian Democratic Party was the main governmental force and, alongside a strong Catholic Church, it helped reinforce traditional family patterns and delayed the reform of family law. The Spanish case was similar: there, a fascist dictatorship, together with the support of the Catholic Church, prevented a change in family-related legislation until the end of the 1970s.

In Italy, the 1970s saw a real process of modernization and secularization: important legislation concerning gender roles and the family was approved; divorce was legalized (in 1970); family law was reformed and modernized (in 1975); and in the same year the age of majority was lowered to 18. Equal treatment at work was introduced in 1977, and abortion was legally authorized in 1978 (Vincenzi Amato 1988). In Spain, after the end of dictatorship, there was a peaceful and gradual transition to a pluralistic, democratic political system from 1975 to 1981. With the reform of the *Código Civil* in 1981, civil marriage became an option for citizens. Questions regarding marital break-up passed from the responsibility of the Church to that of the state. These reforms also led to equality between spouses: wives were no longer legally bound to obey their husbands. Rules regarding finance in marriage, infidelity, paternity, children born out of wedlock and other family matters were also changed (Alberdi and Alberdi 1982). Since the mid-1980s, abortion has been legal in some cases, and cohabiting and homosexual couples can register their unions in municipalities.

In countries like Italy and Spain, where rapid modernization has taken place, incongruencies can be noted in the process of social change: between economic, demographic and family changes, on the one hand, and legislative and welfare-state transformations on the other. The rapidity of change has made adaptation very difficult. In addition, important cleavages in regional economic development have influenced family changes and the development of the welfare state, delaying or even preventing them in the more backward regions (Conde 1982; Paci 1982).

FAMILY CHANGES IN ITALY AND SPAIN IN THE EUROPEAN CONTEXT

In this section we describe the changes which have occurred in the family mainly at the national level[3] and by looking at the different phases of the family cycle. The analysis of family changes can be made at two different theoretical levels. First, the relationships between different societal institutions can be studied, that is, the relations of the family with the state, the Church and the labour market. Second, the 'black box' of the family can be opened, revealing a social unit structured by dimensions of gender and generation or as a unit related to other family units within social networks. We will first focus on the second level of analysis – the functioning of the family – and then try to relate this to other societal institutions.

Changes in the Family Formation Phase: Marriage Patterns and Values

According to Golini (1988), 'one of the most important characteristics of the recent Italian demographic developments is the reduction of the number of marriages'. This change began in the 1970s, later than in other European countries, and is common to all regions but more important in the centre and north. In Spain, the gross marriage rate has decreased in general since 1981 with a certain stability between 1986 and 1990. From 1982 one can also detect regional differences in Spain, but they do not seem to be very important, nor are they clearly structured (Eurostat 1992b; Delgado 1993).

The data seem to support the hypothesis of delayed marriages. While in Italy the total number of marriages has decreased, it is especially the case for young women. At the same time, the marriage rate for women over 25 has increased (Golini and Menniti 1994). The part of the population that has changed its behaviour most rapidly is that of women living in the large towns of the centre and the north (Golini 1988). In Spain, too, the data show that since 1980 the percentage of people marrying before the age of 25 has decreased. The average age of women marrying for the first time rose in 1990, but remains lower than in Denmark, France and Germany although higher than in Britain (Delgado 1993). In Spain and Italy, a number of circumstances favour the delay of marriage: high unemployment rates and increasingly precarious employment for young people, expensive housing, the recent extension of higher education and cultural shifts after 1968 concerning sexual relations before marriage. Another indicator of changing marriage patterns in Italy and Spain is the increase in civil marriages in the last decade.

Can the delay of marriages and increasing civil marriage rates be regarded as indications of a more negative attitude towards the institution of marriage? To answer this question, we will examine attitude surveys in a comparative perspective.[4] In the World Values Survey 1990–1993, people were asked to give their opinion of the statement 'Marriage is an out-dated institution'. Their responses are shown in Table 1.

In most countries, few respondents said that marriage is out-dated, and the differences between countries are not great. Marriage as an institution continues to be highly valued in most countries, with the exception of France.

Another indicator for measuring the degree of institutionalization of marriage is the diffusion of alternative living arrangements. In Italy and

TABLE 1
OPINIONS ABOUT 'MARRIAGE IS AN OUT-DATED INSTITUTION', 1990–1993

Column %	Italy	Spain	Denmark	France	Britain	ex-FRG	Group average
Yes	14.1	16	18	29.1	18.4	15	18.4
No	85.9	84	82	70.9	81.6	85	81.6

Source: World Values Survey 1990–1993: 216

Spain, existing data point to the low degree of cohabitation (Eurobarometer 1991a). Among couple-based families, the percentage of unmarried couples in Italy is comparatively very low, although this number may be significantly underestimated in the Italian case (Sabbadini 1991). Clearly this phenomenon is more common in the Italian north-west, in urban areas and among higher-educated people and employed women. Moreover, peculiar to Italy, most unmarried couples are separated or divorced, and are not found mainly among the young, as elsewhere. In Spain, most cohabitants are young people (18–34), and in contrast to Italy, they are not practising Catholics and live predominantly in urban areas, mostly in the regions of Cataluña, Madrid and País Vasco (Valero 1992).

We have shown that Spaniards and Italians marry later and more often by civil ceremony, following the central/northern European pattern. However, the range of individual choices in family formation is narrower in the south; Italians and Spaniards normally neither cohabit nor live on their own when they are young, but instead stay longer at home. Although the number of single-person households is increasing, very few young people live alone in the south, and, in contrast to other European countries, the elderly predominate in this category (Eurobarometer 1991a; INE 1991; ISTAT 1993). Can this southern phenomenon be explained by the employment/unemployment situation of young people? To answer this, we have correlated the national unemployment rate of young people with their living arrangements. As illustrated in Figure 2 there is a relation between both rates in the case of the youngest age group, especially for Italy, Spain and the United Kingdom.

Unemployment does not explain everything. For France and West Germany, the correlation does not appear to be particularly strong, because despite relatively high unemployment in France, young people seldom live with their parents and, despite relatively *low* unemployment, West Germans live quite often with their parents. More generally, the considerable differences in living arrangements between countries

FIGURE 2

UNEMPLOYMENT AND LIVING IN THE PARENTAL HOME, 1990–91

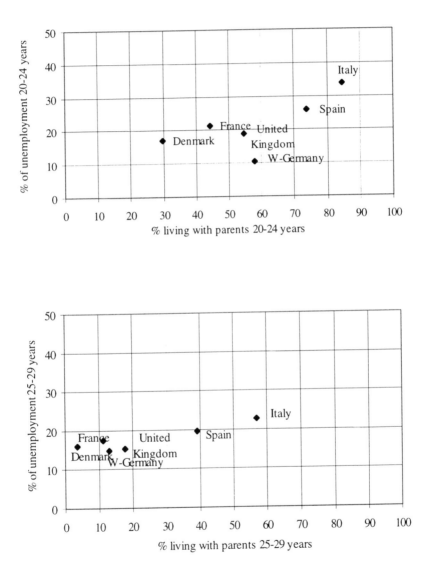

Source: For living with parents: World Values Survey 1990–93: 357, 355. For unemployment: Eurostat 1993

cannot be explained by variations in unemployment rates, because the latter are much smaller than the former. In the case of young people from 25 to 29, variations in unemployment rates between countries are not so large, but variations in their living arrangements are. Recent Italian research shows that a substantial percentage of young women live in their parents' home even when they have a job (Menniti et al. 1992). So is it a cultural peculiarity of Italy and Spain which makes it acceptable and even desirable for young people to stay with their parents for a long time? Cavalli's surveys on this issue argue that young people prefer to remain in their parents' home because of the economic support and social security this supplies, together with personal freedom (Cavalli et al. 1993). In addition, being in school can be a barrier to leaving the parental home, but perhaps more so in some countries than in others. In Italy and Spain, most students stay at home until they finish their education, whereas in other countries the tradition seems to be different. To conclude, it can be said that marriage is more highly institutionalized in Italy and Spain because alternative living arrangements such as cohabitation and single-person living arrangements are not yet institutions, and are still viewed as acts of individual will which break with routine, and may well not be positively sanctioned.

Changes in the Family Expansion Phase

The family expansion phase analysed with national data shows similar changes and features in Spain and Italy. These changes are similar to those of central/northern Europe, although delayed by a few years. In Italy, the decline of fertility began rapidly, in the middle of the 1960s, and before that in Spain. Spain rapidly caught up and reached similar levels (Figure 3). Similarities with other European countries can be found in the increase of the mean age at first birth, in the reduction of childbearing among very young women and in the stabilization of fertility rates after the age of 30.

What makes Italy and Spain similar to each other and different from central/northern European countries? First, Spain and Italy have very heterogeneous fertility patterns between regions, while other European countries are more homogenous (Delgado Pérez and Livi-Bacci 1992). In Figure 3, the fertility rates of the two most disparate regions in Italy and Spain are illustrated. It is curious to see how in both countries the two regions with the highest fertility rates in 1975 have converged over time on the same fertility level in the same way as the regions with the lowest fertility rates. Differences at the territorial level should not be underestimated because they are indicators of different family cultures within a country (Saraceno 1994b).

FIGURE 3
TOTAL FERTILITY RATES AT EUROPEAN, NATIONAL AND REGIONAL LEVEL
1960-1990

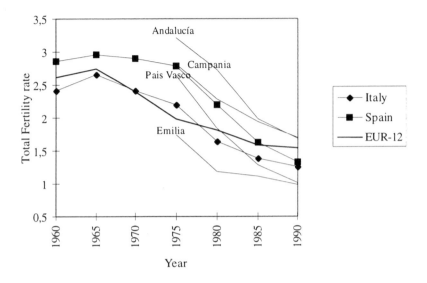

Source: Eurostat, 1992b: E-9. Delgado Pérez and Livi-Bacci 1992

The second way in which Italy and Spain differ from their European neighbours is that the decline in fertility corresponds to declining marital fertility, because birth outside marriage in both countries is uncommon (Eurostat 1992b). In other words, the birth of children is more strongly related to marriage than in central/northern European countries, and has to be seen in relation to the delay in marriages described above.

How can the low fertility rates of Spain and Italy be explained? It is difficult to view them as the result of modernization or by using the explanations given for other west European countries (higher rates of female employment, higher rates of female participation in education, the sexual revolution, and secularization). The reduction of fertility rates in the south occurred and accelerated in the presence of the following factors:

• a lower rate of women in the labour market in comparison with other European countries;

• a gender divergence in education that remained stable until the 1970s (i.e. later than in other countries);

- legislation that up to 1975 in Italy and 1978 in Spain prohibited abortion as well as the dissemination of both knowledge and use of contraception; even after abortion and contraception were legalized, only an incomplete contraceptive revolution took place;

- the strong influence of the Catholic Church on political, cultural and daily life, although to a different degree in Italy and Spain (Saraceno 1994a). Indeed, in Spain the power of the Church was actually restricted during the democratization process.

Could it be that Italians and Spaniards do not like children? Europeans were asked how important it was for them to have a child. The findings confirm the central and fundamental role of children in all countries but with important differences. The percentage of people who consider having a child as essential and very important are 72.9 per cent in Spain, 71 per cent in Italy, 67.3 per cent in France, 63.3 per cent in Denmark, 57 per cent in the United Kingdom and 56.2 per cent in West Germany (Eurobarometer 1993). In addition, in Spain, Italy and France people responded that it was important to have children for marriage to be successful (World Values Survey 1990–1993). One possible conclusion is that Italians, Spaniards and French are more child-oriented than Germans, English and Danes. One could also say that Italian and Spanish people attribute an important role to children in increasing solidarity within the couple, as shown by the higher percentage of Italians and Spaniards who consider that having a young child is a good reason for not getting divorced.

If people in Spain and Italy are comparatively highly child-oriented, then why has the fertility rate decreased? Some Spanish and Italian analysts suggest that the major explanatory factor for the drop in fertility is the late and massive entry of Italian and Spanish women into the labour force since the 1970s. These changes have occurred so fast that the two societies may not have adapted to them rapidly enough: social services, the level of family allowances, labour legislation, housing and social norms inside the family have not changed at the same rate as female employment. It also seems significant that Italy and Spain are among the countries with the least generous child benefits of all European countries (Bradshaw and Ditch 1993). If this analysis is correct, the conclusion can be drawn that childbearing presents greater opportunity costs to Italian and Spanish women than to women in other central/northern European countries, where women's participation in the non-agricultural labour force has a longer tradition, and there are public policies to allow employment and family obligations to be combined (Delgado Pérez and Livi-Bacci 1992). The delay of marriage surely also has consequences for fertility rates delaying and reducing the number of births. As a consequence, the causes of delay in marriage (high youth unemployment rates, a long education phase, housing shortages, etc.) may well influence the fertility level in an indirect way. We should also note that, in contrast to the Irish case, Catholicism has not been able to arrest this decline in fertility in the southern European countries.

Changes in the Family Shrinking Phase

The South also displays specific characteristics in the shrinking phase of the family. In Italy and Spain, as in other Catholic countries of western Europe, divorce laws were introduced later than in other European countries (in 1970 in Italy and 1981 in Spain). When such laws are introduced so late in the socio-economic development of a country, the demography of the people who obtain divorces is rather different from that of other countries which implemented them earlier. Couples who were married and perhaps *de facto* separated for a long time can thus divorce and, as a result, divorcing partners and the children affected by the divorce are older (Goode 1993). In Barbagli's analysis, Italy is distinct from other industrialized western countries in a number of ways, even though the same general tendencies are observable (Barbagli 1990). The most distinctive feature of divorce in Italy (and Spain) is that it is still not a substitute for separation but is simply added to separation as a legal step. This also makes divorce in these countries more costly than in other European countries (Alberdi and Alberdi 1982).

Data analysis reveals that in both countries more people sought legal separation than divorce, at least until 1991. Nevertheless, the divorce rates in the South are still very much lower than those in central/northern countries. In 1989, the number of divorces per 1,000 population was 0.6 for Spain, 0.5 for Italy and 1.6 in the EC12 (Eurostat 1992b). A correct comparison between Italy, Spain and other countries in conjugal instability has to take account not only of the number of divorces but also the number of legal separations, because many couples go no further than the separation stage (Alberdi *et al.* 1994; Golini and Menniti 1994). The evolution of this phenomenon has, and always has had, differential values between North and South, but in both areas there is a tendency to increase. As Barbagli notes, in many northern Italian towns the legal separation rate is not so different from the Swedish divorce rate.

Another difference Barbagli reports for Italy is a clear correlation between the number of children and a reluctance to divorce: fewer couples with many children get divorced than do couples with few children, as opposed to other western countries (Barbagli 1990). A 1993

Eurobarometer survey supports this, showing that for all Europeans the presence of children is the most important reason for not getting divorced, but that the percentage of Italians and Spaniards supporting this argument is higher still. But in an analysis of divorces in Spain from 1981 to 1986, Borrajo found that controlling for the length of marriage, legally separated or divorced couples did not generally have fewer children than married couples, that is, having children did not prevent the marital break-up. An exception was couples married for between two and eight years, of which the separated or divorced had fewer children than those still married (Borrajo Iniesta 1990).

One explanation for the low divorce rate in the South may be the higher institutionalization of life-long marriage in contrast with a more contractual view of marriage elsewhere. However, in order to prove such a hypothesis, the future development of divorce in Italy and Spain will have to be observed, because its legal introduction is still too recent to allow definitive conclusions.

Changes in the Gender Division of Work in the Labour Market

Italy and Spain had a very low rate of female labour participation after the World War II, with Spanish women, over time, less likely to be employed than Italian. During the 1950s and until the mid-1960s, the female activity rate increased in Spain, while in Italy, as a consequence of the first phase of industrialization, it decreased. Since the beginning of the 1970s, female labour force participation has increased in both countries, with a greater acceleration in Italy than in Spain. What has been really new for both countries, however, is that the female labour supply is no longer strictly dependent on market demand but is more and more influenced by women's willingness to enter the labour market. An important historical feature of both countries is the structural shortage of employment, which has affected women's labour force participation in the South in contrast to central/northern Europe. In addition, regional differences in the employment structure were and still are important. Despite the rapid increase in southern female activity rates from around 20 per cent in the 1970s to around 35 per cent in the 1990s, they are still the lowest among the European countries analysed, reaching only two-thirds of the central/northern European activity rates. As well as this difference, women in the Spanish and Italian labour markets are also integrated in different ways than central/northern Europeans.

When considering comparative data on employment in Italy and Spain and especially female employment, it should be noted that labour markets in both countries are characterized by the high number of 'black' or 'grey' jobs. These jobs, mainly held by women, are distinguished by precarious social security, specific time patterns (seasonal jobs, definite time-period contract and part-time work), and low pay (Paci 1980; Muro *et al.* 1988; Solsona 1991). From our perspective, there are three main peculiarities in the recent entrance of women into the labour market in Italy and Spain:

* the growth of female activity rates meant and still means an increase in women's unemployment rates. The gender division of unemployment is much more clear-cut in Italy and Spain than in other countries (Figure 4);

* women's part-time employment is very low. In 1989, 10.9 per cent of Italian women in the formal labour market were employed part-time as against 11.9 per cent in Spain. In France the part-time rate was 23.8 per cent, West Germany 30.7 per cent, Denmark 40.1 per cent and in the United Kingdom 43.6 per cent (Eurostat 1991, Eurobarometer 1991b);

* In Italy and Spain, as shown in Figure 4, there is a generally lower development of the service sector, traditionally occupied by women in central/northern countries, and a higher proportion of employed people in the agricultural sector.

FIGURE 4

ACTIVITY, EMPLOYMENT AND UNEMPLOYMENT

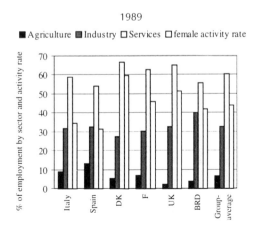

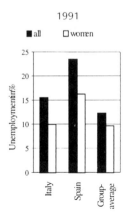

Source: Eurostat 1992a: 41; 1991: 96

To sum up, structural employment shortages, low part-time employment and a less developed service sector can partly explain low female employment rates in these two countries.

As far as the specific career pattern of employed women is concerned, a longitudinal study on employment and the family in the EU carried out for Eurobarometer in 1991 shows clear differences across countries, producing the following groupings: (1) France and Belgium, (2) Denmark, (3) East Germany, (4) Greece, Portugal, Spain and Italy, (5) West Germany and Great Britain and (6) The Netherlands, Luxembourg and Ireland. Women in Spain and Italy enter the labour market relatively late, have a low entry rate, a very high continuity rate and seldom work part time. After the birth of their first child the majority of married women continue to work full time in Italy, whereas in Spain they either stop employment completely or continue with a full-time job. By contrast, in West Germany and Great Britain, women have a high initial entry rate, but low continuity, punctuated by long interruptions and high reliance on part-time work. A very high number of women leave the labour force after the birth of their first child (Eurobarometer 1991b).

As has been shown before, the situation of the labour market in these two countries is crucial for understanding family changes. For Italy, a relationship between the level of female employment and the level of fertility, as well as divorce, can be found by carrying out a regional variance analysis (Barbagli 1990). The low rate of female employment and the high presence of women in the informal sector and among precarious jobs favour an asymmetric relationship between genders in the family.

Solidarity Relationships and Family Values

Demographic behaviour and opinion survey data seem to support the idea that in Italy and Spain familial relations are seen more in terms of obligations than in terms of individual choice. In the following we illustrate the importance of the family in the South in performing welfare tasks, via a brief analysis of family networks, attitudes toward religion and family duties.

An analysis of family networks can be made at two different levels. First, inter-generational family relationships can be analysed by investigating the length of time different generations live together in one household. Second, the family and kinship networks can be described in terms of the extension and intensity of contacts between different households.

As for the first dimension, the specificity of Spain and Italy lies in the lengthier periods of cohabitation between generations. In Italy and Spain – much more so than in central/northern European countries – old people and young people live with their families. In 1993, when asked if old people of 65 years or more lived permanently in their household, 13 per cent of Europeans answered positively. But there were great variations between countries: 8 per cent in France, 9 per cent in Denmark, 11 per cent in West Germany, and 13 per cent in Britain, rising to 19 per cent in Italy and 21 per cent in Spain. A similar picture emerges for young people, but with even greater international variations. An important consequence of these living arrangements is that people necessarily have a great deal of contact with each other – they can help each other and pool incomes more easily if they so choose.

As for family networks, the only comparative study on social networks available (ISSP 1986) does not include Spain, so here we take the Italian and the German cases as representative of two clusters of countries (this data is based on national averages and does not allow for geographical or social differences) (Sabbadini 1994). Both kin and friendship networks are wider in Italy than in Germany. Relatives in Italy live closer together than in Germany and visit each other more often, which means that the degree of individualization is lower. Italian social networks – both kin and friendship – are characterized by strong 'intensity' and 'localism'. A further difference is that the intensity of relationships in Italy frequently extends beyond the relationship with parents (ISSP 1986; Bruckner et al. 1993). The more intense relations between Italians and their relatives is also related to the greater importance of the latter for social and economic support.[5] For help, Italians mostly ask relatives (mother, father, but also sisters and brothers), and the help of the partner is less important than for Germans (Bruckner et al. 1993). Germans have weaker kin and friendship networks, in the latter case in terms both of extension and intensity.

Is Spain similar to Italy in this respect? A Eurobarometer survey of older people in 1992 provides some evidence. People over 60 were asked 'how often do you see your family?' The results support our previous analysis on social networks in Italy and Germany (Figure 5).

The importance of help networks within kinship is also reflected in how young people look for jobs. The results of the Eurobarometer study, 'Young Europeans', show considerable differences from country to country. 'Help from kinship and social networks (relatives and friends) is of primary importance throughout the Mediterranean (Spain, Greece, Portugal, Italy, and even France) [...].' Such help is less important throughout the countries of northern Europe (Commission of the European Community 1988).

Family members in the South interact more closely with each other, and kin networks are more important than elsewhere. The fact that different generations live longer together, along with the high

FIGURE 5

DAILY VISITS OF ELDERLY, 1993

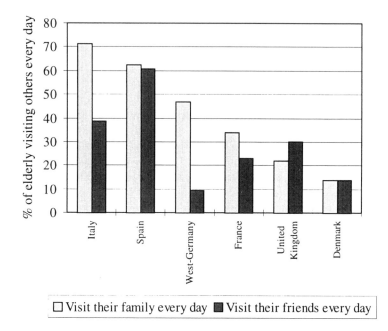

☐ Visit their family every day   ■ Visit their friends every day

Source: Eurobarometer 1992: 37.2

institutionalization of marriage, helps explain the higher density of contacts within and between families. But how can we explain the high level of support and solidarity within these networks? Are they due to the high density of contacts or to other socio-economic characteristics? The level of economic development of a country (measured by the classic indicators of industrialization, urbanization and mobility) can only partially explain the enduring importance of family and kinship relationships in some countries. For example, Höllinger and Haller (1990) have proved that although Italy has a higher degree of urbanization than Austria, kin relationships are much more important. Other possible explanatory factors are historical differences in the frequency of extended families, religious denomination, the strength of the Church, and differences in social policies and housing markets.

Attitudes towards religion clearly display some southern particularities. The Catholic Church in Spain and Italy has traditionally had a great influence on family matters. Despite an important secularization process in recent decades, religion is still very important in both countries. As Greeley has shown in a cross-national study, despite modernization, differences persist between the Catholic and the Protestant ethic and greatly influence family values: while the Catholic ethic is 'communitarian', the Protestant is 'individualistic', because of different preconscious world views. 'Catholics are more likely to visit parents, children, siblings, and other relatives than are other Christians. [...] Net of national differences, then, Catholics do form more intense family networks [...]' (Greeley 1989: 497).

The World Values Survey (1990–1993) confirms the fact that families in Italy and Spain are more often the main vehicle for transmitting religious beliefs than they are in other countries. Virtually all Italians and Spaniards have been brought up with religious beliefs in the home, in contrast to only half in central/northern Europe (Eurobarometer 1993). The importance of the Church in the life of Italians and Spaniards is also supported by the high number of people who attend religious services at least once a week: 37.9 per cent of Italians, 29.2 per cent of Spaniards, but, on average, only 11 per cent of central/northern Europeans. The importance of the Church and religion for family values is also reflected in the ideas people express when asked about family duties.

TABLE 2
LOVE, RESPECT AND PARENTS DUTIES RELATED TO CHILDREN, 1990–1993

Column % How many people mentioned	Italy	Spain	DK	F	UK	BRD	Group average
'Regardless of what the qualities and faults of one's parents are, one must always love and respect them'	82.8	80.8	47	76.9	68.8	61.8	69.7
'One does not have the duty to respect and love parents who have not earned it by their behaviour and attitudes'	17.2	19.2	53	23.1	31.2	38.2	30.3
'Parents' duty is to do their best for their children even at the expense of their own well-being'	78	75.7	51.9	80.5	75.4	53.3	69.1
'Parents have a life of their own and should not be asked to sacrifice their own well-being for the sake of their children'	11.5	15.4	39	19.5	18.8	33.7	23
Neither	10.5	8.9	9.1	0	5.8	12.9	7.8

Source: World Values Survey 1990–1993: 224

Conceptions of duties between generations can be deduced from two questions in the WVS. Over three-quarters of the Spaniards and Italians interviewed felt attached to their parents, independently of their behaviour and attitudes, compared with only about half of the Danes and West Germans. Forty to 50 per cent of the latter tend to support a more differentiated vision.

As for the duties of parents to their children, three-quarters of the Spaniards and Italians interviewed expressed a family-oriented opinion, a somewhat lower percentage than the findings related to the parents.[6] The group average of the central/northern European is still different. These indicators from 1990 to 1991 point to certain cultural qualities that are found not only in Italy and Spain, but which do help to explain considerable differences in behaviour.

The correlation between the indicators of religiosity and family duties suggests that religious heritage is important for family duties, independent of other socio-economic factors. The core of religious heritage in Spain and Italy seems to be the high legitimacy of the Catholic doctrine concerning solidarity and reciprocal duties. But the family is not valued in the same way in all Catholic countries. The differences between countries with the same denomination also have to be related to the history of state–Church relationships and the strength of the state.

THE SOUTHERN FAMILY MODEL

Our findings concerning a theoretical model of the family in Spain and Italy are summarized in Figure 6.

FIGURE 6

THE SOUTHERN FAMILY MODEL

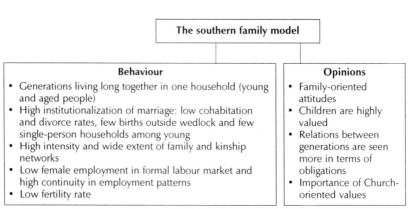

As the model shows, Italian and Spanish families present indicators both of deep change and continuity. The most important change is the increase in female employment which, together with a rapid modernization process, seems responsible for the increase in conjugal instability and for the rapid decline in fertility, which is, in turn, related to the pattern of later marriages. However, we have also found some indicators of permanence in 'traditional' patterns. Marriage as an institution is still very important and, as a consequence, birth outside marriage is still rare and divorce is not (yet) as widespread as in central/northern Europe. To some extent the rarity of cohabitation and living alone as a single young person can be related to the strong institutionalization of marriage. On the other hand, the longer vertical extension of the family unit, together with the relevance of Church-oriented values, can be associated with the high intensity of family and kinship ties as well as to the way in which the obligations are perceived between generations. The longer dependence of young people on their parents is likely to be rooted in the high value attributed to children and in the low importance given to 'independence'. The reverse side of the coin is the propensity of people in the South to offer support to their parents during their old age.

Will this southern family model persist in the future or will it change? Is this simply a question of cultural time lag? Three factors seem to explain and favour the continued reproduction of the southern family model: the socio-economic situation; the nature of social policies in southern Europe; and family culture.

- Social structures in the South will continue to be different from those in central/northern European countries as long as the economies of Italy and Spain continue to be characterized by: the subordinate role of these economies in the international division of labour; the more intensive economic crisis, that is, higher and structural unemployment (affecting a higher percentage of women, young people and the long-term unemployed); a labour market with many precarious jobs held by young people and women in particular, high employment in agriculture, a high rate of self-employed people as well as a higher rate of workers working in small enterprises (i.e. a high proportion of informal jobs); few opportunities for part-time employment in the formal sector; and the concentration of economic and social disadvantages in some areas and regions (OECD 1994).

- In Italy and Spain the entitlement and the level of public social benefits and social services are often related to the family unit and family income. Social assistance, support for agricultural workers, family allowances, help for handicapped persons, scholarships and services for the aged are therefore not institutionalized as individual social rights. Unemployment benefits for young persons seeking their first job are non-existent, as they are supposed to be supported by their families (Jurado Guerrero 1995). This is also often the case in central/northern welfare states, but in Italy and Spain it seems to be more frequent. Similarly, family policies in both countries are not highly developed, and are mainly targeted on families in need and dependent on family income (Neubauer *et al.* 1993). In particular, support for children is 'poor' in comparison with other European countries. The particular institutionalization of some social security laws concerning families must be seen partly as a result of the historical period in which social security was founded and partly as the result of specific socio-political contexts. The current crisis of welfare states will make it difficult to develop more generous family benefits or benefits related to individual rights.

- The family and kinship culture in the South is dominated by the importance of children and family-oriented values, by the importance of obligations, by solidarity between generations and by religious norms. Despite secularization processes, the southern family culture maintains many traditional elements because it adapts well to a context of lasting employment shortage and a scarce availability of social services for families.

FIGURE 7

FACTORS FAVOURING THE REPRODUCTION OF THE SOUTHERN FAMILY MODEL

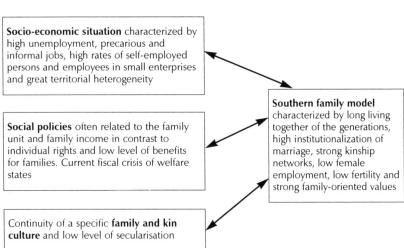

The specific socio-economic development and current situation, the characteristics of social policies and the scarce and regionally-differentiated diffusion of social services all favour the persistence of the southern family model in Italy and Spain, as shown in Figure 7. Family and kinship cultures push in the same direction. These factors encourage solidarity between generations and within kin relationships and make the individualization of living arrangements more difficult. The family-oriented culture is surely a result of this economic and social situation as well as a legitimate factor for the present division of labour between the state and the family, between genders and generations in the labour market and within the family. In turn, the importance of the family and kinship networks is likely to favour social reproduction and inhibit social change, because of the greater probability of social control within the networks. All this favours the persistence of the southern family model.

Nevertheless, certain developments could transform this model. The ongoing processes of secularization, the increasing educational level and the entrance of women into the labour market, together with their wish to be economically independent, will accelerate the re-negotiation of relations between genders in favour of a more symmetrical relationship. The changing population structure, due mainly to a decline in fertility, will have an impact on the potential number of women available to care for the older generation and on the horizontal extension of the kinship networks as well. Therefore, we should also expect a de-institutionalization of family solidarity and of marriage as the dominant family institution.

NOTES

1. By the expression 'family-oriented' countries we mean those characterized by strong family ties and family-oriented values.
2. By degree of institutionalization we mean how far a social pattern is reproduced by routine, is associated with a system of sanctions, is taken for granted, and how far it structures behaviour (Jepperson 1991; Lepsius 1995).
3. Because of the scarcity of regional statistics, national indicators are mainly used to make our comparisons between countries. However, it should be mentioned that while these represent the 'average' of sub-populations, within every country there are many variations at territorial and social levels. Their use is justified only by the same legislative, social and material constraints that citizens meet in their own country (Roussel 1992).
4. The indicators chosen here can be analysed in a comparative way, because questions in this sense have been asked in the same way in international surveys. The interpretation of the results of comparative opinion surveys has to be made carefully, because the same question can produce different meanings across cultures and countries.
5. In the ISSP (1986), people were asked who helps them in their homes and gardens, when they had influenza, suffered from depression, marital crisis, or needed financial help and advice about important changes in their lives.

6. This could be attributed to the technical difference between the two questions: the possibility of answering 'neither' was offered in the question here.

REFERENCES

Alberdi, C. and I. Alberdi (1982): 'La institución matrimonial: Su lugar en la constelación familiar. Aspectos jurídicos y social del divorcio', in R. Conde (ed.), *Familia y cambio social en España*, Madrid: CIS, pp.177–200.

Alberdi, I., L. Flaquer and J. de Ussel (1994): *Parejas y matrimonios: actitudes, comportamientos y experiencias*, Madrid: Ministerio de Asuntos Sociales.

Alcaide Inchausti, J. (1988): 'El gasto publico en la democracia espanola. Los hechos', *Papeles de economia espanola* 37, pp.2–41.

Ascoli, U. (1984): *Welfare State all'Italiana*, Bari: Laterza.

Balbo, L. (1983): 'Il lavoro di servizio delle donne nella società capitalistica', in P. David and G. Vicarelli (eds), *L'azienda famiglia una società a responsabilità illimitatà*, Bari: Laterza, pp.220–39.

Barbagli, M. (1990): *Provando e riprovando. Matrimonio e divorzio in italia e negli altri paesi occidentali*. Bologna: Il Mulino.

Borrajo Iniesta, S. (1990): *La ruptura matrimonial en España*, Madrid: Eudema.

Bradshaw, J. and J. Ditch (1993): *Support for children. A Comparison of Arrangements in Fifteen Countries, Research Report* 21, London: HMSO.

Bruckner, E., K. Knaup and W. Müller (1993): *Soziale Beziehungen und Hilfeleistungen in modernen Gesellschaften*, Working Paper, Mannheim: Mannheim Centre for European Social Research.

Cavalli, A. *et al.* (1993): *Terzo rapporto IARD sulla condizione giovanile in Italia*, Bologna: Il Mulino.

Commission of the European Community (1988): *Young Europeans in 1987*, Luxembourg: Commission of the European Community.

Conde, R. (1982): 'Desarrollo económico y cambio familiar: El impacto del nuevo rol femenino sobre la estructura de la familia', in R. Conde (ed.), *Familia y cambio social en España*, Madrid: CIS, pp.137–65.

Delgado, M. (1993): 'Cambios recientes en el proceso de formación de la familia', *Revista Española de Investigaciones Sociales* 64, pp.123–53.

Delgado Pérez, M. and M. Livi-Bacci (1992): 'Fertility in Italy and Spain: The Lowest in the World', *Family Planning Perspectives* 24/4, pp.162–71.

Eurobarometer (1991a): *Young Europeans*, 34.2., Brussels/Luxembourg: ECSC-EEC-EAEC.

Eurobarometer (1991b): *Employment and Family Within the Twelve*, 34, Brussels/Luxembourg: ECSC-EEC-EAEC.

Eurobarometer (1992): study number 37.2, data file obtained by Zentrum für Europäische Umfrageanalysen und Studien, Mannheim.

Eurobarometer (1993): *Europeans and the Family*, 39.0, Brussels/Luxembourg: ECSC-EEC-EAEC.

Eurostat (1991): *Labour Force Survey, Results 1989*, Luxembourg: Eurostat.

Eurostat (1992a): *Employment and Unemployment*, Luxembourg: Eurostat.

Eurostat (1992b): *Demographic Statistics 1992*, Luxembourg: Eurostat.

Eurostat (1993): *Labour Force Survey, Results 1991*, Luxembourg: Eurostat.

Ferrera, M. (1984): *Welfare State in Italia. Sviluppo e crisi in prospettiva comparata*, Bologna: Il Mulino.

Ferrera, M. (1994): *Southern Welfare in Social Europe*, paper presented at the III International Seminar on Social Policy. Madrid, 24 Oct.

Flaquer, L. (1994): 'La nupcialidad', in M. Juárez (ed.), V. *Informe sociológico sobre la situación social en España. Sociedad para todos en el año 2000*, Madrid: FOESSA, pp.433–45.

Flora, P. (1985): 'On the History and Current Problems of the Welfare State', in S.N. Eisenstadt and O. Ahimeir (eds), *The Welfare State and its Aftermath*, London: Croom Helm, pp.11–30.

Golini A. (1988): 'Profilo demografico della famiglia italiana', in P. Melograni (eds), *La famiglia italiana dall'ottocento ad oggi*, Bari: Laterza, pp.327–81.

Golini, A. and A. Menniti (1994): 'Popolazione e famiglie', in Comitato per l'anno Internazionale della Famiglia, *Per una Politica Familiare in Italia*. Presidenza del Consiglio dei Ministri, Roma: Ministero per gli Affari Sociali, pp.3–26.

Goode, W. (1993): *World Changes in Divorce Patterns*, Yale: YUP.

Greeley, A. (1989): 'Protestant and Catholic: Is the Analogical Imagination Extinct?', *American Sociological Review* 54 (Aug.) pp.485–502.

Guillén, A.M. (1992): 'Social Policy in Spain: From Dictatorship to Democracy (1939–1982)', in Z. Ferge and J.E. Kolberg (eds), *Social Policy in a Changing Europe*, Frankfurt/M. and Boulder, CO: Campus and Westview Press, pp.119–42.

Höllinger, F. and Haller, M. (1990): 'Kinship and Social Network in Modern Societies: a Cross-Cultural Comparison among Seven Nations', *European Sociological Review* 6/2, pp.103–24.

INE (1991): *Encuesta Sociodemográfica Resultados Nacionales, Vol.1, hogar y familia*, Madrid: Instituto Nacional de Estadística.

ISSP (1986): *Social Network and Support System*, Köln: Zentralarchiv für Empirische Sozialforschung. (The participating nations are: Austria, Australia, Great Britain, Hungary, Italy, the USA and West Germany.)

ISTAT (1993): *Indagine Multiscopo sulle Famiglie anni 1987–91*, Vol.2, Roma: ISTAT.

Jepperson, R.L. (1991): 'Institutions, Institutional Effects and Institutionalism', in W. Powell and P.J. DiMaggio (eds), *The New Institutionalism in Organizational Analysis*, Chicago/London: U. of Chicago Press, pp.143–63.

Jurado Guerrero, T. (1995): 'Legitimation durch Sozialpolitik? Die spanische Beschäftigungskrise und die Theorie des Wohlfahrtsstaates', *Kölner Zeitschrift für Soziologie und Sozialpsychologie* 47/4, pp.727–52.

Lepsius, R.M. (1995): 'Institutionenanalyse und Institutionenpolitik', *Kölner Zeitschrift für Soziologie und Sozialpsychologie*, Sonderheft 35, pp.392–403.

Menniti, A. et al. (1992): *Changes in Family Life in the 1980's. The Italian case*. Report to the Working Group Meeting on Family Policy and Family Life, Bonn, April.

Muro, J., J.L. Raymond, L. Toharia and E. Uriel (1988): *Análisis de las condiciones de vida y trabajo en España*, Madrid: Ministerio de Economía y Hacienda. Secretaría de Estado de Economía.

MZES (1994): *OECD Data Base*, Mannheim: MZES, Aug.

Neubauer, E. et al. (1993): *Zwölf Wege der Familienpolitik in der Europäischen Gemeinschaft. Eigenständige Systeme und vergleichbare Qualitäten?* Studie im Auftrag des Bundesministeriums für Familie und Senioren, Stuttgart, Berlin, Köln: Kohlhammer.

OECD (1980)(1989)(1991): *National Accounts of OECD countries*. Paris: OECD.

OECD (1994): *The OECD Jobs Study. Evidence and Explanations. Part I, Labour Market Trends and Underlying Forces of Change*, Paris: OECD.

OECD (1995): *National Accounts. Main Aggregates.Vol. 1. 1960–1993*. Paris: OECD.

Paci, M. (1980): *Famiglia e mercato del lavoro in una economia periferica*, Milano: Angeli.

Paci, M. (1982): *La struttura sociale Italiana*, Bologna: Il Mulino.

Rapoport, R. (1989): 'Ideologies about family forms: towards diversty', in K. Boh (ed.), *Changing Patterns in European Family Life*, London/NewYork: Routledge, pp.53–70.

Roussel, L. (1992): 'La famille en Europe occidentale: divergences et convergences', *Population* 1, pp.133–52.

Roussel, L. (1994): 'La famille en europe occidentale depuis 1950', paper presented at the international conference, Bologna, *Changes in family patterns in western countries*. 6–8 Oct., published by Comune di Bologna Assessorato alle politiche sociali e dell'immigrazione.

Sabbadini, L.L. (1991): 'Le unioni Librere', in A. Menniti (ed.), *Le Famiglie italiane deglianni '80*, Monografie IRP/2, Roma, pp.22–46.

Sabbadini, L.L. (1994): 'Reti di relazioni familiari e tipologia della famiglia', in Comitato per l'anno Internazionale della Famiglia, *Per una Politica Familiare in Italia.* Presidenza del Consiglio dei Ministri, Roma: Ministero per gli Affari Sociali, pp.173–89.

Saraceno C. (1994a) *Family Policy and Family Changes in Italy,* paper prepared for the conference on Family Changes and Family Policy, Mannheim, Oct.

Saraceno C. (1994b): *Ambivalent Familism and Categorial Clientelism in the Italian Welfare State,* paper presented at the Third International Seminar on Social Policy, Madrid, 24–28 Oct.

Solsona, M. (1991): 'The Problem of Measuring Women's Work in Spain', *Iberian Studies* 20/1-2, pp.6–28.

Valero, A. (1992): 'La prevalencia de la familia nuclear en el sistema familiar español', *Revista Internacional de Sociologia. Tercera época* 3, pp.183–210.

Vincenzi Amato, D. (1988): 'Famiglie e il diritto', in P. Melograni (ed.), *La famiglia italiana dall' Ottocento ad oggi,* Bari: Laterza, pp. 629–99.

World Values Survey (1990–1993): Surveys coordinated and documented by Ronald Inglehart, Koeln: Zentralarchiv für empirische Sozialforschung, ICPSR No.6160.

Social Protection in
Contemporary Greece

HARIS SYMEONIDOU

This article provides a general overview of social protection in
Greece in the framework of the southern European welfare model.
The late development of the Greek welfare state is attributed to
institutional and organizational particularities, closely connected
with the country's political history and socio-economic
development after World War II. The principal characteristics of
the Greek welfare state are inadequacy, lack of uniformity and
inefficiency in the benefits provided, an absence of co-ordination
between individual services, centralized administrative and
operating structures and disparities in coverage. A sectoral analysis
reveals the system's weaknesses. Informal care is widely practised
through the family, with women playing the main role. A 'mixed
economy of welfare' and a search for new forms of interaction
between the 'public' and the 'private' are required, while general
reforms are needed in the sector of formal care.

A LAGGING WELFARE STATE

Greece lags behind the other members of the European Union (EU) quite
markedly in terms of spending on social protection. In 1992 the average
amount spent on social protection in the countries of the EU was equal
to 4,348 ECU per inhabitant, but only 1,127 ECU in Greece (see Figure
1). Although an increase in social protection expenditure occurred in all
EU countries in 1980–92, spending grew most in the lower expenditure
countries, including Greece. Nevertheless, Greece still spends less on
health, senior citizens, children and unemployment than any other
member state.

Following Esping-Andersen's (1990) typology, the Greek welfare
regime can be classified as a mix of the 'liberal' and 'conservative-
corporatist' types. The role of private social security schemes and fringe
benefits is rather limited, the state replaces the market only to a certain
extent – since a crucial role in social protection is played by the family –

The author would like to thank M. Rhodes, M. Cavouriaris, I. Emke-Poulopoulou, A.
Sissouras and O. Stassinopoulou for their valuable suggestions.

the benefits provided are contributory and marginal, and non-contributory benefits are restricted to a limited number of the very poor. Welfare services tend to serve the most mobilized social groups. Weakly mobilized sections of the population, which are more likely to need assistance, are on the fringes of the system and the state has traditionally cultivated a policy of dependency for the more vulnerable parts of the population. But the peculiar characteristics of the Greek case are sufficient to contradict the view that the Greek welfare state is simply a 'discount edition' of Esping-Andersen's continental model, and that the lag in its development is not due to 'any specific institutional and organizational features', but 'simply reflects the delay in the construction of the welfare state and more generally the relative economic underdevelopment of the Mediterranean south' (Katrougalos 1996). As argued below, the existing disparities in social protection between Greece and the other countries of the EU *do* reflect key institutional, structural and economic differences which are critical for understanding the nature of the Greek system and its future prospects.

Greece is an example *par excellence* of the southern welfare model, outlined by Ferrera (1996), and is characterized by fragmentation, dualism and ineffectiveness in income maintenance, near universalism in national health care (but with extended scope for private provision), a particularistic-clientelistic welfare state and a peculiar mix between public and non-public actors and institutions. The supportive role of the family counter-balances to an extent the state's inability to satisfy social needs, and the role of women is critical for the care of younger and the older family members. In terms of gender, Greece belongs to the 'male breadwinner model', in which women's social rights are often derived rights (from those of the spouse) or 'second class' benefits and the state does not facilitate women's participation in the labour market, since family obligations are in principle *women's* obligations. Two other features of the 'Latin fringe' – the delay in constructing and difficulties in implementing a social welfare system – are also characteristic of Greece. And as elsewhere in southern Europe (with the partial exception of Spain), the welfare state is highly centralized. Policies on health, social security and other areas of social care are almost exclusively determined by the central state.

One of the essential conditions for the development of a welfare state is the consolidation of dominant ideologies which support the broadest possible application of 'typical rules' to the process of producing value and distributing income. The fact that Greek society is resistant to any weakening of the informal process of distributing resources (in particular, a large and growing 'black economy'), as well as the limited

FIGURE 1

SOCIAL PROTECTION EXPENDITURE BY INHABITANT IN 1985 CONSTANT

PRICES, IN ECU

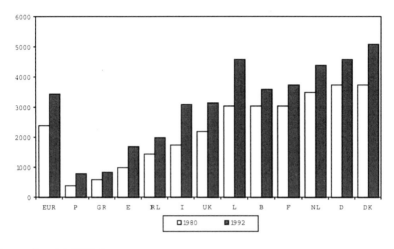

Source: Eurostat 1994: 1

extent of salaried work has, inevitably, affected both the shaping of social interests and the emergence of social needs for commodities and services for collective consumption. It has also determined the degree to which the state is capable of implementing effective social policy or planning (see Petmesidou-Tsoulouvi 1992).

The factors impeding the consolidation of an ideology in favour of rules on social protection and income redistribution are closely connected with the post-war socio-economic development of the country. This, in turn, is inextricably bound up with the passage of power after the Civil War of 1946–49 into the hands of a ruling class which favoured weak, though democratic governments, and had an international orientation in terms of profit making and investment (Symeonidou 1994). The severe social problems of the period were dealt with by repression. The short-lived democratic government of 1964–65 was unable to bring about radical statutory change, and it was not until democracy had been overthrown in 1967, and after the country had experienced seven years of dictatorship, that the legacy of the Civil War began to disappear (Tsoukalas 1987).

But instead of using the large public sector for the development of a welfare state, it was exploited and made the citadel of a new state-affiliated bourgeoisie class which used it to exclude Left-wingers and Communists who were opposed to the regime (Mouzelis 1986). Relations between citizens and the state were regulated by favouritism and other forms of clientelism, and this had a constraining effect on the development of a collective consciousness and a broad consensus on social policy matters. At the same time, the union movement was disorganized and could be manipulated by the authoritarian and patriarchal state.

The massive wave of emigration which saw approximately one million people move to western Europe and more distant destinations between 1955 and 1970 provided a solution of sorts to the problem of unemployment, which has been estimated at 30 per cent during the 1950s (Tsoukalas 1987: 194). The absence of a dynamic section of the Greek population and the fact that emigrants sent remissions home to their families went some way towards filling the enormous gaps in the welfare state and operated as a safety valve to defuse demands on the part of social groups. The wave of return migration which began in the 1970s had the same effect, as returning migrants set up small self-contained businesses in urban and rural areas. Greece has the highest proportion of self-employed persons and the lowest level of salaried workers of all EU countries (Eurostat 1995a). Self-employment tends to favour multiple employment in rural as well as urban areas, and makes it impossible to place individuals in specific social categories and classes.

After 1974, there was increasing interest in the development of collective consumption and the welfare state. This period coincided with the fall of the dictatorship and the development of state benefits in the rest of southern Europe after the overthrow of other dictatorships (Giner 1985; Maloutas and Economou 1988). But it also coincided with economic crisis triggered by the two oil price shocks of 1973 and 1979. The ensuing recession helped delay further welfare development: the flow of revenue from abroad was cut off, exports fell, labour costs increased, the competitiveness of Greek products (even at home) was reduced and foreign borrowing increased. The high rate of internal migration intensified conflicts within the country. Parallel to these socio-economic developments, the clientelistic system expanded to new sections of the middle and lower-middle classes.

The crisis of the social security system illustrates some of the more general problems of Greek welfare. While it is characterized by a great number of insurance funds – 236 in 1995 – the problem is not so much the number of agencies as the way in which they function: the fragmentation of the funds, the complexity of legislation, inequality in contributions and benefits, and organizational and functional difficulties (Rombolis 1991). The extent to which social security funds receive state funding depends more on their political influence – which is linked to the support of pressure groups – than on the real needs of the occupational categories concerned. Nor does the social security crisis involve the entire system but only a small number of funds, above all the Social Insurance Organization (the IKA), a fund with a very wide range of risk cover. This crisis is due to the general problems of the Greek economy, the worsening ratio of pensioners to contributors – because of population ageing[1] – the tendency of insurance funds to borrow from banks at high interest rates and the spending of social security fund reserves by the state for general social policy purposes.

Despite the constantly growing need for social reform, the failure to consolidate new objectives and institutions weakens any effort to bring about significant change. One typical example of this is the reform introduced with the National Health System (see below). Moreover, apart from economic constraints and socio-economic pressures, other problems are due to:

- the diminishing resilience of the 'southern family';

- a clash between the new austerity climate and the wasteful collusive practices involving the public and private sectors in health care and social services;

- a high level of service user dissatisfaction; and

- the need for greater welfare coverage, due to growing social problems (e.g. rising unemployment and the ageing of population).

Together, these create a vicious cycle from which no exit seems possible.

THE 'FORMAL' WELFARE SYSTEM IN GREECE

Health Care

The production and provision of health services is based on a public/private sector mix. Both sectors derive most of their revenue from the social security organizations (health insurance funds). Private services have always been the basic model for out-patient care, and until the late 1970s, private sector provision accounted for more than 50 per cent of hospital beds. In the early 1980s important structural changes to the provision and distribution of health services have been attempted, which are quite similar to those occurring over the last two decades in other southern European countries. The establishment of the National Health System (NHS) was intended to ensure the public provision and distribution of care to the entire population, regardless of income level, social class or social security agency.

The Greek NHS bears numerous similarities to its British equivalent. The two systems have in common the state's responsibility for the health of citizens, the regional organization of health care and the institution of the family doctor. The Greek NHS has also adopted the guidelines laid down by the World Health Organization (WHO) for primary health care, and provision has been made for the development of health centres along Scandinavian lines. According to statutory provisions, all the needs of the population of each region should be met within that region, and primary health care for the rural population is to be provided by health centres. In reality, however, patients are free to move around within the system without any restrictions or geographical commitments. As a result, the country's two main urban centres, which have an extensive inpatient infrastructure, attract patients from all over the country. This can be explained by the unequal distribution of spending on health, by imbalances in regional economic development, by delays in decentralization, by administrative and sociological factors and by the shortage of sufficient numbers of trained medical staff in some specialities and of paramedical personnel.

Between 1984 and 1988, 186 health centres were built and the numbers of hospital doctors and nurses were increased by 60 and 88 per cent respectively. In 1988, one third of hospital beds were transferred from the private to the public sector (European Commission 1994). Despite these provisions, the situation is far from satisfactory. The most important provisions of the NHS law were never implemented, in particular the decentralized health authorities, the institution of the family doctor and the re-organization of the financing of the system. There was an evident breakdown of continuity in health policy (Sissouras *et al.* 1994). The poor economic state of the country, in conjunction with the general opposition to the new system of the medical profession, compelled and/or allowed the central administration to postpone completion of the planned changes in primary health care and in particular the development of urban health centres. The resistance to this of some of the wealthier funds, which can provide above-average packages of services, has also postponed the incorporation of all social security and health funds into the NHS. The incorporation of health funds into the NHS and the establishment of family doctors was only achieved with the 1996 Health Law.

Since the early 1990s, a number of market-oriented innovations have been introduced, including the promotion of privatization, cost controls and the transfer of an important part of health funding to family budgets. Since 1991, the recipient has been obliged to contribute to medical and pharmaceutical expenses (by between 10 and 25 per cent) and to treatment in the out-patient clinics of hospitals. So while expenditure on health services in Greece, at 5.2 per cent of GDP in 1991, was the lowest in the EU, the last family expenditure survey showed that total spending amounts to 8 per cent of the GDP (because of spending in private health sector), which makes Greece stand out as a relatively high spender. In 1991, 42 per cent of health expenditure were financed from private payments, which is the highest proportion of private financing among all member states (Abel-Smith *et al.* 1994; European Commission 1994). But only 18.7 per cent of social protection expenditure is devoted to health care, which is the lowest among the EU countries (see Table 1).

There are numerous other problems. A special characteristic of the health system is the existence of the black economy in the medical profession. Even in state hospitals the payment of 'back handers' is an additional burden on the family budget for health care. More emphasis needs to be placed on health promotion and prevention. One hopes that new reforms will fill the gap and produce more rational mechanisms and a better organized health care system.

Unemployment Benefits

Since the late 1980s, legal innovations have weakened the state's capacity to control private sector salaries, which are now controlled more directly by market forces. These now include increased unemployment, cheap labour offered by illegal migrants and reduced demand for labour due to the general recession of 'ailing' public firms. The official rate of unemployment has risen from 5.3 per cent in 1983 to 8.9 per cent in 1994. The proportion of those who have been unemployed for more than 12 months has also increased, from 32.3 per cent in 1983 to 50.5 per cent in 1994. Unemployment rates (again 1994) are much higher among women (13.7 per cent) than men (6 per cent) and among young people under 25 (27.7 per cent) than among the total active population (Eurostat 1993; 1995a). Unemployment insurance is available for just 12 months. Benefits amount to 40–50 per cent of the most recent salary, with an increase of 10 per cent for each dependent person (up to a maximum of 70 per cent of the most recent paycheck). The Manpower Organization co-ordinates three month courses for the young unemployed (15–18 years old) and there is some vocational training for older workers. Expenditure on unemployment amounted to just 0.3 per cent of GDP in 1991 – the lowest in the EU, alongside Italy, Portugal and Luxembourg. Unemployment benefit, as a percentage of the worker's salary, is also the lowest – together with Italy – among the EU countries (European Commission 1994).

The prospects for employment are far from encouraging. De-industrialization, mass redundancies, the closing of numerous 'ailing' firms and the stagnation of investments are all indications that unemployment will rise and the existing situation will worsen. There is thus a need for corresponding protection of the unemployed and of an adjustment in the system to make the conditions for benefit more favourable and applicable to a larger number of unemployed for a greater length of time.

Pensions

Greece is very much a 'pensioner welfare state'. Pensions in 1991 represented 10.6 per cent of GNP, as against 7.6 per cent in Germany, 5.5 per cent in Portugal and 6.4 per cent in Spain (European Commission 1994: 46) and accounted for as much as 70 per cent of all social benefits (see Table 1). Greece has a higher percentage of pensioners than any other EU country, due primarily to early retirement, large numbers of disability pensions and demographic ageing. Since 1992, however, restrictions have been imposed in granting disability pensions. Nevertheless early retirement is still promoted in some sectors to deal with problems of de-industrialization and unemployment. Survivor's pensions have been extended to women, in accordance with the spirit of equality, but the rights of other dependent family members (e.g. children, grandchildren, etc.) have been discontinued.

The Greek pension system provides benefits to retired persons, their spouses, their dependent children, to disabled workers and dependent members of their families and to surviving spouses and families of deceased workers. Spouses are entitled to a share of social security benefits amounting to 50–70 per cent of the spouses' benefit. Pensions are financed from employer and employee contributions. Although some funds are financed either totally or partially from the state budget (e.g. the Farmers' Pension Fund and the Seamen's Pension Fund), the overall state contribution is low. Recently, the ratio between retired beneficiaries and the active population supporting the social security system has declined. The number of beneficiaries of all funds has increased from 1,210,725 to 2,098,418 during the period 1977–94 (Bamboukas 1995). In order to meet increasing outlays, contribution rates for employers and employees have been increased, benefits have decreased and the age for eligibility has been raised, provoking a deterioration in the living conditions of Greek pensioners.

Social security benefits represent the major source of income of the vast majority of older Greeks. A minority is eligible for 'supplementary' pensions (one among three in the private sector) and very few Greeks receive private pensions (Ministry of Health, Welfare and Social Services

TABLE 1

PERCENTAGE DISTRIBUTION OF SOCIAL PROTECTION EXPENDITURE IN VARIOUS SECTORS, 1980 AND 1992

	Health		Old Age		Maternity Family		Unemployment		Other	
	1980	1992	1980	1992	1980	1992	1980	1992	1980	1992
Europe of 12	37.5	36.6	43.4	44.8	10.5	7.8	6.4	7.2	2.2	3.6
Belgium	34.6	34.4	41.5	44.7	11.3	8.1	11.6	11.4	0.9	1.4
Denmark	35.8	28.5	35.7	35.1	10.8	12.0	12.9	17.2	4.8	7.2
Germany	40.5	41.0	42.7	40.6	9.9	8.9	4.5	6.2	2.5	3.3
Greece	26.0	18.7	61.9	69.0	4.5	1.7	2.5	5.3	5.1	5.3
Spain	36.9	36.6	40.8	41.3	4.4	1.8	16.2	18.5	1.8	1.9
France	35.6	34.6	43.9	44.1	12.7	9.5	5.1	7.7	2.7	4.1
Ireland	42.5	36.0	29.7	27.2	15.1	17.4	7.8	14.6	4.9	4.8
Italy	34.9	31.6	55.1	62.8	7.5	3.9	2.3	1.7	0.1	0.0
Luxembourg	40.4	39.3	47.5	48.4	10.0	11.1	0.9	0.8	1.2	0.4
Netherlands	47.8	45.2	32.9	36.9	9.2	5.4	6.1	8.4	3.9	4.2
Portugal	44.8	45.4	39.4	38.8	8.0	5.6	2.8	5.0	5.0	5.2
England	32.9	36.4	42.8	39.4	13.1	10.9	9.6	6.0	1.6	7.4

Source: Eurostat 1994: 8

1995). Social security benefits were indexed to the cost of living until 1990, but since then they have increased at a lower rate than inflation. Pensions, in any case, are very low, and the lowest are below the poverty level. They are so insufficient that they have been characterized by the prime minister himself as a 'pourboire'. However pensioners pay very high taxes (in 1994 pensioners as a whole paid 14.9 per cent of the total taxes in comparison with 7.0 per cent in 1960). The financial situation of pensioners has deteriorated during the period 1990–95 and is expected to decline still further in the near future.

Social Protection of the Family

Greece has never had an explicit family policy. Nevertheless, legislation on employment, social insurance and other areas of social security, as well as fiscal policy, contains a number of regulations which take into consideration the responsibilities and dependencies within marriage, the duties of parents toward their children and those of adults toward their parents. In some instances these regulations can also have demographic implications in the sense that they can help with the economic and other costs of children.

Until 1983, legislation governing family relationships in Greece dated from 1946 and expressed the social values of a former age. In 1983, as a consequence of the 1975 Constitution and of changing social values, new concepts and provisions were introduced to Greek family law, among which the most important are:

• the introduction of the institution of civil marriage;

• the establishment of equality between men and women;

• the abolition of the dowry;

• the introduction of divorce by mutual agreement; and

• the abolition of the distinction between 'legitimate' and 'illegitimate' children.

Material aid (subsidies, allowances, tax exemptions, etc.) and non-material aid (nurseries, kindergartens, consultative services, etc.) is provided to families (conjugal or mono-parental). Some measures are taken for families 'at risk' (e.g. immigrant families), or for families in crisis (affected by unemployment, handicap, dissolution, etc.), as well as for abandoned children (e.g. adoption). Large families are particularly protected in many ways, a concern which first appeared in the Constitution of 1926: childrens' allowances increase with the number of children and become most favourable for the third child; pensions are given to mothers of more than three children; large families are favoured by housing policy, they have special tax exceptions and they are also provided with some other non-material benefits (Symeonidou 1993; Moussourou 1994).

However, in spite of the increasing concern in the government for the country's demographic situation, family benefits in Greece are very low; together with those of UK and Portugal, they are the lowest among the EU countries (Dumon 1992; Eurostat 1994). Moreover, Greece and Spain have the lowest share of their social protection budgets in this sector (Table 1) and occupy the last position on social expenditure on the family, measured either by inhabitant or as a percentage of GNP (Figure 2). Declining fertility in relation to the increasing economic activity of women makes family replacement services and other measures making family and working life compatible of special importance. There are a number of measures in favour of women, including the protection of working women against dismissal, maternity leave of 16 weeks (paid at 100 per cent of salary), parental leave (3.5 months, for each parent, in the private sector) and a maternity leave of two years for each child in the public sector. Nevertheless, these leave periods are unpaid and, due to a number of severe restrictions, working parents do not make use of them. In the area of child-care, public care facilities are very inefficient in number, especially for children younger than 2.5 years, and are of rather poor quality.

FIGURE 2
SOCIAL EXPENDITURE ON FAMILIES BY INHABITANT, IN ECU, 1992

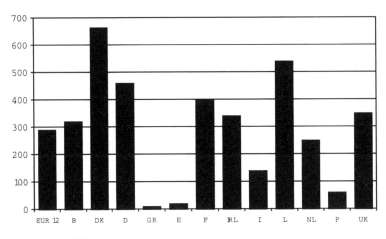

Source: Eurostat 1994: 8

There is also a limited number of services for the elderly. The most important existing service is the institution of the Open Care Centres for the Elderly (KAPI). The purpose of the KAPIs, which are run by local government in all parts of Greece, is to keep elderly people in their homes and at the same time encourage them to be active, independent and equal members of the community. However, they can only provide facilities for elderly people who are capable of looking after themselves and have no particular health problems. In conclusion, family policy in Greece is to a great extent left in the hands of families themselves (see below).

Housing

Housing policy in Greece, especially since 1960, has been rather distinctive by European standards. To start with, housing policy has never been one of the main concerns of post-war governments. While, since 1960, there has been tremendous growth in the building industry – during an intensive and extended period of urbanization – state intervention for provision of ready-built houses and low-interest loans has been very limited. According to the housing survey of the National Centre of Social Research (1986–1987), state loans in urban areas affect a very small percentage of households (0.09 per cent of households acquire their own housing by means of deposits with the Post Office Savings Bank, 0.80 per cent receive loans from housing institutes, and 3.44 per cent buy property out of their own income supplemented by a loan from a housing institute). However, in all cases the level of such loans is far below the sum necessary to purchase a house. Civil servants have better access to such loan facilities than many other population groups who may be in greater need of housing. State intervention in the form of the provision of ready-built housing is even more limited than in the case of loans (1.04 per cent). The situation is essentially the same in rural areas.

Various government five-year plans have set quality targets for housing, the most central of which is to achieve a 1:1 person/room ratio – the internationally recognized standard. Over the last ten years, it has become clear that state policy should aim to improve the quality of existing housing stock (loans for restoration), as is the practice in the rest of Europe. However, beyond recognition of the problem, such action is usually confined to scheduled buildings, whose restoration is intended to preserve the country's cultural heritage.

In recent years, the market for rented accommodation, which until 1986 was relatively stable, has displayed a marked imbalance between supply and demand, leading to state intervention in determining rent levels. Rent is calculated on the basis of the so-called 'objective value' of the property. It is applied to all leases except new ones, an exception judged necessary to prevent a recession in building activity. However, the shortage of housing means that these measures are only applied to a very limited extent, and rents continue, in effect, to be freely negotiable between tenants and landlords. More generally, rent control and land policies have encouraged the spread of home ownership and promoted the building industry whose low costs have kept down prices and rents and have encouraged a large number of people to buy their own house. This explains why Greece has the highest rate of home ownership among OECD countries. However, there have been negative side effects due to the lack of coherent town planning: the lenient attitude of the government and the lack of planning controls has allowed illegal construction in non-officially approved areas quite lacking in basic utilities and infrastructure.

Poverty

Poverty in Greece is defined as households with an income of less than 50 per cent of average disposable per capita income. It has been calculated that the country's very inefficient social protection system diminishes the poverty ratio in Greece by about 18 per cent, but benefits provided are very low and far from covering existing needs. Thus, there is no guaranteed minimum income. The state grants a pension to uninsured elderly persons (Law 1268/82). Individuals aged over 65 years and childless couples of whom at least one is aged over 65 years are eligible for rent allowances. Extra allowances are paid to individuals with special needs. It should be noted that the above poverty allowances (which are extremely low by comparison with the cost of living), are means-tested, while those paid to the disabled are not. Disabled persons are also entitled to some other benefits concerning travel. Those who are not covered by any social security are issued with special 'uninsured persons' booklets after first being granted 'certificates of social protection'. The main issue is the very serious problem of increasing social exclusion.

'INFORMAL' WELFARE

The Role of the Family

There is often talk of a crisis of the family in Greece today. Nevertheless, although the decline of certain demographic indicators (such as the average size of households and the fertility rates) would appear to favour that view, there are several other indicators to suggest the reverse, including the exceptionally low divorce rate (0.7 per cent in 1994, the lowest EU rate along with those of Spain and Italy), and the very low incidence of childbirth outside wedlock (2.9 per cent in 1994)(Eurostat 1995a; Jurado Guerrero and Naldini, this volume).

The Greek family is often described as 'introverted' in terms of the relations among its members (Tsouyopoulos 1981) and emphasis is placed on the important supportive roles played by kinship and the extended family. It could be said that although the family often appears to be nuclear from the outside, its internal form is frequently extended. Women are the basic prop of the family in all forms of care toward all family members. They have internalized their role as carers – a form of 'compulsory altruism' (Land and Rose 1985: 74) – and are the link that keeps the family together.

The centrality of the family can be illustrated in four areas: child care, education, the continuing importance of the dowry and care for the elderly.

• The greater part of child care is provided by the family, as a result of the inadequacy of services available in this area (which can cater to 65–70 per cent of children aged 3–5.5 years but only to 4–5 per cent of children under 3 years)(Symeonidou 1992). Prevailing attitudes play a role as well. One third of all family households in the Greater Athens area enjoy the daily presence and support of grandparents (usually the wife's mother or mother-in-law) in the life of the couple and for the purpose of child-minding or rearing. The results of the National Fertility Survey show that when women work, 44 per cent of child-minding is carried out by the mother or mother-in-law, and most frequently takes place in the family home (Symeonidou *et al.* 1992).

• Greek families make major sacrifices to educate their children (Lambiri-Dimaki 1974). The outflow from Greece of foreign exchange to finance students in universities abroad is greater than the state's total expenditure on tertiary education (Pesmatzoglou 1988). Furthermore, the relatively advanced age at which young people become active in the labour market (due to the scarcity of good jobs) considerably extends the period in which they are financially reliant on their parents.

• The fetish of home ownership is similar to that of education. As already mentioned, Greece has a higher number of houses in proportion to its population than any other OECD country and this is bound up with the institution of the dowry. The dowry may have been abolished by law in 1983 but it continues to exist in practice and reveals the concern of parents that their children should be 'settled' in terms of jobs and marriage, as well as demonstrating the degree to which the family substitutes for the welfare state (Symeonidou-Alatopoulou 1976).

• Apart from looking after young people, the family also has to provide financial support for senior citizens (for whom there are few social services) and for women and men who are not working. It is socially stigmatizing for a Greek family to place a parent or grandparent in an old people's home. A research project carried out by the WHO in 1986 revealed that 86 per cent of persons aged 60 years or more, in rural areas, lived with at least one other person: 58.5 per cent with a spouse, 39.7 per cent with children, 25.2 per cent with grand-children, 2.6 per cent with a sibling and 3.9 per cent with other persons (Triantafillou and Amira 1988). The fact that 47 per cent of the elderly suffered from some chronic health problem gives an idea of the responsibility and burden which families have to shoulder. According to a previous survey, the situation is similar in urban areas (Pitsiou 1986: 43). In Greece the overall population in old people's homes and geriatric clinics is only 0.8 per cent of the total population aged 65 years and over (as opposed to 8–11 per cent in western Europe).

There is an urgent need for the state to provide professional medical and psycho-social support so as to allow senior citizens to live at home. It was for this purpose that the Senior Citizens' Open Care Centres (KAPI) were introduced. The first KAPI opened in 1979 and by 1994 there were 233 of them throughout the country. While senior citizens themselves place great importance on the existence of the KAPI (Amira, Georgiadi and Teperoglou 1987), research reveals that families are often antagonistic towards them, since they indicate that senior citizens may be unhappy within the family framework (Tsaoussis and Hadziyannis 1990). The role played by women in caring for the family is reflected in the rate of KAPI membership among elderly women: while men see the KAPI as a place of recreation, women attend primarily for preventive health check-ups, since the amount of time they devote to caring for their children's households leaves them little scope for leisure (Veniopoulou 1988).

The care of senior citizens in the family may sometimes have a negative impact on the carer's physical and/or mental health, especially in more severe cases (such as severe mental handicap) in which the carer can gain no feeling of having fulfilled a duty or obtain no gratification from a relationship with the patient (Triantafillou and Mestheneou 1991). Moreover, many women stop working to provide care for a dependent family member and thus, become completely dependent themselves, not physically but economically (carers in Greece do not receive any allowances). This situation may reach the levels of social exclusion (Lambropoulou 1993: 725). However, there is an important element of reciprocity in family care. For example, elderly parents contribute to the family budget through their pension or other assets.

The burdening of the family by the state with a task of meeting a whole range of needs of family members (feeding, housing, education expenses, caring for the young and the elderly) often becomes intolerable. A more effective state policy is needed to actively support the role of the family. Having introduced the institution of 'home help' and of 'care at home' in 1992, the real need is to implement them on a larger scale.

The Role of the Church and other Non-governmental Organizations

The most important form of private action for the family and poverty is carried out by the Church of Greece, which has 90 General Poor Funds at bishopric level and 3,194 Parish Poor Funds, which local parishes often call 'Love Funds' or 'Christian Solidarity Committees'. The social work of the Church involves providing a meals service for the elderly and children, making regular or one-off financial payments (e.g. for rent, debts, electricity bills, hospital fees), sending patients abroad for medical treatment, granting special financial support and providing social services (social workers, doctors, counselling services, hostels, orphanages, old people's homes, etc.).

To help families, the Church has set up a number of 'Family Support Centres' in 46 dioceses, which provide counselling, social work, moral support, information, etc., and material assistance in the case of large families. The Church also runs 12 day care centres and 15 orphanages, together with 91 hostels where children from poor families in isolated villages can stay free of charge while attending schools in larger towns. The Church also operates free summer camps for the children of less well-off families. Although the volume of work done by the Church is significant, some criticism could be levelled at the criteria on which those who receive the various allowances are selected. Selection is usually at the discretion of the parish priest, who may well prefer to make payments to those who are frequent church goers rather than those who are really in need.

Apart from the Church, the 'Hellenic Red Cross' runs a number of programmes for care of dependent old people, and there are a number of other private agencies which have developed family-related initiatives. These include the SOS children's villages for orphans, which provide high-level care for the children resident in them and create a real family atmosphere.

CONCLUSIONS

The principal features of the welfare state in Greece are inadequacy and lack of uniformity in the benefits provided, an absence of any co-ordination between individual services and inequality in the coverage of the population. The factors impeding the development of the welfare state are closely connected with the post-war socio-economic development of the country. In most cases funding lags behind, the system is oriented towards curative measures and prevention is ignored. Contrary to present scientific evidence that the quality of life of all citizens ought to be a direct concern of their community, the welfare sector maintains an obsolete, centralized and vertical administrative and operating structure. And this is true not only for the old institutions but for the new ones as well. The sectoral analysis by pensions, unemployment, health care, poverty, protection of the family, education and housing, shows more clearly the system's weaknesses. Generous increases in social expenditure would be needed in order to catch-up with the rest of Europe at least in terms of aggregate expenditure levels. On the other hand the high public deficits 'urge' a restrictive reform of the country's social programmes, as in other southern European countries.

Although there appears to be some room for tax increases – rather than expenditure cuts – due to the size of the informal economy, tax pressure in the formal economy as a proportion of GDP is already relatively high and could provoke a strong reaction from tax-payers. Moreover, labour costs, although relatively low by European standards, do not ultimately offer competitive advantages if productivity is taken into account and this limits the scope for increasing employer contributions. General reforms are needed to the health, education and pension systems, while labour relations have to be reconsidered and unemployment confronted by the creation of new jobs and the re-organization of the labour market.

Given the economic recession and the country's public deficits, some voices have been raised in favour of individual insurance-based provision with collective protection. Nevertheless, and especially in the case of Greece, an important source of state revenue should be mobilized for supporting the traditional welfare state and could be done so with an effective control of widespread tax evasion and tax exemptions. The crisis of social security could be moderated by the creation of Social Insurance banks where the employee's and the employer's contributions could be deposited in order to solve the problem of delayed deposits.

Informal care is becoming an increasingly important issue, especially in Greece and in the other countries of southern Europe, where welfare regimes are of limited nature. In an age of economic recession when western states, with their relatively advanced social welfare systems, are searching for new ways to reactivate the family in its role of carer, it is very important in Greece and other southern European countries to safeguard solidarity among the family members without overburdening women. The family cannot be regarded as a welfare state substitute in the long term. The absence of relevant family substitution services, combined with the inflexibility of the Greek labour market, makes life very difficult for women as 'compulsory altruists'. Moreover, a threat to family solidarity as an essential component of social welfare may come from greater geographical mobility both within Greece and between EU countries, the proliferation of new families formed by mixed marriages and the problems created by multi-culturalism (Symeonidou 1994). It is therefore important to find appropriate forms of intervention which combine financial support for beneficiaries and carers with services in kind, without undermining the structure of family life. Organized voluntarism could also play an important role, while the informal networks which have traditionally sustained the family, should be reinforced and even reconstructed. A number of factors have to be considered in designing a new social policy, including the emergence of an information society and the creation of new forms of employment (more flexible employment patterns, work at home in forms of personal services, etc.). A 'mixed economy of welfare' and the exploration of new forms of interactions between 'the public' and 'the private' are needed.

NOTES

1. Demographic ageing is due to declining fertility (from 2.2 children per woman in reproductive age group in 1980, to 1.38 in 1994, i.e. well below the replacement level). This rate is now among the lowest in Europe, together with Italy, Spain and Portugal. Ageing is also affected by increasing life expectancy at birth (from 72.2 years for males and 76.6 years for females in 1980, to 74.9 for males and 79.9 for females in 1994, which is among the highest in Europe), external migration (particularly amongst the young and productive age groups) and return migration (which adds to the older age groups). The percentage of persons 65 years and older rose from 8 per cent in 1961 to 13 per cent in 1981 and 15.3 per cent in 1995. According to population projections it will rise to 21 per cent in 2020, with all the socio-economic

consequences that this implies (Council of Europe 1995; Eurostat 1995b; NSSG: unpublished data).

REFERENCES

Abel-Smith, B. *et al.* (1994): *Report on the Greek Health Services*, Athens: Ministry of Health Welfare and Social Services, Athens: Pharmetrica.

Amira, A., E. Georgiadi and A. Teperoglou (1986): *Ο Θεσμός της Ανοικτής Προστασίας των Ηλικιωμένων στην Ελλάδα. Έρευνα για τα ΚΑΠΗ*, [The Institution of Open Care for Senior Citizens in Greece. A Research on the ΚΑΠΗ], Αθήνα: Εθνικό Κέντρο Κοινωνικών Ερευνών, Υπουργείο Υγείας Πρόνοιας και Κοινωνικών Ασφαλίσεων.

Bamboukas, G. (1995): '*Το Κοινωνικό-ασφαλιστικό μας Σύστημα σε Κίνδυνο*', [Our Social System in Crisis], Οικονομικός, 6 July, pp.72–3.

Council of Europe (1995): *Recent Demographic Developments in Europe*, Strasbourg: Council of Europe Press.

Dumon, W. (1992): *National Family Policies in EC Countries in 1991*, Vol. 1, Brussels: Commission of the European Communities, Directorate General for Employment, Industrial Relations and Social Affairs.

Esping-Andersen, G. (1990): *The Three Worlds of Welfare Capitalism*, Cambridge: Polity Press.

European Commission (1994): *Social Protection in Europe 1993*, Luxembourg: Offical Publications of the European Community.

Eurostat (1993): *Labour Force Survey, 1983–1991*, Luxembourg: Office of Official Publications of the European Community.

Eurostat (1994): 'Social Protection in the European Union', *Statistics in Focus, Population and Social Conditions, 5*.

Eurostat (1995a): *Labour Force Survey 1993*, Luxembourg: Office of Official Publications of the European Communities.

Eurostat (1995b): 'The Population of the European Union on 1 January 1995', *Statistics in Focus, Population and Social Conditions, 8*.

Ferrera, M. (1996): 'The "Southern Model" of Welfare in Social Europe', *Journal of European Social Policy* 6/1, pp.17–37.

Giner, A. (1985): 'Political Economy, Legitimation and the State in Southern Europe', in R. Hudson and J. Lewis (eds), *Uneven Development in Southern Europe*, London and New York: Methuen, pp.309–50.

Katrougalos, G. (1996): 'The South European Welfare Model: The Greek Welfare State in Search of an Identity', *Journal of European Social Policy* 6/1, pp.39–60.

Lambiri-Dimaki, J. (1974): *Προς μίαν Ελληνικήν Κοινωνιολογίαν της Παιδείας 2*, [Towards a Greek Sociology of Education 2], Αθήνα: Εθνικό Κέντρο Κοινωνικών Ερευνών.

Lambropoulou, K. (1993): 'Οι Γυναίκες ως Φορείς Φροντίδας: Σημασία και Επιδράσεις στην Άσκηση Κοινωνικής Πολιτικής', ['Women as Carers: Importance and Effects on Social Policy'], in *Διαστάσεις της Κοινωνικής Πολιτικής Σήμερα*, [Dimensions of Today's Social Policy], Αθήνα: Ίδρυμα Σάκη Καράγιωργα, pp.715–33.

Land H. and H. Rose (1985): 'Compulsory Altruism for Some or Altruistic Society for All?', in P. Bean, J. Ferris and D. Whynes (eds), *Defence of Welfare*, London: Tavistock, pp.74–96.

Maloutas, T. and D. Economou (1988): 'Εισαγωγή. Κράτος Πρόνοιας: Το "Πρότυπο" και η Ελληνική Εκδοχή του', [The Welfare State: the 'Model' and its Greek Version], in T. Maloutas and D. Economou (eds), *Προβλήματα Ανάπτυξης του Κράτους Πρόνοιας στην Ελλάδα. Χωρικές και Τομεακές Προσεγγίσεις*, [Problems of Welfare State Development in Greece. Special and Sector Approaches], Αθήνα: Εξάντας, pp.13–57.

Ministry of Health, Welfare and Social Services (1995): *Ο Κοινωνικός Προϋπολογισμός του 1995*, [The Social Budget for the Year 1995], Αθήνα.

Moussourou, L.M. (1994): 'Family Policy in Greece: Traditional and Modern Patterns', in W. Dumon (ed.), *Changing Family Policies in the Member States of the European Union*, Brussels: Commission of the European Communities, DGV, pp.88–105.

Mouzelis, N. (1986): *Politics in the Semi-Periphery. Early Parliamentarism and Late Industrialization in the Balkans and Latin America*, London: Macmillan.

NSSG (unpublished data): *Population Projections for 1995*, Athens: Population Direction Section of Vital Statistics of Greece.

Pesmatzoglou, S. (1988): 'Κράτος και Εκπαίδευση στην Ελλάδα', [State and Education in Greece], in Th. Maloutas and D. Economou (eds), *Προβλήματα Ανάπτυξης του Κράτους Πρόνοιας. Χωρικές και Τομεακές Προσεγγίσεις*, [The Welfare State: Problems of Welfare State Development in Greece. Spatial and Sectoral Approaches], Αθήνα: Εξάντας, pp.221–39.

Petmesidou-Tsoulouvi M. (1992): *Κοινωνικές Ανισότητες και Κοινωνική Πολιτική*, [Social Inequalities and Social Policy], Αθήνα: Εξάντας.

Pitsiou, E. (1986): *Life Styles of Older Athenians*, Vol. B., Athens: The National Centre of Social Research.

Rombolis, S. (1991): *Κοινωνική Ασφάλιση. Διαρκής Κρίση και Προοπτικές*, [Social Security. Constant Crisis and Perspectives], Θεσσαλονίκη: Παρατηρητής.

Sissouras, A. *et al.* (1994): 'Greece', *The Reform of Health Care Systems: A Review of Seventeen OECD Countries*, EU 11, Paris: OECD, pp.149–65.

Symeonidou-Alatopoulou, H. (1976): 'Η Εξέλιξη του Θεσμού της Προίκας στην Ελλάδα, 1956–1974', [Evolution of the Institution of Dowry in Greece, 1956–1974], *Επιθεώρηση Κοινωνικών Ερευνών* 36, pp.322–40.

Symeonidou H. (1992): *Family Policy in Greece, Evolutions and Trends in 1990–1991*. Brussels: European Observatory on National Family Policies. Commission of the European Communities (mimeo).

Symeonidou, H. *et al.* (1992): *Κοινωνικό-Οικονομικοί Προσδιοριστικοί Παράγοντες της Γονιμότητας στην Ελλάδα, Τόμος Α, Ανάλυση για την Περιφέρεια της Πρωτεύουσας*, [Socio-Economic Factors Affecting Fertility in Greece. Vol. A. Analysis for the Greater Athens Area], Αθήνα: Εθνικό Κέντρο Κοινωνικών Ερευνών.

Symeonidou, H. (1993): *Family Policy in Greece, 1992–1993. Summary Report*, Brussels: European Observatory on National Family Policies. Brussels: Commission of the European Communities (mimeo).

Symeonidou, H. (1994): 'Le multiculturalisme de la famille immigrée', in P. Popes, C. Presvelou and C. Balsa (eds), *Familie et Humaine dans l'Espace de l'U.E. 1994 Année de la Famille*, Lisboa: Obra Catolica Portuguesa de Migracoes, pp.81–5.

Triantafillou, J. and A. Amira (1988): *Health and Use of Services by the Elderly in Rural Greece*, Athens (mimeo).

Triantafillou, T. and T. Mestheneou (1991): 'Συστήματα Παροχής Υπηρεσιών-Πρόνοιας για τους Ηλικιωμένους στην Ελλάδα' [Systhems of Providing Welfare Services for Senior Citizens in Greece], *Επιθεώρηση Κοινωνικών Επιστημών* 24, pp.301–2.

Tsaoussis, D. and A. Hadziyannis (1990): *Κοινωνικές και Χωροταξικές Προϋποθέσεις Λειτουργίας των ΚΑΠΗ ως Θεσμών Σύνδεσης των Ηλικιωμένων με την Κοινότητα*, [Social and Planning Requirements for the Operation of KAPIs as Institutions to Link the Elderly and the Community], Αθήνα: Πάντειο Πανεπιστήμιο Κοινωνικών και Πολιτιστικών Επιστημών, Υπουργείο Υγείας Πρόνοιας και Κοινωνικών Ασφαλίσεων.

Tsoukalas, K. (1987): *Κράτος, Κοινωνία, Εργασία στην Μεταπολεμική Ελλάδα*, [State, Society and Work in the Post-War Greece], Αθήνα: Θεμέλιο.

Tsouyopoulos, G. (1981): *Το Ελληνικό Αστικό Κέντρο· Δευτερο Μέρος. Η Περίπτωση της Λάρισας*, [The Greek Urban Centre, Vol. II. The Case of Larissa], Αθήνα: ΕΚΚΕ.

Veniopoulou, K. (1988): *Nuclear Norms and Extended Networks. Ideology and Reality in Welfare Provisions*, Athens (mimeo).

Social Exclusion and Minimum Income Programmes in Spain

MIGUEL LAPARRA and MANUEL AGUILAR

This article analyses the ways in which Spanish society is dealing with extreme poverty and social exclusion. Spanish society exhibits a paradoxical combination of widespread precariousness and a limited degree of extreme poverty and exclusion. Social exclusion is still, to a great extent, a remnant of the past rather than a result of recent trends in employment. Some of the social policy actions carried out during the last fifteen years with an impact on this problem are the development of a means-tested benefit system, the setting up of minimum income for social integration programmes targeting the most excluded, and the building of a network of public local social services. We analyse these programmes in the context of economic modernization in Spain in recent years.

POVERTY AND SOCIAL EXCLUSION IN SPAIN

Widespread Social Precariousness that Does not Lead to High Social Exclusion

Spanish society exhibits a somewhat paradoxical combination of high social precariousness and relatively limited exclusion. Spain has some of the highest levels of unemployment, job instability and relative poverty of all European countries. Unemployment rates have been constantly more than 15 per cent of the labour force since the early 1980s, and more than 20 per cent from the mid-1980s until 1992. According to official statistics, one third of the labour force now has a non-permanent labour contract. Relative poverty figures, taken from several different surveys carried out during the 1980s and early 1990s, show that between 15 and 25 per cent of Spanish households are living below a poverty line of 50 per cent of the average equivalent family income.

These figures might lead one to think that, among the developed societies of Europe, Spain is the one that suffers the greatest strains on those mechanisms that assure social integration in modern developed societies: a stable job with a decent level of income, a strong social protection system linked to job-related contributions, etc. Such a degree of instability in these basic integration mechanisms would suggest that Spain has the greatest risk of social exclusion in Europe.

But data, and the daily observation of Spanish society, show that the degree of social exclusion is quite limited, or at least much lower than what one could expect from the levels of unemployment and relative poverty. The number of homeless people, for instance, can be taken as an indicator of extreme social exclusion. It is much lower in Spanish towns than in other big European cities such as Paris or London, and well below the level of New York. Madrid has some 2,000–2,500 people living in the streets or in shelters, less than half the rate of Paris and nearly one-tenth of its equivalent in New York. It is true that Madrid (as well as, to a lesser extent, some other Spanish towns) still has a number of *bidonville* dwellers, but its social meaning is much more complex than a simple case of exclusion from housing. Some 2,000 families live in shacks in the outskirts of Madrid, many of which are actually involved in marginal economic activities that can only survive in such a context (Gaviria, Aguilar and Laparra 1995).

Crime rates also seem to be significantly lower in Spain than in other European countries. The overall crime rates (which certainly have some problems of comparability) given for 1987 by the *Atlas de la criminalité en France* (Atlas 1994) were 34.1 per cent for the whole of Spain, far below the 57.1 per cent in France or the 77.9 per cent given for the United Kingdom. Crime rates have been decreasing in recent years. Spain certainly has a high rate of prisoners, but that has much to do with the inefficiency of the judiciary system. A great number of prisoners are in jail for crimes related to drugs (drug dealing or theft committed by drug addicts), among whom there are non-resident foreigners.

Some other indirect social indicators tend to confirm this view. Infant mortality rates are very low, and the rates of one-person and one-parent households are significantly lower than in other developed European countries. These data are certainly not the result of a in-depth survey of social exclusion, which itself can be defined in different ways. But they tend to support the hypothesis of a relatively low level of extreme social exclusion, and in any case a level lower than one would expect from global indicators of social precariousness.

Some Explanations for Social Integration

Family solidarity is certainly one of the basic factors that explain how Spanish society has been able to reduce the impact of unemployment and job instability. Such solidarity has a very wide meaning. It is not just that people in distress may get some help from their relatives, which is actually a very important role. Spanish families have responded to difficulties by reducing the birth rate and postponing to the late twenties the independence of young people, who are the most affected by unemployment. This means that many Spanish families may integrate in a single household a stable income (in many cases brought home by an adult male breadwinner), a lower and much more unstable income from part-time or short-term jobs or unemployment benefits derived from such jobs (which in many cases will be brought home by the wife and sons and daughters in their late teens or twenties who stay at home), and even an income from a grandparent's old age pension. This means that even if pensions, unemployment benefits or wages are low, they may add up to an acceptable level of family income. At the same time, families are still the chief providers of care for the elderly, the disabled and the ill, as well as of housework. Thus, women add a great volume of non-market work that helps families to cope with the lack of resources that may come from unemployment or job instability.

A second factor that must be taken into account is the expansion of a means-tested sector in the Spanish system of social protection. The development of the Spanish welfare state during the 1980s shows a rather moderate rate of growth. It has been just slightly faster than overall economic growth. But this general trend hides a very strong growth of the means-tested benefits subsystem. This system includes four main kinds of benefits: minimum pension supplements, non-contributory pensions for the elderly and the disabled, assistance unemployment benefits and *salario social* (minimum income) programmes. These programmes will be discussed below.

When seen as a whole, the number of beneficiaries of this subsystem of means-tested benefits increased ten-fold from 1982 to 1992. By 1992 there were 4.5 million beneficiaries – more than 12 per cent of the Spanish population. Although this system certainly has a number of serious problems, such as its limited capacity for protecting the most excluded, it has significantly limited the effects of unemployment. This is especially true in the context of family solidarity, which acts as a mechanism of internal redistribution of income from different sources.

Another factor that has limited the impact of social exclusion is the social housing model, which is based on ownership. Since the 1960s, social housing policy has been mainly oriented towards offering relatively easy access to ownership. The social conservatism of the Franco regime hoped to turn workers into peaceful property owners through this mechanism. The quality of the social housing built in the 1960s and early 1970s was usually very low, and a significant part of the investment in social housing during the 1980s was devoted to rebuilding a great number of obsolete social housing projects.

TABLE 1

EVOLUTION OF SOCIAL PROTECTION EXPENDITURES AND OF MEANS-TESTED
BENEFITS IN SPAIN 1982–1991

	1982	1983	1984	1985	1986	1987
Social protection expenditure (per cent of GDP)	19.4	19.5	19.4	19.9	19.5	19.6
Social protection per capita expenditure (in constant 1985 ECU)	1,050.7	1,068.5	1,080.1	1,130.7	1,162.5	1,238.5
Number of means-tested benefits	464,631	470,066	2,879,448	3,075,603	2,978,894	3,088,838

	1988	1989	1990	1991	1992
Social protection expenditure (per cent of GDP)	19.8	20.1	20.7	21.4	N/A
Social protection per capita expenditure (in constant 1985 ECU)	1,322.3	1,408.4	1,504.0	1,600.5	N/A
Number of means-tested benefits	3,297,999	3,588,472	3,800,560	4,039,260	4,548,084

Sources: Eurostat (SEEPROS) and Ministerio de Trabajo y Seguridad Social, *Boletin de Estadísticas Laborales* (various years) and *Anuario de Estadística Laborales* (various years)

It is true that this housing model based on ownership has limited the development of a rental market, thus leading to relatively high prices. At the same time, when social housing policy weakened during the middle and late 1980s, it turned into a major cause of the difficulties for young people to get a home of their own. But it has limited the processes of spatial segregation of the poorest groups of the population. Although it is true that social exclusion and poverty does appear in higher concentrations in certain places (both in old inner cities and in the peripheral areas), working class families are less prone to abandon these areas and are deeply interested in maintaining the social value and image of their neighbourhoods.

FIGURE 1

EVOLUTION OF SOCIAL PROTECTION EXPENDITURE AND MEANS-TESTED
BENEFITS IN SPAIN 1982–91 (Index 1982+100)

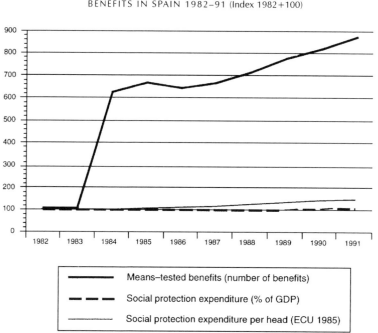

Sources: Eurostat (SEEPROS), Ministerio de Trabajo y Seguridad Social, Ministerio de Asuntos
Sociale, *Boletin de Estadísticas Laborales* (various years) and *Anuario de Estadística
Laborales* (various years)

Limits of the Integrated Precariousness Model

These factors, together with universal education and health care, help to
explain how Spanish society has been able to cope with relatively high
levels of unemployment and job instability. Social analysis and social
policies must take this into account and should be careful to avoid
interpreting Spanish society through simple indicators (such as the
unemployment rate) which may have different social meanings in
different social contexts. But it must also be stressed that this model of
integrated precariousness has some serious limits.

The first problem is that it certainly leaves some people out and
without any kind of protection. A society that relies on family solidarity
may be, at the same time, preventing a great number of people from
falling into exclusion and leaving a small part of the population in a
completely unprotected situation. There is no way of granting a right to
family solidarity. Those who lack a family, or those who live in broken

families may be (and actually are) fewer in number than in other societies, but may also be in a much worse situation. The system of means-tested benefits is aimed mainly at those who already have a (low-level) contributory pension, or at those who have ceased to receive unemployment benefits (but who in any case have had a regular employment experience). This leaves out those in marginal labour-market situations or who lack any job experience.

The second problem is that intra-family redistribution means sacrifices in terms of money, of work (paid or unpaid) and of personal opportunities that bring about conflicts and tensions that may erode family structures. Thus, this form of integrated precariousness may be experienced as a very uneasy situation of insecurity and frustration, even if it does not turn into one of poverty or exclusion. The social and personal costs of this model have fallen chiefly on women and the young.

SOME CHARACTERISTICS OF SOCIAL EXCLUSION IN SPAIN

Research on Poverty in Spain

There is a tradition of research on poverty in Spain, which goes back to the 1960s, but that has mainly developed in the 1980s. This tradition has focused mainly on relative poverty, identified as low family income, and on its measurement. In 1984, a research project carried out by EDIS on behalf of *Caritas Española* (the main Catholic Church social action agency) had a great impact on public opinion. Its estimate of 8 million Spaniards living below the poverty line of 50 per cent of the average per capita family income shook the media (EDIS 1984). It certainly had the virtue of bringing the question of poverty onto the public agenda.

In the following years several other surveys were carried out – some of them at the national level, such as the still unpublished survey carried out by the Ministry of Labour and Social Security in 1985 (or, more precisely, by the *Instituto de Estudios Laborales y de Seguridad Social* and the *Centro de Investigaciones Sociológicas*, both social research government agencies) – and the first official study to offer figures on poverty was carried out by the *Instituto Nacional de Estadística* in 1990–91 (INE 1993). Many others have been carried out at the regional level, usually on behalf of regional autonomous governments or regional *Caritas* organisations. Two of the most interesting are those carried out in the Basque Country (Sanzo 1987) and in Catalonia (GES n.d.). Both studies use several poverty lines, both objective (50 per cent of the average equivalent income) and subjective (basically the CSP–Deleeck and SPL–Leyden methods). All these studies share an approach to measuring relative poverty defined by means of an income (or expenditure) indicator. All of them show that a significant part of the Spanish population lives in relative poverty. When half the average income is taken as the poverty line the results are somewhere around 20 per cent, and when subjective poverty line methods are used, the figures increase substantially.

However, the social and political debate on poverty has always had an ambiguous response to these research projects. The results of these projects have to some extent triggered the debate on poverty, and in the case of the Basque Country, they even produced the IMI (social integration) law (see below). But at the same time, what public opinion, politicians and public and private social agencies consider to be poverty is something very different and much smaller. Public opinion uses the term poor to refer to something much closer to absolute poverty or social exclusion, and thus to something much smaller than one-fifth of the population. Public and private social services agencies focus their programmes (including minimum income programmes) on a much smaller group of the population, somewhere between one and five per cent of the population.

In recent years there has been an attempt to approach this problem from a different perspective. In 1992, a survey on social exclusion in Aragón (Laparra et al. 1994b) carried out an in-depth analysis of the characteristics of the population living in extreme poverty. The excluded population was located through a wide range of public and private social services. It was defined not just by means of an income threshold, but through a combination of economic and social indicators, designed to identify people who experienced the following to a severe degree:

• lack of access to regular employment;

• lack of access to general social welfare systems (health care, education, housing etc.);

• lack of income (i.e., income below social assistance benefit levels);

• problems and/or conflicts in the field of social integration.

It thus concentrated on a much smaller social area, somewhere around three to five per cent of the population. This survey revealed significant differences between what it described as social exclusion and what previous studies termed relative poverty.

The Different Characteristics of the Poor and the Excluded

Whereas relative poverty appears to strongly affect the elderly and people living in rural areas, social exclusion seems to be an urban problem that affects mostly young adults and children. Traditional poverty surveys show that a significant number of elderly people, especially living in rural areas, have a very low level of income. However, most of these people could hardly be termed *socially excluded*. They are socially integrated people with a level of income that, although certainly low, has a very different meaning in a small village than in a large city. Social exclusion occurs mainly in urban areas, and concentrates in some specific parts of these areas, such as old inner cities and some new peripheral neighbourhoods.

All of the following characteristics – old age, a high proportion of women, living alone or in lone couples, in rural areas or small towns and a high rate of illiteracy – which appear in traditional poverty surveys are the result of a high proportion of rural low-income elderly pensioners in relative poverty as a whole. Conversely, when the focus is on social exclusion, a very different image emerges: a high proportion of young adults and of children, and a relatively low proportion of elderly people, as is clearly shown in Figure 2. Exclusion rates are higher than the average both for single people and for large households (five members and above). There is a significant number of very large households, mainly belonging to the gypsy ethnic group. A high birth rate is associated with social exclusion, although what causes what is not clear.

The Excluded and Economic Activity

The social exclusion we have discovered could be characterized as pre-Fordist. It affects mostly people who have never had the experience of secure jobs, rather than those who have lost their jobs in recent years. At the same time, a very significant part of the excluded (although certainly not all of them) do have some kind of economic activity, although they are frequently poorly paid, unstable and in most cases are not offered any kind of social respect. But they certainly help most of the excluded to survive. The survey shows that the potential for economic activity is lower among the excluded, due to the high number of children and the high proportion of people with severe health problems and handicaps. About one-third of the *excluded* adults in Aragón suffered from some kind of handicap or severe health problem. The activity rate for people over 16 is slightly higher than the average for Aragón (53 per cent), while the employment rate is lower (29 per cent among the excluded, 39 per cent overall).

The economic activity of the socially excluded is quite hetero-geneous. Its main characteristics may be summarized as follows:

• unemployment is widespread among the excluded. Not only is the

FIGURE 2
DISTRIBUTION BY AGE AND GENDER OF THE POPULATION OF ARAGÓN
(ACCORDING TO THE 1993 SURVEY)

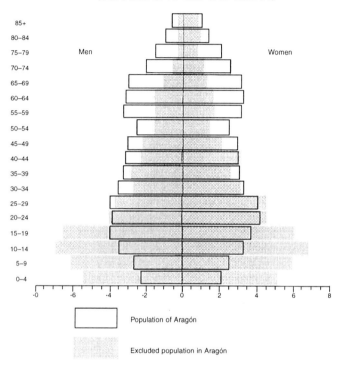

Note: Bars show each age group as a percentage of the whole.
Sources: INE 1991 and Aguilar, Laparra and Gaviria (1996a)

unemployment rate higher (around 43 per cent), but unemployment itself is different. It is what may be called 'exclusion unemployment';

• a large number of the socially excluded are long-term unemployed, whose chances of obtaining even short term contracts are very limited;

• even if many of them are officially registered as unemployed, very few get any kind of unemployment benefit (only 18 per cent of the unemployed among the excluded);

• nor do they receive training or job search support from the official employment agency (INEM).

Even more specific to the socially excluded than 'exclusion unemployment' is what we could call 'exclusion employment'. Many of the excluded actually work and get some kind of income for such work. Half of the excluded households had income from work as the main source of income. Six out of ten excluded households were actually developing some kind of paid work when the survey was carried out. However, the kind of paid work carried out by the excluded is quite particular. It is closer to pre-proletarian or at least pre-Fordist types of work than work as most people would consider it today: a source of stability and social integration. Jobs carried out by the excluded are not only low paid, but in most cases are stigmatizing: street and flea-market selling, cardboard and junk recovery, working as itinerant agricultural or building labourers, as maids or in marginal activities (begging or prostitution) account for two-thirds of all the work carried out by the excluded. Needless to say, practically all of such jobs lack social security coverage. The survey showed that the excluded in Aragón (4.5 per cent of the population) contributed 3.1 per cent of the workers and 2.4 per cent of working hours, but received only 0.9 per cent of the wages paid in the region. That meant around 400 pesetas per hour – gross.

We do not find a passive dependency attitude among the excluded. We rather find very active people who receive only a meagre income and no stability or social protection from their jobs. These jobs provide those who carry them out with a very negative social image. Any strategy for social and economic integration should focus on how this economic activity can be used as a basis to find better jobs, rather than on how allegedly passive and dependent people are pressed into work. As most income derived from such jobs is officially invisible and quite irregular, means-testing for benefits hardly works in a fair and efficient way.

THE GROWTH OF A MEANS-TESTED BENEFIT SYSTEM IN SPAIN

The foundations of Spain's modern system of social security were laid during the 1960s. Those who designed the system foresaw the need for a complementary subsystem of social assistance that would take care of those who were unable to contribute to the social security system, which was initially conceived only for waged workers in industry and the services. Two public agencies were set up: the Fondo Nacional de Asistencia Social (FONAS) (National Fund for Social Assistance) and the Instituto Nacional de Asistencia Social (INAS) (National Institute for Social Assistance). The former was to pay social assistance pensions to the elderly and the disabled and other assistance benefits, while the latter was to provide social services in kind.

However, the whole system (social security and social assistance) did not actually develop until the 1970s. During the second half of the 1970s, the transition to democracy was accompanied by a process of expansion of the social security system (Rodríguez Cabrero 1989). This was partially a consequence of the system's normal development (when the first generations who had contributed arrived at retirement age) but also of an obvious need for building the legitimacy of the new democratic governments. Government-decreed pension increases and – even more importantly – the extension of social security to farmers, the self-employed and other groups brought about a spectacular growth of the system.

By the early 1980s, the social security system was well developed, but the social assistance subsystem barely existed. Actually, the Constitution of 1978 stated that the social security system should reach the whole population, so the original idea of an independent system of social assistance was partially abandoned. The autonomous regional governments retained responsibility for maintaining social assistance services and benefits, although this was established in a very generic way. However, two basic trends changed this situation during the 1980s.

First, the national government wished to limit the growth of expenditure on pensions and unemployment benefits. The pension system was reformed in 1985, in a way that toughened conditions of access, limited the growth and amount of middle and high-level pensions, but at the same time established minimum pension supplements. The unemployment benefit system was reformed in 1984, limiting access to benefits, but establishing a second level of assistance unemployment benefits for those who had exhausted their right to benefits and for certain special cases. Second, there was growing social pressure on regional and national governments to provide some kind of protection for certain groups who were completely outside the social security system, such as the handicapped, certain groups of elderly people and the unemployed. This brought about a somewhat confused process of growth in the non contributory means-tested benefit system. The social assistance old age pensions of the FONAS, which were ridiculous in amount until 1982, began to rise to a low but somehow acceptable level. A special social assistance minimum income benefit for the handicapped was established in 1984. In 1991, both programmes were integrated into a non-contributory means-tested social security pension system. Since 1989 regional governments began to establish minimum income levels for social integration programmes.

Nowadays in Spain there is a series of means-tested benefits aimed at ensuring a minimum level of monthly income for different groups of the population. These benefits barely constitute a system, since they are not well integrated, frequently overlap and suffer from an incoherence of design (Aguilar, Laparra and Gaviria 1996b).

There are four basic minimum income benefit groups:

1. social security minimum pension supplement (*Complementos de mínimos de pensiones de la Seguridad Social*);

2. social assistance pensions and non-contributory social security pensions for the elderly and the disabled (*Pensiones Asistenciales* and *Pensiones No Contributivas*);

3. social assistance benefits for the unemployed (*Subsidio asistencial por desempleo*);

4. minimum income for social integration programmes (*Ingresos mínimos de inserción* or '*salario social*').

All of these benefits are means-tested, but their respective means-testing criteria, and the way in which they work, are quite different from one another in several aspects:

- some of them are means-tested benefits that are paid to people already receiving social security pensions (1) or to unemployed people who have finished their contributory benefit period (3). In these cases, people with no previous contribution at all cannot claim benefits;

- benefits in groups 2 and 4 can be claimed with no previous contribution;

- some are differential benefits that raise existing income to the minimum, whereas other benefits have a fixed amount;

- benefits in groups 1 and 2 are claimed mostly by elderly and disabled people who are, therefore, outside the labour market. Exceptions in these groups are widow pensioners (some of whom are under 65 and able to work), orphans (most of them under 18) and social assistance sickness pensioners (who in some cases are *socially disabled* people);

- benefits in groups 3 and 4 are claimed by people who are unemployed or in extreme poverty, and who are mostly of working age but with different real levels of working ability.

The differences between these programmes are fully illustrated in the table in Appendix 1.

The data available on people receiving social minimum benefits in Spain has several limits. The data refer to the number of benefits, not people or households/families. It is therefore difficult to calculate the population living with the support of these benefits. It is very unlikely

TABLE 2

NUMBER OF MEANS-TESTED SOCIAL MINIMUM BENEFITS IN SPAIN
(DECEMBER 1992)

	Under 60		60 and older	Total
	In the labour market	*Disabled/ not in the labour market*		

1. *Complementos de mínimos de pensiones* (social security minimum pension supplements)

Jubilación (retirement–old age)	–	–	1,164,845	1,164,845
Viudedad (widows)	–	134,000	723,000	856,948
Invalidez (disability)	–	126,000	301,000	427,251
Orfandad y familiares (Orphans and other relatives)	–	100,000	8,000	108,363

2. *Pensiones asistenciales y no contributivas* (social assistance and non contributory pensions)

Pensiones asistenciales de enfermedad (sickness)	–	92,014	80,889	172,903
Pensiones asistenciales de vejez (old age)	–	–	140,295	140,295
Subsidio LISMI (disability)	–	102,438	123,091	225,529
Pensiones no contributivas jubilación* (old age)	–	–	134,298	134,298
Pensiones no contributivas invalidez* (disability)	–	79,410	–	79,410
Prestación por hijo minusválido a cargo	–	257,681	–	257,681

3. *Subsidios asistenciales por desempleo* (assistance unemployment benefits)

Subsidio por desempleo (assistance unemployment)	789,412	–	35,760	825,172
Subsidio eventuales agrarios (agricultural labourers)	205,524	–	–	205,524

4. *Programas de salario social* (minimum income for social integration benefits)

Prestaciones periódicas y empleo social	40,237	–	–	40,237

1. Complementos de mínimos de pensiones	0	360,000	2,196,845	2,557,407
2. Pensiones asistenciales y no contributivas	0	531,543	478,573	1,010,116
3. Subsidios asistenciales por desempleo	994,936	0	35,760	1,030,696
4. Programas de «salario social»	40,237	0	0	40,237
Total	**1,035,173**	**891,543**	**2,711,178**	**4,638,456**

* June 1993

that any single person will be receiving more than one benefit. It may happen (though it is not too likely) that the same person will receive some kind of social assistance pension and a minimum income benefit. However, it is much more common to find two (or even more) benefits in the same household. Non-contributory pensions are actually paid to both spouses, and a son or daughter may be on assistance unemployment benefit. It therefore does not make much sense to try to estimate from these figures the number of *ayants-droit*, for double counting would be strongly increased with no basis for correction.

The distribution of pension supplement claimants (under/over 60) is a rough estimate. We have assumed that the distribution of minimum pension supplements by age groups in each type of pension follows the same pattern as all pensions of each type. It is likely that minimum pension supplements are more frequent among the eldest groups (who contributed during the low wage and contribution period of the 1950s and 1960s). So our estimate of pension supplements under 65 should be taken as a maximum. A number of widows and orphans are able to work and in the labour market, but one can assume that most of the social security pensioners under 60 are actually out of work.

SALARIO SOCIAL: MINIMUM INCOMES FOR SOCIAL INTEGRATION PROGRAMMES IN SPAIN

Among the various means-tested benefit programmes mentioned in the previous section, the *salario social* deserves specific discussion (Aguilar, Laparra and Gaviria 1995). The name *salario social* (social salary or wage) is actually a very inadequate term, which has been used to designate very different programmes. The name *salario social* does not actually appear in any of the official designations of such programmes.

In 1988, the Basque regional government decided to establish a limited form of minimum income for social integration, to some extent based on the French RMI (*revenue minimum d'intégration*). The regional government of Navarra had already established a similar programme in 1985 with a strong workfare component, quite unnoticed outside the region. The central government reacted strongly against the Basque initiative, on the grounds that benefits were not the correct solution to poverty, and that it might violate the constitutional right to equality of treatment for all Spanish citizens. The subsequent debate did not, unfortunately, focus on whether this kind of benefits-for-social-integration programmes were the best policy against severe poverty, but rather on the political identity of regional governments and their ability to set up their own social policy measures and establish their own agreements with the trade unions, who saw in these programmes an indirect way of extending unemployment benefits. *Caritas* (the catholic social action agency) supported the establishment of these programmes for they were the first explicit social policy measure aimed at helping the poorest.

By 1992, all regional governments had decided to establish a *salario social* programme (except the Balearic Islands that only did so in 1995). But although the origins were the same and in most cases the overall design is quite similar, these programmes are actually quite different from one another.

All the *salario social* programmes share some elements:

- they include benefits in cash that are paid to an individual but take into account all the members of the household, who in most cases may not claim a benefit of their own;

- they establish an income level that is to be taken as a criterion of lack of sufficient income, at around 30,000–45,000 ptas for the claimant, plus a much smaller quantity for each additional member of the household;

- they set a minimum time of residence (one to ten years) in the region to qualify for the benefit;

- benefits are always granted for a specific period of time. In some cases they may be renewed, as long as the circumstances are the same, whereas in other regions there is a strict time limit.

Although these elements are common to all programmes, it is possible to establish some clear differences. In some regions benefits can be legally claimed as a right, while in most cases the regional government grants the benefit at its own discretion. A few regions have developed a workfare model in which most claimants actually get a six month public utility job instead of benefits in cash. Some regions have established wide programmes that reach most of the severely poor population, while in other cases the programme barely exists. Taking all these differences into account, we can identify several types of *salario social* programmes:

- the only programme that resembles a minimum income benefit as conceived in other European countries is the Basque *Ingreso Mínimo de Inserción* (IMI). It is actually provided as a right and is received by all those who claim and qualify for it. The French RMI is certainly the closest model;

- three regions (Madrid, Catalonia and Navarra) have limited versions of the same idea, in which only some claimants actually get the benefit, usually due to budget limitations;

- three regions (Andalusia, Asturias and Castilla-La Mancha) have workfare programmes, under which some of the claimants are hired for a short-term job, chiefly in local councils. Access is discretionary and relatively limited;

- the rest of the programmes are actually discretionary social assistance benefits, of some importance in certain regions, but very limited or barely existent in others.

The size and importance of these programmes is set out in Table 3.

TABLE 3

MINIMUM INCOME BENEFIT CLAIMANTS IN 1993

Region	Population aged 25–64 in 1991	Households 1990–91	Households receiving monthly salario social benefits 1993	Per cent of total households
Basque Country	1,121,960	610,787	11,786	1.93
Navarra	263,882	145,964	1,460	1.00
Madrid	2,538,726	1,418,768	10,996	0.78
Castilla-La Mancha	789,453	512,489	2,391	0.47
Canary Islands	723,760	393,564	1,683	0.43
Asturias	570,241	339,884	1,375	0.40
Catalonia	3,100,219	1,806,184	5,872	0.33
Castilla y León	1,268,845	802,853	2,495	0.31
Andalusia	3,275,671	1,876,388	5,000	0.27
Rioja	134,154	75,561	205	0.27
Galicia	1,355,989	780,266	1,476	0.19
Murcia	490,490	283,349	500	0.18
Comunidad Valenciana	1,904,362	1,141,993	1,873	0.16
Extremadura	503,380	329,150	441	0.13
Cantabria	265,123	151,305	100	0.07
Aragón	598,981	384,009	106	0.03
Balearic Islands	352,263	212,106		
Ceuta and Melilla	57,558	35,232		
Spain	**19,315,057**	**11,299,852**	**47,759**	**0.42**
Regions with minimum income	18,905,236	11,052,514	47,759	0.43

Source: Aguilar *et al.* (1995)

Minimum income regulations usually include some measures aimed at encouraging labour market integration:

- the most widespread of these is the obligation to sign a *social insertion contract*. Its contents are actually very different for each region and each case, but as a general rule consist mainly in social support/ treatment and some labour market integration oriented activities;

- the general obligation of accepting (not refusing) job offers, as occurs with unemployment benefits. This condition can be found in five regions: Andalusia, Asturias, the Canaries, Castilla y León and the Basque Country;

- in some regions claimants may be asked to help social services by assisting the elderly or handicapped (with no labour status);

- regions have legally established (and four actually enforce) social interest temporary jobs (*empleo social protegido*) as a compulsory alternative to benefits;

- limits placed on the period of for the receipt of benefits, which is very short in most regions, as well as the possibility of removing benefits in certain circumstances.

No region has actually established any work encouragement mechanism (such as partially taking into account labour-related earnings), although the Basque Country IMI Law is open to such a possibility.

It is very difficult to find precise data on what is actually done to help and encourage labour market integration for claimants of minimum income from social integration programmes (IMI – *salario social*). In most cases, insertion actions and plans are designed and managed by social services departments, with a limited capacity for action in this field. It is possible to identify four main types of actions:

- there is a very large supply of training courses (*Formación profesional ocupacional*) funded by the *Instituto Nacional de Empleo* (INEM), regional governments, local authorities and the European Social Fund. This has become the standard labour market integration action for the unemployed. As it is fairly easy to find room for someone in such courses, social services departments have frequently sent their IMI claimants to them. These courses may have proven useful for some of the less excluded or marginalized IMI claimants. Nevertheless, they do not seem to be too useful for the majority of them. The previous education and training level required is usually too high for most IMI claimants. Standard training courses are inadequate to cope with the difficulties of people with poor work experience and habits, thus appearing quite useless to the claimants themselves. This problem has developed into a perverse mechanism of using training courses as a punishing and control method, regardless of its insertion value, and of claimants passively attending such courses with no effective results (except that of keeping benefits). These courses, seen as useless by claimants, are at the same time a strong obstacle to poor people's economic survival strategies (working in irregular jobs). Conversely, IMI-style benefits are quite helpful in such cases, offering a stable (although very low) income that acts as a support basis for somewhat higher (but much less reliable) income from marginal economic activities;

• some local social services and labour agencies have developed specialized training activities which usually combine basic education, (pre)professional training and social support, specifically oriented to IMI claimants and other social services' clients. These experiences (still very limited in number) have proven much more adequate and effective than traditional training courses;

• the *empleo social protegido* (temporary social labour contracts) has attained an important level in certain regions. Navarra, Asturias, Andalusia and Castilla-La Mancha put most of their minimum income benefit claimants into such temporary jobs. This approach is much closer to real-world work experience. Nevertheless, in many cases such programmes are not actually designed as a path towards better opportunities in the labour market, but rather as a more legitimate way of paying benefits. Temporary contracts tend to be too short to be helpful, and claimants are transferred to the responsibility of central government labour market agencies at the end of the contract.

• Some experiences of specialized professional training have evolved into something quite similar to the *Entreprises d'insertion* in France. These experiences are still limited in number and have to face the lack of legal regulation. Subsidies are usually discretionary and irregular.

During the last six years, the Spanish social services administration, especially at the regional and local levels, have made the strongest effort ever in the field of social integration anti-poverty programmes. Its effect on the poorest groups of the Spanish population has certainly been important. It has also brought about some interesting changes in local social services, which have tried to adapt themselves to the needs of a population to which they previously had very little to offer.

TABLE 4
RELATIVE SIZE OF *EMPLEO SOCIAL PROTEGIDO* IN THE REGIONS WHERE IT IS AN
ALTERNATIVE TO IMI-STYLE BENEFITS

Region	A Claimants of *salario social* (as a whole) 1993	B People who are offered a social utility employment 1993	B/A per cent
Andalusia	5.000	3.200	64
Asturias	1.375	1.300	94,5
Castilla-La Mancha	2.391	1.167	48,8
Navarra	1.460	393	26,9
Total (4 regions)	10.226	6.060	59,4

Source: Aguilar *et al.* (1996b)

TABLE 5

SOME FIGURES ON IMI/*SALARIO SOCIAL* CLAIMANTS' PARTICIPATION IN
LABOR MARKET INTEGRATION ACTIVITIES 1993

Community of Madrid
IMI claimants 1993   10,996
- No. of «Proyectos IMI» (training and workfare projects)   33
- People taking part in «Proyectos IMI»   1,334
- People taking part in «Proyectos IMI»/IMI claimants   18
- per cent of total Programa IMI expenditure   9.7%

Catalonia
RMI claimants 1993   7,000
- People taking part in «Proyectos de motivación laboral»   1,185
- People receiving vocational counseling   1,926
- People taking part in vocational training   580
- People taking part in job search activities   228
- per cent of RMI claimants who take part in employment oriented actions   46.6%

Basque Country
IMI claimants 1993   11,756
- Of the claimants who have ceased to receive RMI,
  per cent that has found a job   52.2%
  per cent that receive a pension   19.0 %

Comunidad Valenciana
PER claimants 1993   1,873
- People taking part in Talleres de Integración social (training)   544
- People taking part in Centros de Integración Sociolaboral (workfare)   127

Source: Aguilar *et al.* (1995)

Nevertheless, this experience has several limits and problems. The first weakness is the very irregular development of *salario social* programmes, which accounts not just for certain differences between regions but for their practical inexistence in some areas. This tendency has been strengthened by the lack of a central government policy in the field, either to take the whole policy area in hand, or to establish certain minimum levels for the whole country. Most regional governments do not have the budget required.

The result is not only the existence of regional differences, but also the imbrication of *salario social* and other means-tested benefits whose regulations takes no account of each other. Co-operation between national and regional agencies is practically non-existent. This is especially important when it comes to unemployment benefit, vocational training and labour market agencies. As a result, in some cases, *salario social* programmes are limited to low level in-cash benefits with little in the way of accompanying social integration measures, which was what the central government was originally supposed to be afraid of.

THE DEVELOPMENT OF LOCAL SOCIAL SERVICES

Finally, a few words must be said about the role of local social services in Spain during the last 15 years. Their importance derives not only from the strong and rapid development of such services during the 1980s, but also from the role they are supposed to play in the struggle against poverty.

Local social services have different names in different Spanish regions. *Servicios sociales generales, servicios sociales de atención primaria, servicios sociales de base* or *servicios sociales comunitarios* (i.e. *general, primary care, basic* or *community social services*) are some of the names given to these non-specialized local services. The basic design is, however, quite similar in most places. Small teams of social workers, social educators, family workers and others run local services that offer information on social problems, access to some social benefits and some community work activities (Casado Pérez *et al.* 1994). The forerunners of these services can be traced back to the 1960s. They began to operate properly in 1979 in large towns and spread through most of the country during the 1980s. They were set up by local councils, with the support of regional governments, especially in rural areas. Since 1988, central government, regional governments and local councils agreed to finance these services together.

By the early 1990s there was a widespread network of local services, that covers most of the country, with one social worker for every

10,000–20,000 inhabitants and one employee for every 4,000–9,000 inhabitants. These rates vary from one region to another and from rural to urban areas (Laparra, Aguilar and Gaviria 1994a). These services were initially conceived as local offices that would offer an easier and closer access to social benefits. This explains some of the problems local social services are facing, especially in the fight against poverty. On the one hand, access to information and benefits (and to a certain degree, home help) have absorbed most of the resources and effort, while community action and social casework have lagged behind (social casework is actually not recognized as a specific service). On the other, the benefit catalogue is rather limited in Spain, so it is not unusual to see local public services sending claimants to private agencies (the private agencies that public local services were supposed to supersede) in order to obtain financial support.

This changed to some extent in the early 1990s when minimum income programmes were set up and, in most regions, access to such benefits was to be achieved through local social services. Not only were they supposed to offer access to benefits, but they were also to establish a social integration contract that was expected to include social casework, access to training and rehabilitation services, etc. This challenge has revealed some of the limits and problems of local social services, that may be summarized as follows:

• the system of local social services is not sufficiently integrated. It is not unusual to find different services from local, regional and even in some cases national agencies acting in the same field on the same problems. Although efforts have been made to simplify this structure, in many regions services for the handicapped, people with drug problems and children have their own independent structures. And, of course, co-operation with private agencies is still complicated, obscure in many aspects and quite inefficient;

• although local services started to develop in large towns, nowadays their structures are stronger in rural areas than in metropolitan districts, especially in poor neighbourhoods. The aim has been to offer a basic coverage for the whole country, so a significant part of resources have been devoted to cover under-populated rural areas, where there is a high rate of low income, socially integrated elderly people. As a result, urban areas in which the socially excluded poor population is concentrated have much more limited per capita resources;

• the inability of local social services to develop an empowering action, flexible enough to reach the excluded, enabling in the sense of giving people chances to improve their situation, and supportive in the sense of being able to help and follow people through their social integration process. The design of these services has been highly bureaucratic and rigid. They have stressed all the features that helped to break with the traditional charitable image of services for the poor. They have defined themselves as universalistic in the sense of not being aimed at the poor. But finally it is the poor and the excluded, with those who need strong enabling help in integrating, that they must deal with.

CONCLUSION

The way in which Spanish society has dealt with the growth of unemployment and job instability has kept social exclusion at very low levels. The social cost of fast economic modernization has been unevenly distributed among a significant part of the Spanish population, in a way that has allowed families, in most cases, to manage it through intra-familiar redistribution. Whatever the costs (which are certainly high) in terms of personal opportunities and economic difficulties for many people (chiefly women and the young), extreme poverty and social exclusion are very limited.

This has kept the issue of severe poverty off the policy agenda. Spanish public agencies have avoided facing the problem directly, expanding social security programmes towards those who were not reached by them and using means-tested differential benefits in a society where means testing is extremely difficult. The significant amount of resources devoted to means-tested programmes during the 1980s has failed to fully reach the most excluded, mainly because they are conceived as means-tested extensions of contributory programmes. Thus, the ill-targeting of benefits, together with the weakness of the *salario social* programmes and a bureaucratic development of local social services have limited public action towards the most excluded. Means-tested benefits have helped to maintain people living in precarious conditions rather than to integrate the excluded.

This process has not prevented the system, especially in the field of income maintenance, from retaining its traditionally fragmented structure. It is possible to point to several lines of fragmentation. Labour market status differentiates a core contributory social security system associated to a stable job, a national non-contributory income maintenance system for those outside the labour market (the elderly or handicapped), and regional or local (in most cases discretionary) social assistance benefit programmes for the able-bodied excluded from the labour market core. But regional differences are also very strong in the field of social assistance benefits and personal social services, the two key mechanisms for countering social exclusion.

In the coming years, anti-exclusion policy in Spain will have to improve its minimum income schemes and personal social services network and rethink the roles of public programmes and the non-profit sector. The development of such a strategy will be helped by the relatively small size of the problem and the fact that the excluded have not evolved into a locked-in underclass. This would help Spanish society to manage more effectively the growing process of immigration from North Africa and the difficulties faced by family structures in playing their present role in the long run.

APPENDIX 1
CHARACTERISTICS OF MEANS-TESTED SOCIAL

Name of benefit	Type of benefit	Differential/fixed amount	Maximum amount 1994
1. Social security pensioners' minimum supplement (*Complementos de mínimos de pensiones de la Seguridad Social*)			
	A monthly supplement paid to any social security pensioner whose pension (plus other income) falls below a certain level. This level is fixed every year in the General Budget Law, and the minimum pension levels vary according to the type of pension. All of these levels are below the SMI.	Differential	Retirement or disability (with dependent spouse): 807.520 pta/year\n\nAmounts for widows, orphans or retired people under 65 are lower (456,890–686,280 pta/year)
2. Social assistance pensions and Social Security (non contributory) pensions (*Pensiones asistenciales/ pensiones no contributivas de la Seguridad Social*)			
2.1 Social assistance illness pension (*Pensión asistencial de enfermedad*)	A monthly means-tested pension paid to sick people who are unable to work and whose income is below the pension.\n\nIt cannot be claimed any longer, but people who receive the pension may keep it.	Fixed	24.935 pta/month = 349.090 pta/year
2.2. Social assistance old age pension (*Pensión asistencial de vejez*)	A monthly means-tested pension paid to elderly people (over 65) and whose income is below the pension.\n\nIt cannot be claimed any longer, but people who receive the pension may keep it.	Fixed	24.935 pta/month = 349.090 pta/year
2.3. Minimum income guarantee benefit for the disabled (*Subsidio de garantía de ingresos mínimos de la LISMI*)	A monthly means-tested benefit paid to people with a disability above 65% and whose individual income is below 75% of the minimum wage.\n\nIt cannot be claimed any longer, but people who receive the benefit may keep it.	Fixed	24.935 pta/month = 349.090 pta/year
2.4. Social Security non contributory retirement pension (*Pensión No contributiva de jubilación de la Seguridad Social*)	A monthly means-tested pension paid to elderly people who are not entitled to social security contributory retirement pensions.	Differential	32.635 pta/month = 456.890 pta/year

MINIMUM BENEFITS IN SPAIN (1994)

Previous contribution required	Claimant population	Who manages	Who pays
Claimants must already be Social Security pensioners	Retired people (mostly aged) Disabled people Widows (mostly aged)	National Institute for Social Security	Tax funded. Central government transfers the amount to social security administration.
None	Disabled (defined as people that suffer from an illness that makes them unable to work). Criteria are flexible and vary from one region to another	Regional Social Services/Social Assistance administration	Tax funded. Central government transfers the amount to regional governments
None	Elderly people (over 65)	Regional Social Services/Social Assistance administration	Tax funded. Central government transfers the amount to regional governments
None	Disabled people (certified disability above 65%) who are absolutely unable to work	Regional Social Services/Social Assistance administration In some regions it is managed by the National Inst. for Social Services	Tax funded. Central government transfers the amount to regional governments
None	Elderly people (over 65)	Regional Social Services administration	Tax funded. Central government transfers the amount to regional governments

APPENDIX 1

Continued

Name of benefit	Type of benefit	Differential/fixed amount	Maximum amount 1994
2.5. Social Security non contributory disability pension (*Pensión No contributiva de invalidez de la Seguridad Social*)	A monthly means-tested pension paid to disabled people (disability above 65%) who are not entitled to social security contributory retirement pensions.	Differential	32.635 pta/month = 456.890 pta/year

3. Social assistance unemployment benefits (*subsidios asistenciales por desempleo*)

3.1 Social assistance unemployment benefit (*subsidio asistencial por desempleo*)	A monthly means tested benefit paid to registered unemployed people who have finished their contributory unemployment benefit period or have payed social insurance contributions for a short period (not enough to claim unemployment benefit). Also paid to migrants returning from abroad and prisoners leaving jail.	Fixed	75% of the Minimum Wage It also includes old age pension contributions which are paid to social security.
3.2. Special unemployment benefit for agricultural labourers	A monthly means-tested benefit paid to unemployed agricultural labourers in Andalucía and Extremadura. (Agricultural workers are not usually entitled to unemployment benefits)	Fixed	75% of the Minimum Wage It also includes old age pension contributions which are paid to social security.

4. Minimum income for social integration programmes (*rentas mínimas de inserción* or «*salario social*»)

	Monthly means-tested benefits payed to people under 65 (usually over 25) with very low income. Conditions vary from one region to another.	Differential	Varies from one region to another. 30.000–42.000 pta/month for a single person 0–6.000 pta/month for each additional member of the household

Previous contribution required	Claimant population	Who manages	Who pays
None	Disabled people (certified disability above 65%) who are absolutely unable to work	Regional Social Services administration	Tax funded. Central government transfers the amount to regional governments
a) Unemployed who have previously received unemployment benefit (they had to contribute for over one year to claim it) **b)** Unemployed who cannot claim contributory benefit (contribution for over 3 months and less than a year) **c)** Migrants returning from abroad and prisoners leaving jail need no contribution	Unemployed people with dependants	National Institute for Employment (Social security administration)	Tax funded. Central government transfers the amount to social security administration
60 days of contribution during the last 12 months	Unemployed agricultural labourers in Andalucía and Extremadura	National Institute for Employment (Social security administration)	Tax funded. Central government transfers the amount to social security administration
None	People between 25 and 65. Main groups: • Lone mothers • Long-term unemployed with no right to unemployment benefits • Marginal groups	Regional Social Services/Social Assistance administration	Funded by regional governments

REFERENCES

Aguilar, M., M. Laparra and M. Gaviria (1995): *La caña y el pez. El salario social en las comunidades autónomas 1989–1994*, Madrid: FOESSA.

Aguilar, M., M. Laparra and M. Gaviria (1996a): 'Peculiaridades de la exclusión en España', in *Pobreza, necesidad y discriminiación*, Madrid: Fundación Argentaria-Visor.

Aguilar, M., M. Laparra and M. Gaviria (1996b): 'Programas de renta mínima de inserción en España 1989–1995', in *Pobreza, necesidad y discriminación*, Madrid: Fundación Argentaria-Visor.

Atlas (1994): *Atlas de la criminalité en France*, Paris: La Documentation Française.

Casado Pérez, D., M. Aznar López, D. Casado de Otaola, A. Gutiérrez Resa and C. Ramos Feijóo (1994): 'Acción social y servicios sociales', in *V Informe sociológico sobre la situación social de España. Sociedad para todos en el año 2000*, Madrid: FOESSA.

EDIS (1984): *Pobreza y marginación*, Madrid: Caritas Española.

Eurostat (various years): (SEEPROS) (Statistical System on Social Protection).

Gaviria, M., M. Aguilar and M. Laparra (1995): 'Exclusión social y políticas de integración en la Comunidad de Madrid', *Economía y Sociedad* 12, pp.217–32.

GES (Gabinet d'Estudis Socials) (n.d.): *Mapa de la pobresa a Catalunya*, Barcelona: Generalitat de Catalunya.

INE (1991): *Censo de Población*, Madrid: Instituto Nacional de Estadística.

INE (1993): *Estudio de los hogares menos favorecidos segœn la Encuesta de Presupuestos Familiares 1990–91*, Madrid: Instituto Nacional de Estadística.

Laparra, M., M. Aguilar and M. Gaviria (1994a): 'Iniciativas locales y comunitarias en la lucha contra la exclusión' in III Seminario Internacional de Política Social 'Gumersindo de Azcárate', Madrid.

Laparra, M., M. Aguilar and M. Gaviria (1994b): *La exclusión social en Aragón*, Departamento de Bienestar Social y Trabajo-Gobierno de Aragón.

Ministerio de Asuntos Sociales (various years): *Boletin de Estadísticas Laborales*.

Ministerio de Trabajo y Seguridad Social(various years): *Boletin de Estadísticas Laborales*.

Rodríguez Cabrero, G. (1989): 'Orígenes y evolución histórica del Estado de bienestar espa–ol en su perspectiva histórica. Una visión general', *Política y Sociedad* 2.

Sanzo, L. (1987): *La pobreza en la Comunidad Autónoma Vasca*, Vitoria-Gasteiz: Gobierno Vasco.

Regional Decentralization and Health Care Reform in Spain (1976–1996)

ANA RICO

This article analyses the evolution over the last twenty years of two important interrelated policy changes involving a major restructuring of Spanish political institutions: regional decentralization and health care reform. Focusing on (1) the political decentralization of health care policy; (2) the formulation and implementation in Spain of the British NHS model; and (3) the 'reform of the reform' undertaken in the Spanish health care system in the 1990s, the main conclusions are that major policy reforms are especially difficult when they involve substantial transfers of powers to subnational governments or private agents. The successful completion of such ambitious reform seems to require a combination of political elites' *intense* preferences and citizens' *extensive* preferences for the reform model. Generally, the historical coincidence of intense and extensive political preferences depends on the existence of a common cultural heritage concerning the ways in which different institutions work.

This article analyses the determinants and consequences of the process of regional health care decentralization in Spain. Health care decentralization is the result of two related institutional changes: the reform of the public health care sector and the territorial decentralization of the state. Both took place in a context of the general restructuring of political institutions that coincided with the emergence of a new democratic regime. The model of *Estado de las Autonomías* designed by the 1978 Constitution involves the introduction of some important features of the federal model. In addition, it responds to the long-standing aspirations for self-government of traditionally nationalistic regions, such as Catalonia and the Basque Country. The nature and content of the legislative powers devolved to the regional tier of government are unique characteristics of the Spanish case that are not

I am grateful to the European University Institute and the Mission Researche Experimentation (MIRE) for supporting the research reported in this paper, presented at the Conference on *Comparing Social Welfare Systems in Southern Europe*, Florence, 22–24 February 1996. I am also grateful to Martin Rhodes for his extensive revision of the article.

shared by other southern European countries, with the partial exception of Italy. The process of decentralization is a central element of the health care reform that was initiated in the second half of the 1970s and culminated in 1986 with the enactment of the General Health Law, which also involved an important institutional shift from the Social Security model to a National Health Service. Health care reform is distinctive in this respect, for neither universal coverage nor regional decentralization were embraced by other welfare policies such as retirement pensions or unemployment benefits (Guillén 1996).

The argument proceeds from a conceptual introduction, which sets out a theoretical approach to the Spanish reform process, before analysing how health care reform in Spain can be understood in terms of the coincidence or non-coincidence of elite and public preferences, mass mobilization and the presence of a supportive international policy paradigm. This particular policy context also helps explain the differences in health care reform between Spain and other southern European countries, an issue explored in the final section.

POLITICAL PREFERENCES AND POLICY PARADIGMS

The main analytical concern of the paper is to criticize functional explanations of territorial decentralization – which see the latter as an elite response to growing complexity and policy overload – by stressing the important role played by public preferences and broadly shared cultural traditions. Two explanatory tools are important here. The first is a distinction between *extensive* and *intense* public preferences derived from the work of Jacobs (1992) and Tarrow (1995). While Jacobs emphasizes the influential role of extensive, widespread public preferences, Tarrow stresses the impact of mass mobilization, implicitly pointing to another dimension of public preferences which make them politically influential: intensity. I argue that the main influence of social movements and mass mobilization, as well as organized groups' pressures, derives from their expression of especially intense political preferences. The simultaneous coincidence of intense and extensive political preferences greatly reinforces their separate impact on policy and institutional change, while also constituting a necessary requirement for the success of attempts at institutional reform.

The second explanatory element is the impact on mass and elite preferences of *international* ideas about, and experiences of, state and social institutions. Shared cultural understandings of institutions evolve from the interaction between national experiences and international ones. Spanish health reform and decentralization has taken place in a period of change in the dominant international paradigm on state intervention, which has shifted from Keynesianism to neo-liberalism. This shift has influenced the model of health care reform finally adopted, thus acting as an important constraint on policy formulation and implementation. Adapting Hall's (1990) analysis of policy learning and paradigm shifts, I argue that successful paradigm shift requires the simultaneous concurrence of two necessary factors: the compatibility of the new international paradigm with broadly shared public understandings derived from past experiences of national institutions, which enhances its electoral appeal; and the intensity of political leaders' preferences for the international policy paradigm, which might depend not only on ideology and electoral calculations, as Hall argues, but also, as the Spanish case suggests, on the strength of their international commitments. The combined effect of these two broad factors greatly facilitates change: while the former guarantees a latent majority disposition to accept new ideas, the latter increases the mobilization capacity of political leaders to transform latent acceptance into open public support. Hall suggests that far-reaching change in policy goals will be neither easy nor complete in countries or policy sectors that do not meet one or both of those requirements. Indeed, I will suggest that social policy reform in Spain is a paradigmatic example of an incomplete and partially failed paradigm shift, precisely because neither of those two requirements was fully met.

THE POLITICS OF TERRITORIAL DECENTRALIZATION IN SPAIN

The existence of language and ethnic communities in Spain with distinctive cultural identities and nationalist claims is well-known. As a result, conflict over the building of a centralized state produced two broad cultural traditions: the first defending centralism, and suspicious of the separatist and belligerent attitudes of the nationalist regions; and the second proposing the devolution of political rights to those regions, and suspicious of the traditional centralist positions of central political authorities. Confrontation between these cultural traditions proved especially disruptive during the Second Republic, contributing to the tragic episode of the Spanish Civil War (1936–39).

The political solution to this long-standing regional cleavage during the democratic transition that started in 1976 was also marked by the conflict between the two traditions. At the beginning of the transition, the general attitudes of central political leaders with respect to regional claims to self-government were divided but generally dubious. Regional decentralization, it was feared, might pose two important threats to democratic stability: the strong opposition and animosity of the military towards any solution resembling federalism, and the possibility of hidden hostile and separatist intentions on the part of nationalist parties. In fact, both threats became real during the transition period, as the persistence of the terrorist group ETA, and the attempted coup of February 1981, clearly show.

Even so, the violent repression of regionalist sentiments under Franco was viewed negatively, and inclined leftist central political parties to consider claims for regional self-government as politically legitimate (Pérez Díaz 1987). A majority of the population tended to agree. In 1975, 60 per cent of Spaniards were in favour of conceding more freedom to the regions, and only 15 per cent against, while the debates in the press between 1976 and 1978 also reveal general support for giving broad political autonomy to nationalist regions (Granja 1981). These attitudes were fostered by the intensity of nationalist sentiment in Catalonia and the Basque Country, where the considerable mobilizing capacities of the regional political parties allowed an effective exertion of pressure on central political leaders. In turn, this capacity was built on the intensity of political claims in the Basque and Catalan communities: in 1976, around 65 per cent of Catalans and 75 per cent of Basques supported demonstrations in defence of regional political rights (García Ferrando 1982: 373, 445). Between 1981 and 1982, a total of 48 demonstrations took place in support of regional autonomy under the leadership of Basque and Catalan political parties (Aguilar 1997), which reinforced their electoral support.[1] The central political elite was forced to abandon its initial resistance to regionalist demands and to build them into the constitutional settlement.

But the constitutional decentralization formula was ambiguous and contradictory, due to unresolved differences between proponents (mainly on the right) of traditional state centralism and advocates (mainly on the left) of a quasi-federal solution (Bonime-Blanc 1987). The lack of agreement on the range of powers to be devolved, and on the degree of hierarchical control to be retained by the central state, created two functional problems:

- an unclear distribution of competencies between central state and regional governments, which made the implementation of the decentralization formula problematic;

- the uneven distribution of competencies between different types of regions, which allowed for the costly maintenance of a central state bureaucracy, still in charge of policy formulation and implementation in several policy sectors in the standard regions. The Constitution recognized two types of region: 'special' regions (mainly those with intense majority claims to self-government) and 'standard' regions (which were given different political rights in terms of the range of powers they could assume and the time period in which they could acquire rights to autonomy).

In the field of health care services, the constitutional differences in the distribution of powers among special and standard regions are especially significant. There were initially four special regions with constitutional rights to assume full political competencies (Andalusia, the Basque Country, Catalonia and Galicia) and later on Navarre, Valencia and the Canary Islands also obtained those rights by delegation from the central government. The ten standard regions do not have constitutional powers in the field of health care services, and remain under the legislative and administrative auspices of central state agencies. As a result, in 1992, by when around 60 per cent of Spanish population were served by special region health bureaucracies, the number of health care bureaucrats in Madrid (about 6,000) remained the same as in 1982 (Girón Sierra et al. 1988).

THE REFORM OF THE HEALTH CARE SYSTEM (1976–1986)

The Transition to Democracy (1976–78)

Public coverage of individual health care needs in Spain was initiated in the 1940s but remained a means-tested and largely residual system until the beginning of the 1960s (Guillén 1996). Between 1962 and 1972 a series of social security laws introduced three important changes: the inclusion of health care within the social security system, a remarkable increase in public coverage[2] and the creation of a large network of social security-owned hospitals in charge of public health care provision.[3] However, these incremental moves did not respond to a parallel change in broader policy goals, but rather evolved as a result of the combined influence of bureaucratic pressures, economic expansion and mounting opposition to the authoritarian regime. An important determinant of those changes was the occurrence of several conflicts and strikes within the public health care sector from 1971 on, led by groups of young doctors with communist and socialist allegiances. Between 1976 and 1977, the critical years of the transition to democracy, the process of reform continued, in a context of wider involvement of political parties, technical and corporate associations and the general public.

The First Democratic Government and the Frustrated Attempt at Health Care Reform (1979–82)

In October 1979, the centre-right government of UCD made an important, but unsuccessful, attempt to initiate health care reform, responding to repeated pressures from communist and socialist representatives in Parliament. Instead of launching the long expected legislative reform, the UCD presented a non-binding document, the *Resolution on Health Care Reform*, which was approved in Parliament despite attempts by the opposition to delay it.

The resolution established an eight-year launch period, justifying the delay by referring to the financial problems affecting the social security system. In fact, the impact of the economic crisis and parallel national socio-economic changes had dramatic consequences for the Spanish social security system. Global social expenditure increased by 39.7 per cent in real terms between 1975 and 1982, and from 9.9 per cent to 15.5 per cent as a percentage of GNP between 1975 and 1980. Also between 1975 and 1982, the number of pensioners increased by 31.6 per cent and public expenditure on pensions increased in real terms by 29.3 per cent; unemployment rates escalated from 3.1 per cent to 16.3 per cent, while expenditure in real terms multiplied by 13 between 1974 and 1981. In contrast, health care expenditure increased by just 8.3 per cent in real terms – due, according to the UCD Minister of Health, Manuel Núñez, to the fact that the health care sector was considered secondary to income transfers (Maravall 1992; Guillén 1996).

The First Socialist Government and the Enactment of the General Health Law (1982–86)

The process of health care reform was finally launched in December 1983, less than a year after the first socialist health minister, Ernst Lluch, was appointed. The reform had four broad political goals, which had been present on the socialist and communist political agendas since 1976:

• the separation of the health care services from the system of social security, with the central aim of financing the services through general taxation;

• the introduction of universal health care coverage for all Spanish citizens;

• the unification of the fragmented, overlapping networks of public providers, and the clarification of the future role of the sizeable sector of (mostly) non-profit-making private providers contracted out by the public system; and

- the enactment of the basic state legislation and the institutional framework for regional decentralization.

The socialist reform model, inspired by the British National Health Service, could count on the support of international health care institutions such as the WHO and was perfectly compatible with the social-democratic ideology of the party in office. In addition, with the exception of the public/private mix in health care provision, the other major policy goals were generally shared by all the central political parties, except for the right-wing Popular Party (*Partido Popular*), which backed a scheme of user co-payments as a complementary source of public financing.

Disagreements between the socialist party and the centre-Right Basque and Catalan regional parties, on the other hand, mainly focused on the institutional model of decentralization: two-thirds of the amendments proposed by Basque and Catalan political parties in the parliamentary debate of the General Health Law referred to the territorial distribution of power. However, there was also a minor disagreement between the Catalan parties and the socialists about the role of non-profit providers, which will be mentioned in more detail below.

Finally, the broad agreement among the central political parties on universal, free-of-charge access, finance by the public budget and regional decentralization was also shared by the general public and, to some extent, by the medical profession. Opinion polls showed that in 1975, 96,6 per cent of the population considered that the state should provide health care for all (INP 1977: 756); while roughly two-thirds of the hospital doctors favoured socialized medicine in 1978 (González Rodríguez 1979: 154). Also in 1978, two-thirds of the population thought that employers paid too much under the social security system, while almost 80 per cent thought that the state should pay the bulk of health care costs instead. Finally, two-thirds of the medical profession favoured a regionally decentralized health care organization, which was supported by more than one half of the population (Servicio de Estudios Sociológicos del IESS 1979a, b). Public opinion did not support the decentralization of other welfare policies such as pensions (REIS 1989), which may explain why decentralization was only carried out in the health care sector.

However, the issue of public/private provision was far more controversial. On the one hand, the main right-wing parties, the UCD and PP, exerted considerable parliamentary pressure on the socialists to include private hospitals within the National Health Services, yet preserving property rights and regulatory discretion. In fact, almost 60 per cent of the UCD and PP amendments to the General Health Law focused on the role of the private sector. However, the centre-Right party UCD was eager to accept increased government regulation of private hospitals in exchange, while it put more emphasis on non-profit hospitals and less on the professional power of the medical class than the right-wing UCD. In addition, both the medical profession and the general public were fairly divided on this issue, although they generally favoured mixed public/private provision: 70 per cent of the medical profession and 40 per cent of public opinion was favourable to the maintenance of some private provision (Servicio de Estudios Sociológicos del IESS 1979a: 130), while the quality of private provision was considered higher by 40 per cent of doctors and almost 60 per cent of public opinion (INP 1977: 789). The only forces against the creation of a public health service on the NHS model were the elites of the Medical College Organization, the employers associations of private providers, a section of the pharmaceutical business association and financial sectors interested in launching complementary health insurance schemes.

The positions of the actors involved emerged during the long process of health care reform, which began in December 1983 and ended in April 1986 with the enactment of the General Health Law. The draft of the law remained basically unchanged until October 1984, when a meeting of the Council of Ministers revealed significant divergences among the socialists themselves concerning the capacity of the state to finance the reform. There were four main issues at stake: the shift from social security funds to general taxation, free-of-charge access to the public system for those high income groups still uncovered, the future role of private providers contracting into the public system and the scope of regional decentralization.

The first three issues involved a confrontation between the Ministry of Finance and the Ministry of Social Security, on the one hand, and the Ministry of Health on the other. The former defended the need to control public expenditure and stressed the inability of the state to undertake a policy shift as ambitious as the building of a National Health System. This position was congruent with the dominant neo-liberal positions of the socialists on economic policy as well as with the international compromises whereby Spain was integrated into the European Community, which was negotiated at the same time as the health care reform. Such international commitments were widely supported by public opinion: two-third of Spaniards supported EC membership in 1986 (Maravall 1991). An agreement was reached in the Council of Ministers in early April, a couple of days before the initiation of the parliamentary discussion of the law. As a result, financing from the public budget and the extension of public provision were to be pursued gradually, while the pace of change was subordinated to the economic circumstances of the country. In addition, access to the system by high income groups was guaranteed, but was to be paid for by them at market prices.

The fourth issue at stake – the scope of regional decentralization – was much more radically transformed during the policy-making process. This was the result of the extensive and influential intervention of regional political parties during the policy-making process, and especially during parliamentary debates. The internal divisions among the socialists were in this case successfully exploited by the Catalan and Basque nationalist parties. As a result, most of the latter's amendments were, in fact, introduced by the socialists, and the final version of the law gave almost full legislative and planning powers to the special regions as well as important financial and self-organizational discretion. It is worth noting that the prominent intervention of regional political parties in the making of the General Health Law, and the recognition given by the socialists to their claims, was extended neither to other affected social groups nor to the other opposition political parties (Rodríguez and de Miguel 1990: 110).

DOES DECENTRALIZATION MATTER?: CENTRAL HEALTH CARE POLICY AFTER THE REFORM (1986–1996)

The Implementation of the Health Care Reform (1986–90)

The implementation of the 1986 reform was initiated by the second socialist government in 1987, in a context of economic expansion and public expenditure growth. In the second half of the 1980s, the average annual growth rate of GNP was higher than 4 per cent. Moreover, the tax reforms of the UCD and PSOE governments, undertaken during the first half of the 1980s, considerably increased the fiscal capacity of the state and provided favourable conditions for the implementation of the health care reform. In fact, tax revenues increased by 6.6 per cent of GNP between 1982 and 1990, while more than 2 million new taxpayers were brought into the system between 1982 and 1987 as a result of the socialist government's anti-tax evasion policies (Maravall 1992: 36–7).

As a result, important advances were made towards the unification of public health care networks by both central and regional governments from 1987. Furthermore, from 1989, 70 per cent of public health care expenditure was financed from the public budget, while the process of decentralization was extended to five additional regions: the Basque

Country and Valencia in 1987, Galicia and Navarre in 1990, and the Canary Islands in 1994. As a consequence, regional political authorities directed the implementation of the reform in a territory comprising 60 per cent of the Spanish population. The new health care authorities soon proved their ability to respond quickly to the implementation challenge as well as their capacity to introduce policy innovations at a faster rate than the central state. A significant example is the Basque Decree 26/1988, enacted just six weeks after the devolution of health care powers, which extended universal coverage to all the inhabitants of the Basque Country (Freire 1993: 75). The Basque initiative was followed by several Autonomous Communities as well as by the central state between 1989 and 1991.

However, the crucial paradox of the implementation of health care reform in Spain after 1990 is that the policy paradigm on which it was based – the British NHS model – was already being thrown into question in its land of origin. There, a new policy paradigm was being developed along the principles of *managed competence* proposed by Alan Enthoven in the mid-1980s, and introduced by the British government from 1989 onwards under the label of 'internal market' reforms. The core of the proposals, which involve a major policy shift in the health care sector, is to maintain public financing and universal access, but to divide up financing, purchasing and the provision of health care, encouraging new competencies among health care providers and recognizing a new and extended role for private providers and managerial techniques within the public health care system. As a result of this paradigm shift, the early 1990s represents to some extent a turning point for Spanish health care policy as well.

The Second Wave of Reforms (1990–95)

As the new ideas were progressively adopted in Britain (and, more slowly, elsewhere in Europe) the Parliament of Catalonia passed the Catalan Law of Health Care Reform (*Ley the Ordenación Sanitaria de Catalunya*) in May 1990, only a month after a similar reform, the quasi-market reforms, began to be applied in the British NHS. The law tries to make the principles of the 1986 General Health Law compatible with new reform proposals. As in Britain, those proposals included the division of financing and purchasing functions from the provision of services, shared by private (mostly non-profit-making) hospitals contracted out of the public system and by public hospitals and primary health care centres. The reform also involved some operational measures such as the regulation by private law of the top public institutions responsible for policy formation and direction; the decentralization of planning and priority setting to the local level and health care centres; and the introduction of a public/private mix in the management of health care centres, although public control in such managerial joint-ventures was guaranteed.

Two factors account for the change of policy paradigm in Catalonia:

- the unique institutional features of the Catalan health care sector, in which private non-profit-making hospitals provide two-thirds of public hospital care (Coll 1981: 308);

- the intensity of Catalan policy-makers' preferences for the reform proposals, derived from positive national experiences of non-profit health institutions, combined with the emergence of the new policy paradigm at the international level, which reinforced long-standing aims of Catalan reform.

Although there is no data on Catalan public opinion on this issue, the unanimous consensus (involving employers associations, trade unions, the medical professions, and all political parties in the opposition, including the communists) achieved by the Catalan government in passing the 1990 law is illustrative of the widely shared positive view of private health care in this region (Cernadas 1994).

The Catalan reform was to prove highly influential for regional and central policy-making during the first part of the 1990s. With respect to central health care policy, the 1990 Catalan law was often quoted during 1990 and 1991 by central health authorities and the press as the model to follow in the rest of Spain. In a highly sensitive political atmosphere, the Parliament appointed a committee of experts in January 1991, on the initiative of a new Health Minister, with the objective of evaluating the performance of the National Health System, and designing the subsequent 'reform of the reform'.

The Committee of Analysis and Evaluation of the National Health System (*Comisión de Análisis y Evaluación del Sistema Nacional de Salud* 1991), reported in July 1991. The report opened a process of wide public debate and contestation. In contrast with the broad social and political consensus achieved in Catalonia on the new policy paradigm, the committee's recommendations faced strong opposition from trade unions, professional associations, interest groups, the public opinion, the press and the parties on the Left (including a significant sector of the socialist party). The debate ended with the socialist government's declaration that it would not introduce the reform proposals, and the dismissal of the socialist Minister of Health who had been in favour of most of them.

However, a major shift in policy goals was only partially prevented.

An interesting example at the central level is Royal Decree 858/1992, which introduces a new policy instrument, namely an explicit, detailed contract with public and non-profit-making hospitals responsible for public provision as a pilot experiment, which was then more generally launched in two-thirds of the regions by the central government a year later. The contract involves a limited managerial decentralization to health care centres, while specifying the expected levels of hospital activity (for this reason, it is called a *contract-programme*) as well as the expected costs for each broad category of expenditure (González López-Valcarcel *et al.* 1995). The explicit policy goals of the contract-programme are to promote the separation of financing and provision functions and to foster competition among public providers in the medium term. The Basque Parliament adopted the same reform goals in June 1993 (Fernández 1996).

An additional, remarkable feature of the 1992 Decree is that it involves the explicit legitimation of the role of private, especially non-profit providers within the public sector, which contradicts the formal content of the General Health Law (although it should be noted that the Decree intended to legally enforce the *maintenance* of the role and size of the private sector, rather than its expansion). In fact, 15 per cent of public central health care expenditure had gone through private centres in 1975, rising to 22 per cent in 1980, but declining to 15 per cent at the end of the 1980s, where it remained until 1993 (Coll 1980; López Casasnovas 1993). This suggests that there was, in fact, no firm commitment to implement the gradual substitution of private provision as formally stated in the law. This is especially significant if we remember that this was the only element of the socialist reform proposals not supported by the general public.

It is also important to note that both the contract and the system of prospective funding included in the Decree were first launched by Catalonia in the second half of the 1980s, and subsequently adopted by several autonomous regions from 1991.[4] In addition, the 1990 Catalan law had a remarkable impact at the regional level. Apart from the Basque reform proposals already mentioned, the regulation of some of the activities of the Catalan Health Care Service through private instead of administrative law was emulated by several other regions between 1992 and 1994 (Viñas 1993). Finally, several reform proposals were launched in Andalusia during this period, under the socialist government, which aimed to introduce private management practices and regulations in limited areas of the region's public health care sector. It is interesting to note that such proposals were partially blocked due to the opposition of the Communist Party, the trade unions and professional associations, while the Catalan reform, which was much more ambitious, was passed with their explicit agreement.

Recent Trends and Future Reforms in the National Health System

The second half of the 1990s has been characterized in Spain by the opening of several parallel debates on the role of the private sector and the introduction of innovative organizational measures. In this respect, the first measure enacted is the reform of the Catalan 1990 Law, passed by the Catalan Parliament in September 1995. The most interesting measure included in that reform is the possibility of contracting out public primary care with co-operatives of General Practitioners, a change that is currently being discussed in the Basque Country as well.

The second measure adopted is the contracting out of hospital care to a private company in a couple of Valencian counties, a reform undertaken by the new Valencian government, controlled by the Popular Party (PP) since the regional elections of 1995. Such companies will enjoy monopoly rights over a twenty year period to provide hospital care. This measure provoked strong opposition and a rapid mobilization of the trade unions, user associations and the socialist and communist parties. Previous attempts by the Valencian government to introduce open competition into senior managerial appointments was considered unconstitutional by the courts.

Both measures acquired special significance when the PP spokesperson on health care at the central level announced in February 1996 that the Valencian model would be extended to the rest of Spain if the PP won the national elections held in March that year. However, the first months of PP government suggest that those programmatic goals will not be enacted in the medium term, partly due to the strong social and political opposition to them. Only two limited attempts have been made up to now, and both of them have been partially blocked:

- Royal Decree 10/1996, passed on 7 June, which allows the management of public health care centres on a private law basis. The original text of the Decree, copied from the 1990 Catalan reform law, was modified two days later to eliminate all explicit references to private companies, as a result of the fierce opposition from leftist parties in Parliament. In addition, the Minister provided further evidence of moderation when he declared to Congress on 28 June that the management of centres would remain public.

- the Popular Party opened a public discussion in September 1996 on two schemes of user co-payments proposed by the Catalan Party, the CiU. Those proposals attracted strong political and social opposition as well, while two thirds of Spaniards were against them according to the public opinion polls released in the press.

These two moves suggest that any reform proposal that goes beyond those measures already approved in the first half of the 1990s will require the formal modification in the Parliament of the General Health Law, and, apart from encountering important political obstacles, will endanger the narrow electoral support enjoyed by the Popular Party.

EXPLAINING HEALTH CARE DECENTRALIZATION AND REFORM IN SPAIN

Both the general constitutional decentralization of the state, and the decentralization of health care powers to the regions, can plausibly be explained by the same set of factors:

• the existence of an intense and distinctive identity and set of preferences in nationalist communities, which were eager to mobilize in defence of their nationalist claims;

• the emergence of political organizations able to exert active pressure on the centre in defence of their constituencies' interests;

• the fact that a majority of the general public, and an important part of the central political elite, tended to consider these intense preferences as politically legitimate due to the historical coincidence of repressive centralism with authoritarian governments, and regional decentralization with democratic regimes.

An important role is played by intense political preferences in determining institutional change. The failure of health care reform between 1976 and 1983 illustrates that extensive national and international preferences for increased intervention of the state in the health care sector were insufficient to foster policy change. Such preferences were not defended with sufficient intensity by the centre-Right party in office, the UCD, for two main reasons: because such extensive preferences for public health care were not fully compatible with the ideology of the centre-right governing party, which tended to favour the role of the private sector;[5] and because the economic crisis and the parallel fiscal crisis of the social security system weakened the capacity of the state to undertake major institutional reforms, especially in a context in which all the efforts were focused on the building of democratic institutions, which was logically considered the political priority of the period.

The same negative view of the financial and institutional capabilities of the state to launch major institutional reform in health care was also expressed by the first socialist government, explaining the limited version of the NHS model introduced in the General Health Law. In this case, however, financial considerations did not fully block the reform due to the intensity of preferences of a significant section of central health care authorities, and the compatibility of both public preferences and the dominant international policy paradigm with their own ideological positions. In addition, the success of the Catalan health care reform illustrates that major institutional reform does not automatically follow from strong state structures. Rather, positive national experiences with private institutions, combined with a coherent and widely shared international paradigm stressing the role of the private sector, can also lead to major institutional change. In other words, it may be precisely the weakness of state structures, rather than their strength, which promotes institutional reform.

The Catalan case also illustrates the role of ideology in facilitating a major shift in policy goals. In this respect, the centre-Right ideology of the party in office fostered the early enactment of the internal market paradigm, while the social democratic positions of the Socialists, together with their positive national experiences with state institutions, helped prevent central attempts at reform during the 1990s. Furthermore, the success of the Catalan reform, in contrast with the failure of UCD's attempts, emphasizes that the availability of a coherent international paradigm compatible with the ideology of the party in office helps achieve institutional change. In this respect, the absence of a consistent and appropriate paradigm in the early 1980s blocked the UCD's reforms while also delaying the Catalan reform until the end of that decade. Finally, the recent failure of the Popular Party's attempts at reform suggests that intense government preferences for institutional reform backed by a widely accepted international paradigm are not sufficient to foster change in the absence of extensive public support for a new institutional model.

The dynamics of health care policy during the 1990s also allow us to draw some conclusions as to the consequences of regional decentralization for efficiency and equity in health care policy. As for efficiency, empirical evidence suggests that the Spanish regions are much more dynamic than the centre in reforming previously inefficient services, and in introducing policy innovations.[6] As for equity, in contrast to pessimistic forecasts of increasing differences in policies and in the treatment of citizens across territorial boundaries, the evidence indicates a diffusion of policy innovations which may involve a redistribution of knowledge and expertise from the richer to the poorer regions.

Such trends are not only perceptible in the field of health care, but also in social services, both in Spain and in Italy (Fargion and Aguilar and Laparra, this volume). Although formal policy shifts may not affect all regional health care services equally, because of varying political circumstances, evidence from Spain suggests that a substantial amount of convergence takes place through informal processes such as intergovernmental co-operation, electoral pressures, professional socialization, imitation of models of best practice and the sharing of experts across territorial administrations. The relative influence of those factors remains an open question for future research.

CONCLUSIONS: THE SPANISH CASE IN COMPARATIVE PERSPECTIVE

Does the Spanish case shares some of the specific traits of other southern European welfare states? Ferrera (1996) has argued that a common feature of the reform of health care systems in Greece, Italy, Portugal and Spain has been a formal commitment to the British NHS model, 'characterized by open and free access to all residents, standardized rules and organization, and tax financing'. According to Ferrera, this has been the result of pressure exerted by strong communist and socialist parties, backed by deeply-rooted leftist subcultures. This is confirmed by the Spanish case. An additional explanatory factor in Spain is the wide support given by public opinion, the medical profession and the trade unions to the reform proposals.

The second common characteristic of southern European health care sectors is the implementation gap in actually applying these formal commitments to institutional change. Ferrera argues that, despite the enactment of constitutional and legal measures, the commitment of southern European governments to applying reform has been 'half-hearted', mainly due to politico-institutional factors such as the weakness of state institutions and the absence of 'an open, universalistic culture'. However, there seem to be marked differences among the countries of the region in this respect. Universal access to health care was completed in Italy, and nearly completed in Spain, while a dualist health care system seems still to be dominant in Portugal and Greece (Symeonidou and Guibentif, this volume). Also, at least in the Spanish case, an important and successful effort to standardize the rules and organization of health care institutions was made from the late 1980s on, while the percentage of tax-based financing rose from 25 per cent in 1976 to roughly 95 per cent in 1996. This is hardly a case of 'half-hearted' reform.

The Spanish case suggests that the limited implementation of institutional change may have more to do with contextual factors prevalent at the international level than with the politico-institutional factors specific to southern Europe. In particular, the change in the dominant policy paradigm at the international level that took place in the mid-1980s probably contributed to the failure to fully implement reform in these four countries, all of them latecomers with respect to the adoption of the NHS model. The theoretical approach developed above suggests that a change in the dominant policy paradigm would decrease the intensity of political leaders' preferences for the institutional change, possibly accounting for the half-hearted approach to implementation referred to by Ferrera. National differences in public opinion would then explain the degree of implementation of the reform.

A second contextual factor may be the change in the economic cycle. While the enactment of reforms requires a favourable political context, their implementation requires favourable economic conditions. The expansion of the state's role in health care occurred in most west European countries in a favourable political and economic climate. However, in southern Europe, the implementation of the same reforms was initiated in a period of economic recession, while their growing international compromises, linked to membership in the European Community, set clear political limits on expansive macroeconomic policies.

Changes in the international context may also help explain the maintenance of a sizeable private health care sector contracted-out of the public system in southern European countries, despite the adoption of the formal NHS. In this respect, the Spanish case seems to be different in that only 15 per cent of the public health care expenditure is channelled through private health care centres in the 1990s, while the equivalent figures for Portugal and Italy are 40 per cent and 37.5 per cent respectively (Ferrera 1996). Also, the percentage of total health care expenditure financed privately was below 15 per cent in Spain in the late 1980s (Murillo et al. 1996), while the equivalent figure in Greece was more than 40 per cent (Symenonidou, this volume). This may be due to the fact that the expansion of the public network of health care centres took place in Spain during the 1960s and 1970s, in a context of unprecedented economic growth and the dominance of a policy paradigm that favoured the expansion of state institutions.

In the same vein, the Spanish case seems to be deviant regarding the most recent wave of reforms in southern European health care systems. A notable feature shared by Italy, Portugal and Greece is their rapid incorporation of some of the reform measures recently launched in other western welfare states, which tend to expand the role of private providers and financing (Granaglia, Guibentif and Symeonidou, this volume). This seems especially surprising given the fact that these countries were latecomers to the former policy paradigm. Again, a potential explanation here might be the combination of political leaders' intense preferences for the new international model of change, together with extensive public preferences for a deep reform along the same lines, reflecting negative national experiences with the operation of public health care institutions.

However, similar reform proposals have been blocked in Spain until now. Spanish reform in the 1990s is much more moderate, and seems to be oriented towards increasing the efficiency of the public sector rather than decreasing its size and role *vis-à-vis* the private sector. According to the theoretical arguments developed above, a potential explanatory factor here may be the higher preferences for public health care institutions by the Spanish public compared with other southern European countries: in 1996 the percentage of citizens stating that health care runs well or needs only minor changes was 47.2 per cent in Spain, but just 19.1 per cent in Italy, 24.1 per cent in Portugal and 29.7 per cent in Greece (Le Grand 1996).

This may also imply that the challenges facing southern European public health care systems in the near future will also be different in Spain. In particular, the structural crisis of the welfare state pointed to by Ferrera might affect the Spanish health care sector less profoundly than in other parts of southern Europe. An additional factor that may mitigate the pressures to dismantle the public health care system in Spain is political decentralization. In fact, the empirical evidence suggests a remarkable commitment of regional authorities to improve and expand public welfare services, both in the field of health care and in the related field of social services and minimum income programmes (Fargion and Aguilar and Laparra, this volume). This trend is especially noticeable by way of contrast to recent central government policies, which have been focused on cost-containment and cutting back welfare services.

NOTES

1. The electoral share of the Catalan Nationalist Party (CiU) increased from 23 per cent in the 1983 local elections to 47 per cent in the 1984 regional elections, while the Basque Nationalist Party (PNV) increased its share by just two percentage points during the same period.
2. Public coverage increased from 25 per cent in the 1940s to 50 per cent in 1965. The changes introduced from 1962 on, which eliminated the condition on low-income groups gaining access to the system, were applied from 1967, and expand the part of the population covered to 80 per cent in 1975 (INP 1977; Guillén 1996).
3. While in the 1940s only 3 per cent of public health care was provided by state-owned health care centres, in 1975, 75 per cent of the public health care budget was spent by public providers (INSALUD 1978). This is a distinctive feature of the Spanish health

care system, for social security systems do not usually develop their own network of centres.

4. The contract was also introduced in Andalusia, the Basque Country and Galicia, while the system of prospective funding was introduced in these three regions plus Valencia.

5. In fact, the role of private providers in public health care increased substantially under UCD governments, the percentage of public expenditure spent by private centres increasing from 15 per cent in 1975 to 22 per cent in 1980.

6. In this respect, the results of a Delphi survey conducted among a small sample of health care experts in 1995 support the main conclusions of this article: 80 per cent of the experts consulted considered that health care transfers had positive effects in improving policy innovation and dynamism as well as health care management (Herce *et al.* 1995).

REFERENCES

Aguilar, P. (1996): 'La amnesia y la memoria: manifestaciones a favor de la amnistía en la transición española a la democracia', in M. Pérez-Ledesma and R.Cruz (eds), *Cultura y acción colectiva en España*, Madrid: Alianza editorial.

Bonime-Blanc, A. (1987): *Spain's Transition To Democracy: The Politics of Constitution-making*, Boulder, CO: Westview Press.

Cernadas, A. (1994): 'Análisis del proceso de elaboración, discusión y aprobación de la Ley de Ordenación Sanitaria de Cataluña, en el marco de la política sanitaria catalana', Masters Thesis in Political Science at the Universidad Autónoma de Barcelona.

Coll, P. (1980): 'Problemática actual de los conciertos con instituciones sanitarias', *Revista de la Seguridad Social 6*, pp.185–213.

Coll, P. (1981): 'El previo conocimiento de la bases para una propuesta de ordenacion sanitaria regional', *Revista de la Seguridad Social 10*, pp.307–9.

Fernández, J.M. (1996): 'Estrategia de cambio en el Servicio Vasco de Salud', in *Mercados internos y reforma sanitaria*, XIII Jornadas de Economía de la Salud, Madrid: Fundación Maphre.

Ferrera, M. (1996): 'The "Southern Model" of Welfare in Social Europe', *Journal of European Social Policy 6/1*, pp.17–37.

Freire, J.M. (1993): 'Cobertura sanitaria y equidad en España', in *I Simposio sobre Igualdad y Distribución de la Renta y la Riqueza*, Madrid: Fundación Argentaria.

García Ferrando, M. (1982): *Regionalismo y autonomía en España*, Madrid: Centro de Investigaciones Sociológicas.

Girón Sierra, B., *et al.* (1988): 'Niveles de salud y gasto sanitario en España', *Revista de Sanidad e Higiene Pública 63*, pp.25–38.

González Rodríguez, P. (1979): 'Médicos hospitalarios y no hospitalarios: sus opiniones sobre la reforma sanitaria', *Revista de la Seguridad Social 1*, pp.147–214.

González López-Valcarcel, B., Pellisé, L. and Barber, P. (1995): 'La financiación pública de los servicios sanitarios en España', *Documento de Trabajo 95-13*, Madrid: FEDEA.

Granja, J.L. (1981): 'Autonomías Regionales y Fuerzas Políticas en las Cortes Constituyentes de 1931', *Sistema 40*.

Guillén, A.M. (1996): 'Citizenship and Social Policy in Democratic Spain: The Reformulation of the Francoist Welfare State', *South European Society & Politics 1/2* (Autumn) pp.253–71.

Hall, P.A. (1990): *Policy Paradigms, Social Learning and the State: The Case of Economic Policy-making in Britain*, CEACS working papers, no.1990/4, Madrid: Centro de Estudios Avanzados en Ciencias Sociales.

Herce, J.A., J. Cabasés and G. López Casasnovas (1995): 'Los problemas de la sanidad pública en España: una encuesta rápida entre los expertos en economía de la salud', *Documento de Trabajo 95-01*, Madrid: FEDEA.

Instituto Nacional de Previsión (INP) (1977): *Investigación sobre la asistencia farmacéutica en España. Estudio socioeconómico sobre el conjunto de la asistencia sanitaria española*, Madrid: Ministerio de Trabajo.

Instituto Nacional de la Salud (INSALUD) (1978): *Memoria estadística*, Madrid: Ministerio de Sanidad y Consumo.

Jacobs, L. (1992): 'Institutions and Culture. Health Policy and Public Opinion in the U.S. and Britain', *World Politics* 44/2.

Le Grand, J. (1996): 'Health Care Reform and the Market: the British Experience', paper presented at the Conference on the Modernization of Public Health Care in the World, Madrid, 23–24 Sept.

López Casasnovas, G. (1993): 'Estructura y regulación del sistema sanitario español', *Documento de Trabajo 93-10*, Madrid: FEDEA.

Maravall, J.M. (1991): 'Economic Reforms in New Democracies: the Southern European Experience', CEACS Working Paper no.1991/22, Madrid: Instituto Juan March de Estudios e Investigaciones.

Maravall, J.M. (1992): 'What is Left? Social Democratic Policies in Southern Europe', CEACS Working Paper, no.1992/36, Madrid: Instituto Juan March de Estudios e Investigaciones.

Murillo, C., S. Calonge and Y. González (1996): 'La financiación privada de los servicios sanitarios', FEDEA Working Paper 96-10, Madrid: FEDEA.

Pérez-Díaz, Víctor (1987): *El retorno de la sociedad civil*, Madrid: Instituto de Estudios Económicos.

Revista Española de Investigaciones Sociológicas (REIS) (1989): *Datos de Opinión*, in REIS 46, pp.227–64.

Rodríguez, J.A. and de Miguel, J. (1990): *Salud y Poder*, Madrid: CIS y Siglo XXI de Editores.

Servicio de Estudios Sociológicos del IESS (1979a): 'Estudio comparativo entre profesionales sanitarios y opinión pública sobre organización y reforma sanitaria', *Revista de la Seguridad Social* 1, 113–40.

Servicio de Estudios Sociológicos del IESS (1979b): 'Encuesta nacional a la opinión pública sobre la organización sanitaria española y su posible reforma', *Revista de la Seguridad Social* 3, 259–91.

Tarrow, S. (1995): 'Mass Mobilization and Elite Exchange: Democratization Episodes in Italy and Spain', *Democratization* 2/3 (Autumn) pp.221–45.

Viñas, M. (1993): 'Estudio comparativo de los servicios de salud configurados en las leyes autonómicas , *Puntexpress Sanidad* 114, pp.1–4.

Social Assistance and the North–South Cleavage in Italy

VALERIA FARGION

This article discusses the effects of regional decentralization on the Italian welfare state, focusing on the development of social assistance policies in the different parts of the country. The analysis of the legislation passed by the regions over the past twenty years suggests, first, that the North–South cleavage obtains and, second, that politics matters. While in most southern regions an archaic system of poverty relief is dominant, the centre-north is characterized largely by a modern system of social services. However, the differences in the performance of regional governments cannot be fully explained by referring exclusively to historical legacy. It must also take account of political variables. In the final section these findings are discussed in a comparative perspective.

Research on the welfare state has largely concentrated on income maintenance and health care. In western countries most social expenditure is in fact funnelled to these policy areas. Therefore, it is not surprising that scholars pay special attention to these particular sectors, especially in light of current financial difficulties. Nevertheless, there are good reasons not to confine ourselves to the analysis and/or the reformulation of social transfer schemes and health care systems. As Jens Alber has recently pointed out, 'social services have become increasingly important ingredients of welfare state production. Hence it will be necessary to shift the research agenda accordingly' (1995: 132).

If we consider the socio-demographic changes which have occurred during the last two decades in all advanced industrialized countries, the reasons for such a statement become quite clear. Population ageing, coupled with increasing female labour force participation and the virtual disappearance of the extended family have created a new kind of problem, especially with respect to the needs of the elderly, but also for the care of children and the disabled. The growing inability of women to perform traditional caring functions, due to their increasing commitments in the labour market, has fuelled a widespread demand for social services. What is most needed is help for persons who are dependent on others due to long-term illness, disability or old age. This entails in the main providing domestic help and nursing services as well as residential care facilities.[1]

How crucial these services are for our society quickly becomes clear if we refer to some data on the aged. During the past thirty years, the number of people over sixty almost doubled in the EU member states to 20.7 per cent of the population (100 million people). However, our knowledge about the actual supply of services for the aged in the different countries is extremely limited. We know even less about other types of social services dealing with a wide variety of issues such as vocational training and social integration of the handicapped, foster care of children without family support, rehabilitation of drug addicts, maternity and child care. In short, the whole range of benefits and services falling into the broad category of social assistance has been largely neglected by comparative studies on the welfare state.

Similar neglect has characterized the development of programmes for the poor and the most needy, who originally represented the core beneficiaries of social assistance. Only recently have these programmes acquired greater political visibility in the face of mounting unemployment and increasing poverty. According to official data, there are currently seventeen million unemployed in EU countries and over fifty five million people living below the poverty line. As Ian Gough (1995: 1) argues, 'there is at present a mismatch between the salience of means-tested social assistance in policy practice and in academic study'.[2]

In addition to the structural changes occurring within the economy and the labour market, we also need to consider the climate of austerity in which the current debate on the welfare state is embedded. The cash benefit side of social assistance is coming under scrutiny also because of the new emphasis on means-testing stemming from the restrictive orientation of the early 1990s. Political discussion about targeting, selectivity and income-testing has spurred interest on this policy field, given its traditional linkage with these concepts.

Actually, the scope of social assistance considerably broadened during the 1960s and 1970s, with universal principles creeping in, especially with respect to the kinds of services illustrated above. Nevertheless, the primary role of the sector with respect to poverty and social exclusion – dating back to its origin – was never really superseded. In sum, over the past thirty years each European country has developed a specific blend of selectivity and universalism within its own system of social assistance.

Shedding some light on the profile of social assistance policies in Italy is of broader comparative perspective for a number of reasons. Southern European countries have recently come to the forefront of the international debate on the welfare state, with a number of scholars claiming the distinctiveness of their social policies with respect to other continental and northern countries. Ferrera (1996) usefully discusses the traits which, according to him, constitute a specific Mediterranean model, suggesting that Italy 'has in many respects led the way for the whole area'. Ferrera draws particular attention to social assistance. In contrast with all other European countries (MISSOC 1996), Italy, Spain, Portugal and Greece have in fact no national minimum income scheme for individuals and families with insufficient resources. However, in Italy and Spain regional and local authorities can and to a certain extent do step in to fill this gap, making an investigation into social assistance schemes, especially at the sub-national level, important for these countries.

Turning to the other side of the coin, that is from cash subsidies to the provision of services, the scanty evidence we have points again to a much lower level of development within the Latin countries as compared to the rest of Europe. The arguments advanced to explain why these countries appear as latecomers usually refer to the prominent role of the family and the Church in society. But overall our knowledge on the subject remains inadequate. Moreover, if we consider that responsibility for this policy area lies primarily with regional and local authorities, we can surely expect subnational variations to make the picture even fuzzier.

In the Italian case this issue is especially relevant, given the deeply rooted dualism of the country, which is also reflected in the different social problems prevailing in the centre-north and the south. Whereas in central and northern Italy the needs of the elderly are at the fore, in the south poverty and unemployment definitely take priority. But it is not just a matter of difference in the problems being faced. According to Putnam's well-known (1993) study on the institutional performance of Italian regional governments, we can expect to find divergent policy orientations between centre-north and south even with respect to the same issues.

This article concentrates on regional policies. We shall present data from a broader research project covering social assistance legislation and expenditure for the fifteen ordinary statute regions over the first twenty years of their activity.[3] To justify our emphasis on the regional level, we should recall the crucial role the regions play in this particular area with respect to both national and local levels of government. According to the Constitution, the regions (first established in 1970) are entrusted with legislative power in this field, whereas the role of central government is limited to setting the guidelines for regional regulations. Within the framework of regional legislation, local authorities have complete responsibility at the operating level. This means they are responsible for providing public social services as well as co-ordinating the public sector with the non-profit and the private sector.

Our analysis clearly does not allow for an evaluation of the actual impact of social assistance policies, since it does not consider the implementation process at the municipal level. However, it does provide basic information for further research in this direction. Our purpose is to identify the institutional setting of social assistance in the different parts of the country and to examine how this impinges on the local administration of the system. Our main concern is to investigate the effects of decentralization on the actual substance of social rights. This is an increasingly relevant issue which goes well beyond the boundaries of the Italian welfare state.

THE POLICY LEGACY

In order to understand the ideology underlying Italian social assistance policies and their make-up, we must go back to the historical role played by charitable institutions in Italy. The power of the Church and the strong catholic tradition of the country meant that there were a greater number of these institutions than in other European countries. Up until the end of the nineteenth century, charities provided the only response by society to the problems of the poor: a response which consisted primarily in confining the needy to different kinds of institutions (orphanages, mental hospitals, old age homes, etc.).

The unification of Italy and the establishment of a monarchy did not change this state of affairs.[4] Indeed, the first law on charity discharged the state from any direct responsibility for providing assistance to the poor. A step forward was made with a law of 1890 which brought a large number of charitable bodies under state control, giving them the status of public agencies. However, on the whole, the shortcomings of the act – still in force – certainly outweigh the advantages. Charitable institutions were placed under the supervision of provincial authorities for administrative and financial matters, but no clear provisions were set to control the scope and the content of their action. As a result, throughout this century these institutions have carried out their functions with maximum independence, operating in effect as private bodies despite their public legal status.[5]

If we consider how public assistance policies developed during the twentieth century, it is evident that state action in favour of the underprivileged sectors of the population increased enormously. Nevertheless, the legal right of citizens to receive social assistance was formally sanctioned only by the 1948 republican Constitution and remained little more than a verbal commitment in the years which followed. The extension of state activities occurred in a piecemeal way. No attempt was made to redefine the scope of social assistance or to provide consistent guidelines and co-ordination of the wide range of benefits and services. Social assistance functions were distributed among an impressive number of public bodies. Significant resources were channelled into group-specific agencies which enhanced the labelling, categorizing and discrimination of beneficiaries, while offering an alluring opportunity for clientelistic manipulation (Bonaccorsi 1979). The importance of such agencies increased especially under the Fascist regime, but the process was not reversed in the post-war period when, indeed, a variety of new agencies was established.

Local government played a marginal role within this framework. The relevant legislation constantly limited direct provision of social services by the municipalities and the provinces. As a result, the role of local authorities in the field was confined mainly to funding institutional care provided by the charities or private bodies.

During the 1960s, public assistance was still a system geared to the poor, largely discretional and characterized by backwardness and inefficiency. Wide gaps existed in the coverage of social needs accompanied by an overlapping of public functions and the dispersion of resources among an extraordinary number of agencies. The approach to social demands emphasized institutional care and relied heavily on charitable and private bodies. In short, the institutional setting of this policy area until the early 1970s was that of a wasteful and chaotically organized, residual welfare state.

SOCIAL ASSISTANCE DURING THE FIRST PHASE OF REGIONAL GOVERNMENT

The establishment of the Regions in 1970 (more than 20 years late with respect to the relevant constitutional provision) was a watershed in the development of Italian social assistance policy. As noted earlier, the Constitution entrusted the regions with legislative power in the field of public assistance within the guidelines set by national framework legislation. During the first stage of the devolution process central government opted for a very restrictive interpretation of what the Constitution originally envisaged. The transfer of powers enacted in 1972 (by Legislative Decree No. 9) did not consider the policy sector as a whole, but gave the regions responsibility only for specific and detailed issues. Moreover, no guidelines were provided as to how the regions were to perform the new functions.

As a result, until 1977 the regions could really only play a promotional role. In that year, the national government finally provided for a comprehensive shift of power from centre to periphery in the field of social services. But despite these severe limitations, regional policy-making during the 1970s significantly altered the policy legacy in the field, primarily in the northern and central part of the country.

Table 1 provides information on regional legislation for the elderly. This highlights a clear difference between the northern/central and southern regions. While the first group of regions promotes community care for the elderly, the latter group disregards the issue completely. Three southern regions lack any sort of legislation at all, which suggests they are quite satisfied with the policy they inherited from the state, that is, the institutional care approach.

TABLE 1

REGIONAL LEGISLATION FOR THE ELDERLY (1972–1978)

	Institutional Care	Community Care
Piedmont		L.29.7.1974 n.21
		L.4.5.1976 n.19
Lombardy	L.22.1.1973 n.10	L.3.4.1974 n.16
		L.12.4.1975 n.50
		L.24.8.1977 n.39
Veneto		L.9.6.1975 n.72
Liguria		L.15.1.1974 n.1
E. Romagna		L.7.5.1975. n.27
Tuscany		L.3.1.1973 n.3
Umbria		L.23.2.1973 n.12
		L.14.2.1978 n.6
Marche		
Lazio		L.3.2.1976 n.11
Abruzzo	L.6.6.1975 n.56	
Molise	L.20.12.1972 n.22	
Campania		
Puglia	L.4.7.1974 n.22	L.12.8.1978 n.36
Basilicata		
Calabria		

Table 2 presents data on regional laws for the handicapped. A similar pattern emerges. Regions in the north and centre appear intent on establishing a network of open social services for the rehabilitation and social integration of the disabled. On the contrary, southern regions concentrate exclusively on funding a wide variety of traditional public and private agencies providing categorical assistance.

TABLE 2

REGIONAL LEGISLATION FOR THE HANDICAPPED (1972–1978)

	Funding of categorical agencies	Rehabilitation services
Piedmont	L.3.6.1975 n.37	
	Lombardy	L.20.6.1975 n.10
	Veneto	L.31.1.1974 n.17
L.30.5.1975 n.57		
Liguria		L.9.6.1975 n.32
		L.31.1.1977 n.10
E. Romagna		L.7.5.1975 n.27
Tuscany		L.3.8.1973 n.46
Umbria	L.26.4.1974 n.29	
Marche		
Lazio		L.19.9.1974 n.62
Abruzzo	L.17.4.1973 n.17	
	L.18.4.1975 n.36	
	L.15.5.1975 n.44	
	L.3.9.1976 n.44	
Molise	L.13.1.1975 n.2	
	L.31.5.1975 n.42	
Campania	L.9.8.1974 n.38	
	L.5.6.1975 n.49	
Puglia	L.30.12.1974 n.46	
Basilicata	L.9.6.1975 n.49	
Calabria	L.16.12.1974 n.18	
	L.3.6.1975 n.28	
	L.27.7.1977 n.19	
	L.12.3.1977 n.10	

In short, northern and central regions stimulate the expansion of a wide range of community services: home help for the elderly, rehabilitation and training for the handicapped, day-care centres, home nursing for sick and the disabled. Indeed the list lengthens if we consider the implementation of national laws on maternity services and day-care facilities for small children. It is true that northern-central regions are helped by their interaction with a strong system of local government, with municipalities already playing an active role in the 1960s in experimentation and innovation in social services. Quite the opposite holds true for southern regions, given the traditional weakness and inefficiency of local government in the south. Nevertheless, the institution of a new level of government – endowed with legislative powers – offered southern political forces opportunities which they did not even attempt to consider.

A break-down of regional expenditure in the field confirms this picture. During the early years of their activity, northern and central regions shifted major resources from traditional to innovative functions, for example by cutting back expenditure on institutional care in of community care. Southern regions instead continued to spend most of their budget on the old system of public assistance. The difference between the two areas of the country is quite striking: in 1978, southern regions spent only about 20 per cent of total expenditure on innovative services, whereas the north and centre spent 48 per cent and 69 per cent respectively.

The question goes beyond the geographical location of the regions, however. Table 3 suggests that a further distinction can be drawn within the centre-north of Italy, depending on the political majority in the region. Emilia Romagna, Tuscany and Umbria had governments headed by the Italian Communist Party (PCI) during the first and the second term of the regional legislature (1970–75; 1975–80) and Piedmont, Liguria and Lazio elected left-wing majorities, including the Communist Party, after the elections of 1975, while the remaining regions were all run throughout the period by coalitions centred on the Christian Democratic Party (DC).

TABLE 3

NUMBER OF TIMES THAT EACH CATEGORY OF BENEFICIARIES IS INDICATED IN REGIONAL LEGISLATION ON SOCIAL ASSISTANCE (1972–1978)

	individuals	private institutions	public agencies	municipalities	provinces
Piedmont	1 *	1 *	1 *	2* 3	
Lombardy		4	5	6	1
Veneto	1	2	3	3	
Liguria	1 *			2* 3	
E.Romagna				5	
North	3	7	9	24	1
Tuscany		1		7	
Umbria	1	1		4	1
Lazio	1 *	1 *		3* 3	1 *
Marche	1	1			
Centre	3	4		17	2
Abruzzi	1	4	5		2
Molise	3	2	4	1	1
Campania	3	3	3	1	
Puglia	3	1	1	1	1
Basilicata	2	1	2	3	
Calabria	3	2	4		
South	15	13	19	6	4
Italy	21	24	28	47	7

* Number of financial provisions passed during the first regional legislature for the three regions that changed political majority after the elections of 1975.

Referring to the allocation of regional funding, Table 3 sheds some light on the welfare mix created by regional voluntary legislation[6] for the period 1972–78. Five major categories of beneficiaries are identified: individuals, private organizations, public agencies, municipalities and provinces. We should also recall that, according to the Constitution, the regions are not supposed to be involved in direct management, which is a responsibility of the local level. They should concentrate on planning and co-ordination of the benefits and services provided within their jurisdiction.

The profile of southern regions contained in Table 3 is unequivocal. In only six cases (out of a total of 57) are municipalities taken as a reference point by southern legislation. The bulk of attention is devoted to traditional public agencies and private institutions (19 and 13 provisions, respectively). Moreover, if we look at the distribution of the provisions of the legislation granting benefits directly to the citizen, 15 of such provisions (out of 21) are concentrated in the south. In brief, southern regions – with the exception of Basilicata – ignore local authorities in favour of direct provision of benefits whenever possible and of financial support for the intricate network of agencies traditionally operating in the field.

Left-wing regions behave in exactly the opposite way. Their legislation focuses almost exclusively on local authorities and, in particular, on municipalities. Practically all spending for social services is channelled to the local level of government, with only marginal attention paid to other public agencies and private organizations. Central and northern regions run by centre or centre-left coalitions fall between the two previous groups. The cases of Lombardy and Veneto are emblematic. Their funding is more or less evenly distributed among private institutions, municipalities and other public agencies, and attempts to maintain a pluralist system of social assistance where local government, public agencies and private institutions are placed on an equal footing. The two latter groups are left free to decide as to the scope and the content of their activities.

Based on this evidence, the decentralization process in the 1970s clearly did not contribute to redressing historical disparities between the north and south of Italy, at least as far as social needs are concerned. Indeed, it may have increased them.

FROM EXPERIMENTATION TO THE CONSOLIDATION OF REGIONAL POLICIES

The institutional context of regional intervention in all areas, including social assistance, was dramatically changed by the passage of Legislative

Decree No. 616 of 1977. First of all, the marginal role of municipal government within the maze of public assistance was completely reversed. Municipalities were given full responsibility for the management and co-ordination of all social services operating at the local level. The decree also provided for the abolition of a wide range of public agencies granting benefits and services to specific categories. The functions of these organizations were transferred to local government, as were personnel, financial resources and assets. As a result, local authorities were suddenly overloaded with new responsibilities, but once again no consistent directives were given by central government.

The three major parties submitted different reform bills providing guidelines for the exercise of the functions transferred to the municipalities. However, Parliament never approved any of them and has still to pass a comprehensive reform of public assistance. In consequence, the regions were put under great pressure to take over the task by passing their own legislation for the reorganization of local social services. Further pressure came from the health reform of 1978, which provided for the creation of health districts and required the co-ordinated management of social and health services at the local level.

How did the regions fulfil the new task? The fundamental differences over welfare issues between regional governments and the central government are quite striking. During the second part of 1980s, decisions taken at the national level completely reversed the direction of policy set out by the 1978 health reform (Ferrera 1984). For whereas the 1970s ended with a consistent injection of universal principles into the Italian welfare state, the restrictive reforms inspired by selective criteria were a key feature of the 1980s. During this period, practically all government measures on social policy revolved around budgetary matters. This emphasis on cost-containment was perhaps not surprising, considering the size of the total public debt and annual deficits. Nevertheless, by imposing rigour on spending, such an approach clearly compounded the traditional difficulty in using equity criteria for the allocation of costs and benefits.[7]

Whilst central government was intent on scaling back the welfare state, albeit in makeshift and contradictory fashion, at the regional level there was a widening of horizons. Regions run both by left-wing majorities by the same (centre-right) coalition as in national government expanded social programmes and sought a thorough re-organization of the local service network. This was largely done by using the goals and the principles of the previous decade at a time when national policies were already moving away from them. During the third and the fourth regional legislatures (1980–85; 1985–90), as many as ten out of fifteen regions approved reform laws covering the entire system of social assistance. As might be expected the regions missing from the list are mostly southern regions. To be exact, four out of six regions in the south did not pass a reform law (Abruzzo, Molise, Puglia, Campania), whereas in the centre-north only Lazio failed to do so (see Table 4).[8]

TABLE 4
REGIONAL LEGISLATION FOR THE REORGANIZATION AND THE PLANNING OF
SOCIAL SERVICES (1978–1990)

	Reform laws		Regional plan for social services	
	1980–1985	1985–1990	1980–1985	1985–1990
Piedmont	L.R. 20/1982		L.R. n.7/1982	L.R.n.59/1985
Lombardy		L.R.n.1/1986		D.C.R.87/1987
Veneto	L.R.n.55/1982		L.R.n.13/1984*	L.R.n.22/1989
Liguria		L.R.n.21/1988		L.R.n.8/1989
E.Romagna	L.R.n.2/1985			
Tuscany	L.R.n.35/1978**		L.R.n.70/1984	
Umbria	L.R.n.29/1982		L.R.n.11/1985	L.R.n.9/1990
Lazio				
Marche		L.R.n.43/1988		
Abruzzo				
Molise				
Puglia				
Campania				
Basilicata	L.R.n.50/1980			
Calabria		L.R.n.5/1987		

In order to fully appreciate what the inaction of these five regions actually entails for a large part of the centre-south, the content of the reform laws requires some discussion. Interestingly enough, the ten laws are virtually alike, regardless of the region and its political orientation. Starting with the basic goals and principles laid down in the laws, social assistance is supposed to help individuals to fully develop their potential and participate in social and family life. Social assistance should not only provide a minimum level of subsistence, but should also help promote physical and emotional well-being. This is clearly based on the post-material conception of needs developed during the 1970s and is linked to a further concept: the prevention and removal of economic, cultural, environmental, social and psychological barriers that exclude the individual from everyday life, study and work. Needless to say, these goals are far too ambitious. Yet we would be wrong to under-estimate the implications of this approach.

The regional reform laws state that the differentiation of benefits and services according to category must be overcome. This means rejecting one of the original pillars of the Italian welfare state, deeply rooted in an impressive number of group-specific schemes. In its place we find the principle that each individual has the right to the same level of treatment and service. They also reject the strategy of institutional care, establishing the right of the individual to remain within his or her own background and local community. Priority is therefore given to the development of community services which are to be integrated with health, education and other services to provide a global response to social needs. The laws also take a similar approach to specific aims. For example, they all stress the importance of:

- the rehabilitation and reintegration into the community of the mentally ill and handicapped;

- the insertion of needy children into foster care; and

- the provision of auxiliary social services for working mothers and their children.

The regions examined are still involved in the development of an ambitious global plan, despite changes in the prevailing political and cultural tendencies and increasing financial difficulties. The changed context of the 1980s did not seem to influence markedly the horizons set by the reform laws. The goals are virtually the same as those established a decade earlier, but the means to achieve them are quite different. Having passed a reform law on social services, the regions maintained that the public sector should not bear all the responsibility for meeting the legitimate needs and expectations of citizens; it should be shared with the private and non-profit making sectors.

More specifically, all reform laws aim at integrating non-profit with public service providers; non-profit organizations are required to conform to the spirit and guidelines of regional legislation in order to become a part of the social services system. The regional level of government retains a role in planning and co-ordinating both public and private non-profit service providers. The latter, provided that they meet certain requirements, are also included in all public decision-making procedures.

Overall, the reform laws blur the differences detected in the legislation of the 1970s between the regions run by left-wing governments and regions with centre or centre-left governments. What seems to have occurred is a cross-fertilization of the ideas produced by the two sets of regions in the previous decade. Centre and centre-left regional governments come to share an emphasis on planning which was formerly restricted to leftist regions which, in turn, fully acknowledge the valuable contribution of the third sector – originally the product of the catholic subculture.

The basic cleavage which surfaces in the 1980s is once again territorial. Regional policy-making divides Italy into two quite distinct areas on either side of the line joining the southern borders of Tuscany and Marche. To the south of this imaginary boundary line, we can certainly detect interesting signs of institutional diffusion, but overall regional policies on social assistance remain backward and fragmented. Almost ten years behind the rest of the country, southern regions finally began to pass legislation on community care for the elderly and social integration of the handicapped. Yet it looks like a drop in the ocean. For despite the dramatic number of institutionalized children and adolescents in all southern regions (particularly in Puglia and Campania), nothing has been done to promote alternative solutions. Also, while central and northern regions strictly control the quality of the services provided by the public and private sectors, especially with respect to residential homes, the issue is almost completely ignored in the south.[9] As a result it is left to the judiciary and/or media to uncover the numerous cases of ill-treatment of mentally ill patients and the aged in private and public institutions.

Nevertheless, we should guard against overvaluing social assistance policies in central and northern Italy where there has been a definite slowdown in intervention, especially in the 1990s. Even the more active regions have not reviewed their social service plans in the past few years (cf. Table 4) and have failed to update the service standards and goals established in the late 1980s. Moreover, the traditional marginalization of social assistance vis-à-vis the health sector has increased markedly in this part of the country as well, especially as a consequence of the recent reorganization of the health system promoted by central government. The new regulations provide for a clear separation of health and social assistance, contrary to the twenty-year attempt to integrate them. Above all, the difficulties stem from the shortage of financial resources which more easily affects the social assistance area where entitlements are less difficult diminish.

This explains the fate of the minimum income scheme. All regional laws on social assistance reform refer to the concept of a minimum income or a minimum level of subsistence when setting guidelines for the provision of cash benefits by municipalities. However, the phrasing is generally vague, deferring the actual definition of relevant standards to subsequent regional legislation and, in particular, to regional social plans. Interviews with regional officials show that practically all regions have avoided this further step, preferring not to formally sanction a minimum income standard, leaving the task to the local authorities responsible for the administration of the benefits and services. To our knowledge, the only regions in the centre-north setting a specific standard (and linking this to size of household) are Lombardy, Tuscany and Umbria. But interestingly, these regions have not updated their standards during the last few years.

Nevertheless, most local authorities in the centre-north do operate minimum income schemes (*minimo vitale*), the vast majority of them providing cash benefits to individuals and families with insufficient resources, usually taking the minimum contributory pension for private employees as a reference point. However, the lack of regional regulation and the shortage of financial resources at the local level result in marked variations in coverage and benefit levels,[10] even in the same region.

How should we interpret regional inaction in this policy area, given so much detailed regional regulation covering practically all aspects of social service provision? The question is a delicate one. First of all, it is an issue that should certainly be settled also at the national level in order to avoid possible clashes between regional regulations and other directives coming from the centre, such as the income threshold established by the national government for exemption from co-payments for health care services. Obviously, regional minimum income standards with different bases increase the confusion, creating a complex set of different poverty lines. Also, giving legal status to any standard of minimum income might create excessive pressure on regional budgets to provide funding for local schemes. Municipalities would face a commitment to a certain level of entitlements, irrespective of the resources available in their budgets.

But even given these limitations, the overall picture of social assistance policies in northern and central Italy remains radically different from that in the south, where the concept of a minimum income is excluded from social assistance, despite the fact that this is precisely where poverty and unemployment are highest. As the second official report on poverty bluntly reminds us: 'whereas 63 per cent of the total population lives in the centre-north and 37 per cent in the south, the poor are distributed in just the opposite way: 37 per cent are in the centre-north and 63 per cent are in the south' (1992: 35). Among the elderly (aged 66–75), the report documents that the poor represent 14.9 per cent in the centre-north compared with 34 per cent in the south. Southern local governments ignore minimum income schemes, including the two regions – Basilicata and Calabria – which, surprisingly, set the standard in the second half of the 1980s.

THE TERRITORIAL CLEAVAGE AND THE SOUTHERN MODEL OF WELFARE

How can we explain such wide geographical variations? The structure of social needs definitely differs in the two parts of the country. If we consider factors such as the ageing of the population, female labour force participation and changes in family structure, the centre-north of Italy looks very much like the rest of continental and northern Europe. The situation of southern Italy seems much closer to Greece, Portugal and certain southern regions of Spain, where the basic problem is a high dependency ratio and insufficient wage income for substantial number of families. We would therefore expect to find a quite different cultural perception of social needs in the south compared to the more prosperous parts of the country, that is, how can we expect people to be particularly sensitive to psychological and emotional needs when basic material needs are unmet for such a large number? Under these circumstances it is not surprising that institutionalization of children without family support is not openly stigmatized.

Yet, it is misleading to focus exclusively on social needs and their cultural perceptions. We also need to look at the kind of constraints and opportunities faced by southern regions, starting with the political-cultural context in which the new institutions were embedded. Until recently, the emphasis on the catholic as opposed to the communist subculture obscured a deeper cleavage in our political system. There was, it is true, a large literature on southern clientelism, but this was not integrated into the broader framework of the different relations between civil society and political institutions in the two parts of the country.

As Farneti suggested long ago, 'the political system can be dynamically interpreted as a historical formation which emancipates itself from civil society especially with respect to the two aspects of legitimacy and effectiveness' (1971: 60). As Graziano (1980) also suggested, we can interpret the southern question in terms of missed political emancipation. Clientelism, as both a privatization of politics and the colonization of civil society, has 'frozen' the confusion of roles between state and society and created a structural weakness in the political system. As a result, the political process in southern Italy displays remarkably different features to the centre-north:

- pre-political particularism;
- an instrumental approach to politics;
- an absence of collective action; and
- vertical channels of articulation and aggregation of demand.

These are all elements that go to create a vicious circle.

Given these premises, we can safely assume that for most of the southern political elite the new regional level of government primarily represented an alluring opportunity to allocate a constant flow of resources according to particularistic criteria. Our research suggests that a large number of policy choices in the field of social assistance are quite consistent with this assumption, one of many examples being the very limited use of legislation and the clear preference for administrative instruments allowing for greater discretion.

The syndrome we have outlined certainly represents a heavy burden for all southern regional governments. Putnam (1993) argues that the roots of the southern question can be traced as far back as the Middle Ages. But while recognizing the importance of the historical legacy, we also find variations *within* the south (and also within the centre-north) that call for further explanation. In contrast to all other southern regional governments, Basilicata and Calabria do re-organize their systems of social assistance along the same lines as the centre-north: there is a universalistic approach in their legislation as well as the definition of rules and procedures for controlling public and private service provider. Contextual variables and historical legacies cannot explain these two cases. But if we introduce political variables, the picture becomes clearer. According to evidence collected by Putnam, Leonardi and Nanetti (in their twenty-year study of Italian regions), Basilicata is an 'over-achiever' with respect to contextual factors. This outcome is explained by local political factors (namely a very low level of intra-party and intra-coalition conflict which helped produce high political stability and continuity in political leadership) (Putnam *et al.* 1985; Leonardi *et al.* 1987) although Putnam makes no mention of this in his latest book (1993).

We cannot refer to the same set of variables in the Calabria case. Quite the opposite holds true for this region, which has had twelve different governments between 1970 and 1990, ranking it top of the list for political instability along with Campania, Lazio and Molise (Fedele 1990). However, it should be noted that the approval of the reform law and subsequent regulations coincided with the establishment of the first left-wing government in a southern region. This element requires careful consideration before we can arrive at any definite conclusion. Certainly what is striking is the break with all previous legislation, which appears exclusively interested in distributing resources, disregarding any general regulation of regional policies.

Obviously, a real change in the existing system of social assistance requires far more than the mere passing of a law. Unlike northern and central municipalities, southern ones have no tradition in the provision of social services and depend almost exclusively on regional funding. So it is not surprising that very little change can be detected at the local level using available indicators (Censis 1995: 100–1). More attention should be paid to the symbolic dimension of the message that an institution conveys to the citizen. This is particularly so in a context such as southern Italy where the concept of citizenship and the rights and responsibilities of the individual have been so dramatically downgraded. Just as the daily experience of mismanagement, clientelism and corruption reinforces people's distrust in their political institutions, a reversal of the trend can interrupt the vicious circle. Administrative transparency, the use of universalistic versus particularistic criteria in the allocation of funds, emphasis on social needs, equality of treatment, efficiency and effectiveness can gradually erode traditional distrust and overcome negative expectations. Obviously, this cannot be done overnight. It is a long-term process requiring stability and a firm stance by the leading political majority. Unfortunately, this is not the case for Calabria.

CONCLUSION

Our research suggests that the territorial dimension has to be taken into consideration if we want to give an accurate picture of the Italian welfare state and understand what it effectively means for the citizens of that country. If we examine health services and income maintenance programmes,[11] the distance between the two parts of Italy appears even greater. Just keeping to social assistance, our results show clearly that whether we look at cash subsidies or at the provision of services, average figures can be highly misleading.

The actual situation of minimum income schemes looks much bleaker than that described by MISSOC in its annual report on the development of social protection in the EU. The comparative tables contained in the 1995 and 1996 editions point to the range of established *minima* but disregard the fact that this programme is virtually non-existent in southern Italy.[12] Gough (1996), however, paints a picture which is perhaps *too* gloomy by including Italy alongside Spain, Portugal, Greece and Turkey in a distinct south European 'rudimentary assistance' *regime*. In this system 'national categorical assistance schemes cover certain specific groups, mainly elderly and disabled people. Otherwise there is local discretionary relief provided by municipalities or religious charitable bodies' (1996: 13). This may be an accurate description of the archaic public assistance system still prevailing in the south but seems inappropriate for other parts of the country. The development of quite divergent policy approaches at the subnational level suggests that the model should be qualified, at least in the case of Italy.

In fact, Rico and Laparra and Aguilar (this issue) suggest that this also holds for Spain. Their discussions of health policies and minimum income programmes both emphasize the importance of the territorial dimension and related differences in the level of social protection. For example, means-tested benefits can be legally claimed as a right in the Basque Country whereas in other regions the scheme is very limited or barely existent. In sum, although Italy and Spain share the basic traits of the southern model of welfare with Portugal and Greece (Ferrera 1996), these two countries also display distinguishing features. Apart from having reached a more mature stage in the development of welfare policies, during the past two decades both countries engaged in a substantive transfer of functions to regions and local authorities. Moreover, the devolution process was complicated by the uneven distribution of powers between special and ordinary regions. The Spanish health system is emblematic for that matter, resulting in a complex of institutional arrangements differing from region to region.

In short, the dynamics of centre-periphery relations in the area of social policy have exacerbated the contradictions between prosperous and more backward areas in Spain as well as Italy. Unfortunately, this is unlikely to change in the near future. Indeed in the present climate of austerity, European integration goals are heavily influencing social policy choices in all southern European countries. In this context Spain and Italy appear to be confronted with an additional problem: inter-regional tensions over the different levels of benefits and services available within their national boundaries. We should perhaps pay more attention to these geographical disparities. Because while impinging on the kind of equity dilemmas currently being faced by all welfare states they might also trigger a mobilization of interests with deeply delegitimizing effects: hardly a welcome prospect for either country!

NOTES

1. In many cases home care does not represent a viable solution and appropriate residential care becomes the only, albeit more costly, solution.
2. According to Gough, 'we have little comparative knowledge of the number of schemes, their categorical benefits or beneficiaries, how benefits are calculated, whether they are rights-based or discretionary, the conditions attached to benefits, the levels of government responsible for financing and operating them, or of their effectiveness in reducing poverty or their efficiency in targeting those in need' (1995: 1).
3. The five regions under special statute (Valle d'Aosta, Trentino Alto-Adige, Friuli

Venezia Giulia, Sicily and Sardinia) have not been considered because they are in a quite different position compared to the other regions. First, they were established much earlier; second, they have greater powers and they receive substantially larger state transfers. All of these differences make it inappropriate to include the five regions in a comparative study of subnational policy development in exploring what happens when the same institutional reforms occur in different socio-economic and political contexts.

4. The development of public assistance policies in Italy from 1861 to the fascist regime is treated in greater detail in Fargion (1983).

5. The Italian Constitutional Court recently reversed the legislative approach to charities based on the 1890 law. According to sentence No. 396 taken by the Court on 24 March 1988, the first provision of the 1890 law which conferred public status to the charities contrasts with article 38 of the 1948 Constitution and is therefore illegitimate. As a result, after a hundred years in the public sphere, the charities that meet certain requirements are entitled, upon request, to be privatized. It is interesting to note that only ten years earlier, Government Decree No. 616 envisaged the extinction of all public charities (IPAB) and the transfer of their properties, personnel and funds to the regions and the municipalities. Instead of defining the procedures for their extinction, the regions are now involved in providing the necessary regulation for the privatization process.

6. Regional regulations enacting national laws are not considered here, i.e. provisions stemming from the law on crèche facilities (Law 107/1971), on maternity and child services (Law 405/1975) and on the prevention of drug addiction (Law 685/1975).

7. More detailed information on the measures taken by the central government with respect to health care and family allowances in particular can be found in Fargion (1995: 11–12). For an overview of restrictive reforms in more recent years, see Saraceno and Negri (1994).

8. As of January 1996, the four southern regions had not yet approved a reform law and in fact had not even prepared a first draft. The regional council of Lazio recently approved such a bill, which, however, is not yet in force.

9. With the exception of Calabria, which has established a regional register for residential homes and a regional commission for ensuring that regional requirements are met. Calabria's regulations in this area closely follow legislation in the centre-north.

10. More specifically, differences refer to conditions of eligibility; severity of means-testing; extent of family obligations; and adjustments for size of household.

11. Over the eighteen years of its operation, the National Health Service has not been able to redress territorial disparities in terms of infrastructure and the level of services inherited from the pre-existing insurance system. In income maintenance, the literature has highlighted a dualistic system in which high benefits are provided for privileged groups with strong attachment to the formal labour force, alongside low and discretionary benefits for the rest of the population (see Ferrera 1996). However, the formal labour force is largely concentrated in the north and this results in overall higher levels of social protection in that part of the country.

12. Cf. MISSOC (1996) Table XII, p.393.

REFERENCES

Alber, J. (1995): 'A framework for the comparative study of social services', *Journal of European Social Policy* 5/2, pp.131–49.

Bonaccorsi, M. (1979): 'Gli enti pubblici del settore della sicurezza sociale', in F. Cazzola (ed.), *Anatomia del potere DC*, Bari: De Donato, pp.57–149.

Centro Studi e Investimenti Sociali (CENSIS) (1995): *I confini del welfare. Logiche di decentramento e logiche di riequilibrio*, Roma (unpublished report).

Commissione d'indagine sulla povertà e l'emarginazione (1992): *Secondo rapporto sulla povertà in Italia*, Milano: Angeli.

Farneti, P. (1971): *Sistema politico e società civile. Saggi di teoria e ricerca politica*, Torino: Giappichelli.

Fargion, V. (1983): 'L'assistenza pubblica in Italia dall'unità al fascismo: Primi elementi per un'analisi strutturale', *Rivista Trimestrale di Scienza della Amministrazione* 30/2, pp.25–70.

Fargion, V. (1995): *The territorial cleavage in Italy and the Welfare mix in social services*, paper presented at the conference on 'Comparative Research on Welfare State reforms', ISA RC 19, Pavia.

Fedele, M. (1990): *La forma di governo regionale*, Camera dei Deputati, X legislatura, rapporto di ricerca no.416.

Ferrera, M. (1984): *Il Welfare State in Italia*, Bologna: Il Mulino.

Ferrera, M. (1996): 'The "Southern Model" of Welfare in Social Europe', *Journal of European Social Policy* 6/1, pp.17–37.

Gough, I. (1995): *Diverse Systems, Common Destination? A Comparative Study of Social Assistance in OECD Countries*, paper presented at the conference on 'Comparative Research on Welfare Reforms', ISA RC 19, Pavia.

Gough, I. (1996): 'Social Assistance in Southern Europe', *South European Society & Politics* 1/1 (Summer) pp.1–23.

Graziano, L. (1980): *Clientelismo e sistema politico. Il caso dell'Italia*, Milano: Angeli.

Leonardi, R., R. Putnam and R. Nanetti (1987): *Il caso Basilicata*, Bologna: Il Mulino.

MISSOC (1996): *La protection sociale dans les Etats membres de l'Union européenne*, Bruxelles.

Putnam, R. (1993): *Making Democracy Work*, Princeton: PUP.

Putnam, R., R. Leonardi and R. Nanetti (1985): *La pianta e le radici*, Bologna: Il Mulino.

Saraceno, C. and N. Negri (1994): 'The Changing Italian Welfare State', *European Journal of Social Policy* 4/1, pp. 19–34.

The Italian National Health Service and the Challenge of Privatization

ELENA GRANAGLIA

The aim of the paper is to analyse the main policies of privatization of the Italian NHS, now partly under implementation and partly under discussion. To do so some prior attention is given both to the development of a taxonomy of the different meanings of privatization and to a brief description of the context in which privatization proposals have arisen. The conclusion is that these policies, though very similar to the ones under discussion (and, partially under implementation) in continental and northern Europe, still continue to be accompanied by the persistence of many of the traits of the so-called Mediterranean welfare state, above all a poor administrative culture.

Privatization is a very vague term that may have different meanings. In the industrial context, it usually coincides with denationalization, that is to say, the expansion of private supply through a particular procedure, the selling of public enterprises to private producers.[1] These latter tend to be identified as profit-based enterprises, be they proprietor-owned or investor-owned, or in rare cases, co-operatives of ex-public employees. Especially within the social (and more generally the public) services, many other meanings can be found. Privatization may imply the expansion of private supply through entry liberalization, that is to say through the breaking, rather than the selling, of public monopolies. In this perspective, financing and productive responsibilities would be separated. The former would remain public, while the latter could become private and there would be competition among the different producers.

There are many specific options available and they vary according to:

- whether public financing occurs through direct payment of producers, that is to say, through public contracting, or through reimbursing consumers for expenditure made;

- the degree of freedom of choice given to consumers, which could

I would like to thank L. Arcangeli, from the Italian Department of Health, for the information given. As usual, all errors and omissions are mine, as are the critical remarks.

range from being totally unrestricted as in the traditional model of economic competition to being variously restricted as in the different versions of managed competition, whereby consumers' choice is structured by some sponsors, be they public or private;

- the private producers chosen: besides profit-based enterprises, there can be non-profit organizations, voluntary associations and families.[2] Privatization could also imply the expansion of private financing, either through the introduction of cost sharing, as in co-payments, co-insurance and deductibles, or in the use of wholly private prices, as in the case of a freeze or an outright reduction in public expenditure.[3] Furthermore, privatization could be the reduction of any public activity, including any kind of deregulation of the private sector.[4]

Finally, a more general meaning could simply be the introduction, within the public sector, of market-like behavioural rules. In other terms, supply and financing would remain public, but their organization would mimic private firms and markets. Such a policy could be applied both to the remuneration schemes adopted within the different organizations and to the overall relationship among producers: in the health case, it would involve the development of competition.[5] If the public sector is characterized by a private–public mix, the competitive game could vary according to the same variables indicated in the case of the expansion of private supply through entry liberalization.[6] A further possibility, in this perspective, could be to auction the management of organizations that would remain publicly owned.

Despite their diversity, all of the above meanings share a common qualifying element: privatization has to do with the introduction of incentives (and disincentives); different actors have to be made responsible for their performance. The main idea is that institutions provide each individual with the mix of opportunities and costs associated with the pursuit of the different objectives. Individuals, being utility maximizers (satisficers), try to maximize (satisfice) their personal benefits, minimizing the costs they have to bear. The problem, within a great deal of the public sector, is that costs, instead of being borne by those who engender them, tend to be shifted onto the collectivity. The essence of privatization consists in shifting ('internalizing') these costs back onto those who generate them (see De Alessi 1989). The various conceptions of privatization also share a common set of objectives: efficiency in production and freedom of choice and, through it, quality of care.[7] Even though equity does not lie among the major objectives of privatization, it is worthwhile noticing that, in many instances, it is held to be perfectly compatible with privatization.

However, another meaning could be given to privatization that is exactly to the contrary of those indicated above. It could stand for the pursuit, within the public sector, of the private preferences of the different actors, independently or even against all consideration of collective goals. Within an NHS context, for example, doctors could privately decide how to allocate resources, irrespective or even contrary to public health goals.[8] In other words, privatization could imply the privatization of benefits and the collectivization of costs. To avoid confusion, I call this last kind of privatization 'n-privatization' (where n stands for negative).

This paper concentrates on the description and discussion of some policies of privatization of the Italian National Health Service (NHS), now partly under implementation and partly under discussion, which have the intent of coping with n-privatization. Before doing this, some background information on the Italian NHS is necessary.

THE ITALIAN NATIONAL HEALTH SERVICE

The Italian NHS was established at the end of the 1970s, replacing the old social insurance system which was crippled with deficits and overburdened by inefficiencies, poor quality and barriers to access for those excluded from the labour market. The reform was highly ambitious. Great emphasis was put not just on the realization of universal access with no distinction among citizens, but also on results, namely the promotion of physical and mental health, within the constraints of efficiency in provision and patients' satisfaction.[9]

Today, after about twenty years, these promises are largely still unfulfilled. Universal access has certainly been achieved, but with respect to equity, recent studies show that 'if, during the 1980s, individuals aged 18–74 and with school degrees equal or inferior to the elementary degree had had the same mortality rates of individuals in the same age group, but with University degrees, there would have been around forty-thousand fewer deaths each year' (Costa et al. 1994: 29). With respect to efficiency in production and quality, the evidence is equally discouraging.[10] After years of continuous increases, public expenditure fell from 6.1 per cent of GNP in 1993 to about 5.8 per cent in 1994. Between 1992 and 1993, it even decreased in absolute value.[11] As will be argued below, the fall in public expenditure has not, however, brought an end to deficit financing.

Understanding the context of privatization in the Italian health system requires a further specification of the original institutional design of the Italian NHS. Three elements are important: the organizational model, financing and private elements within the system.

The Organizational Model of the NHS

There was a serious under-valuation in the law instituting the NHS and in the health policy community supporting it, of some of the basic requirements necessary for the working of any organization. The inspiring model is that of rational-synoptic planning, the limits of which are today well-acknowledged. All attention is focused on the setting of objectives, as if the attribution of the objectives to the different actors is a sufficient condition for having them satisfied.[12] No attention is therefore given to the (transaction) costs of the different organizational solutions. It was decided to delegate all major health policy decisions to a National Health Plan to be promulgated by Parliament. Recurrent political crises apart, Parliament has proven totally inadequate in legislating on such specific matters. The first health plan to see the light of day was in July 1994, more than 15 years after the founding of the NHS.[13] Incentive compatibility was equally ignored. Take the distribution of resources within the NHS. Territorial distribution was based on so-called 'transfer' finance: higher levels of government resources were transferred to poorer regions, without any control on their use. More specifically, the state distributes resources to the regions on the basis of a capitation fee. The regions transfer these resources to the Local Health Authorities (USL – Unità Sanitarie Locali). The most common method been global retrospective budgeting based on historical costs, a method that wholly dispenses with any evaluation of performance. Public hospitals are reimbursed through a mix of global retrospective budgets and fees per day of hospitalization. Should any surplus be produced anywhere, it should be returned to the centre.[14]

Similarly, regarding the organization of USLs and public hospitals, both were to follow the traditional bureaucratic model. This meant that, among other things, controls could only concern the legitimacy (rather than the merit) of different activities, no economic accounting was required, employees could not be dismissed, career advancements are substantially automatic and so on. Furthermore, politicians were put in charge of the USLs, that is actors more interested in building consensus, which, especially in the local context, has frequently coincided with the pursuit of clientelistic politics.[15] In short, the organizational context was highly conducive to the spread of behaviour typical of 'n-privatization'.

Finally, the information requirements necessary for the working of any organization were also overlooked. By information requirements I refer to the fact that not only does personnel have to be trained, both formally and informally through peer group practices, but information has also to be developed and diffused on the best means of meeting the stated objectives. This last point may seem trivial, but according to the most optimistic estimates, no more than 30 per cent of health care services have proved effective (see Light 1991).

Financing

The law establishing the NHS provided for the abandonment of the old system of contributory financing in favour of a budgetary coverage, more in line with the redistributive goals of universal access and with the realization of the public goods typical of a national health service. The system of payroll tax financing has yet to be abandoned. Furthermore, a new contribution was introduced in 1986, the so-called health tax, that is imposed on the difference between taxable personal income and the sum of wages and pensions with some exemptions. The rate amounts to 5 per cent for the first 40 million lire and 4.2 per cent for incomes between 40 and 100 million lire. In 1993, overall contributions covered just over 42 per cent of NHS expenditure, while 44 per cent was financed from the general budget. The share covered by contributions, according to estimates, increased to 47 per cent in 1994 (see Dirindin 1993; 1995).

Finally, among the sources of financing, both deficits and cost sharing in the field of pharmaceutical, specialist and diagnostic services have to be mentioned. Deficits have been recorded every year since the inception of the NHS: in 1993 and 1994, they amounted respectively to 7.5 per cent and an estimated 8.6 per cent of total NHS outlays. Deficit financing can, in part, be explained by the more general difficulties of Italy's public finances, in the sense that estimated expenditure has been consciously underestimated in order to arrive, at least formally and certainly with a short-sighted outlook, at a balanced budget. Cost sharing (another system of payment based on the benefit principle) provides only 2.5 per cent of the receipts of the NHS. The many changes introduced almost every year and the constant attempts to widen cost-sharing, with the only result of spurring popular protest until these attempts are abandoned, have been quite anomolous.[16]

Private Elements within the System

Cost sharing is a form of private financing and it is important to stress the wider role played by the private sector since the inception of the NHS. All GPs are independent contractors paid on the basis of capitation fees established at a national level. Most facilities providing specialist and diagnostic assistance are private and sell their services to the USL on a fee-for-service basis. Similarly, 90 per cent of private hospitals are providers of the USL, mainly in the less capital intensive sectors of general medicine, rehabilitation and psychiatric assistance. Payments are based on fees per day of hospitalization established at the national level.[17] Doctors who are employees of the NHS have long been allowed to practice in these private hospitals as well. Such a possibility is now forbidden, but the ban is often overridden. The decision to send a patient to a private facility is made by the USL on a case-by-case evaluation. Private pharmacies are reimbursed for the cost of drugs subsidized by the state. Finally, since 1985, the regions have been allowed to select a list of services that can be privately provided and then publicly reimbursed at prices established by the regions themselves. In short, the NHS can be described as a private–public mix.

It should also be stressed that the relationship with the private sector is characterized by the same lack of attention towards incentive compatibility as in the purely public side of the NHS. For example, capitation fees favour the shifting of assistance from lower-cost general services to the higher-cost specialized ones. Fees per day of hospitalization are based on the global (again historical) costs generated by private production, with no reference to the specific output produced, creating an in-built incentive to increase the length of stay. The possibility for doctors who are employees of the NHS to practice in private hospitals selling their services to the USL has contributed and still contributes to the malfunctioning of public hospitals. The overall cost of private sector utilization can, any way, be shifted to the national level, given the system of 'transfer' finance previously described.

Finally, 4.5 millions of citizens have private insurance, in the form of individual or group insurance, both enjoying fiscal benefits.[18] Private expenditure has been constantly increasing. In 1992, it amounted to about 2 per cent of the GNP. Estimates for 1994 show a further increase of 0.2 per cent.

This background is important for understanding the context in which the challenge of privatization is taking place – one in which the NHS has constantly undervalued the role of organizational requirements, where financial costs are highly visible, thus making pressures for change high, and where a considerable proportion of services are already produced by private actors.[19]

THE PRESENT CHALLENGE OF PRIVATIZATION

The present challenge of privatization takes place along two directions.[20] On the one side, there is the challenge, sanctioned by Decree 502 of 1992, Law 724/1995 and by the National Health Plan, of abandoning the old system of remuneration for hospitals, based on a mix of retrospective global budgeting and fees per day of hospitalization. From then on, all hospitals, regardless of their nature, would be paid through prospective rate-setting based on DRGs (a system of fixed prices for clearly specified diagnostic treatment categories), while the regions would become responsible for any deficit they might experience.[21] All hospitals, with the exception of general hospitals belonging to the USL – for which the provisions are still unclear – would have the right to retain any surpluses they generate. Competition among producers would then be fostered, even though in which particular way is not clearly specified.

While the model of public contracting appears privileged, the role for consumer choice is unclear. The managed competition version has certainly been chosen; and consumer choice is somewhat restricted by public sponsors. But to what extent? One possibility is to follow the British contracting-out version. In this case, public managers would have a great role in structuring patients' choices: acting as agents of the patients, they would both choose the producers and specify the services mix to be provided. Consumer choice would then be restricted and competition would be concentrated mostly on the prices, it being in the interest of producers to lower prices in the contract. In the Italian case, the national level would provide a set of maximum rates, while regions and USLs would be free to contract lower ones.

There is, however, another possibility – the Swedish example of public competition. To be more precise, in the Italian case we could call it public sector competition, given the presence, in that country, of a plurality of private producers.[22] In this perspective, consumers would be free to select the producers themselves. Producers would be paid directly by the USL according to the number of patients they are able to attract: thus, rather than on price, competition would develop along the quality dimension (especially in its non-technical aspects). Competition would remain managed because public managers would both establish the packages of services to be financed and select the private hospitals which consumers could attend, namely those which accept certification, that is, meet certain quality standards and accept reimbursement by the USL at the same rates charged by public hospitals.

A second model of reimbursing consumers directly, instead of resorting to public contracting, is under consideration. In this case, competition would cease to be managed. All hospitals could be utilized and consumers could be reimbursed for the services acquired, with the reimbursement set equal to the rates utilized in the NHS (obviously, provision is limited to the services that are also publicly provided). The only influence on consumers' choice would be indirectly exerted by the comparison with what the NHS produces and with the prices that it charges. In the view of its supporters, the incentives would be a mix of those operating in both the above models. There would be competition on quality, but also on price if tariffs cover only part of total costs. On the other side, there is the challenge posed by another and more radical version of this model: to give citizens the possibility of opting out completely from the NHS, using vouchers to buy private insurance. Such a possibility, which again implies dispensing with managed competition, is contemplated in an article of Legislative Decree no. 502 of 1992.[23] The amount of the vouchers would be equal to a percentage of the capitation fee distributed to the regions, to be decided at the national level. Although this article has recently been cancelled, proposals of this kind have been present since the institution of the NHS and have lately acquired growing support, even among sections of the left and the trade unions, who simply place more emphasis on the social aspect of the market and regulation, including:

- the development of a social market where non-profit organizations, voluntary services and self-help are present together with profit-based organizations;

- a guarantee that access to the system remains truly universal; and

- the need for an authority to secure equality of access and quality of care.[24]

Thus, we have privatization according to different meanings. Rate-setting, together with the fostering of competition, represents a form of privatization by introducing, within the NHS, market-like rules for the remuneration of the single producer and in the relationship among different producers.

To present rates as a form of privatization may seem strange, since rates are nothing but administered prices. But unlike global budgeting, rates mean that each producer is paid according to what he does and that, if surpluses are be retained, he has an incentive to minimize costs, the net remuneration being the difference between the rate and the costs sustained. Furthermore, rates based on DRGs, unlike those previously utilized and based on cost per day of hospitalization, have the advantage of stimulating cost-minimization for each episode of illness, with the positive effects of reducing inappropriate length of stay and increasing occupancy rates and turnover.

Privatization as an expansion of private supply could also occur. This is obvious in the case of public reimbursement of private expenditure and of vouchers. Some further privatization of supply could, however, also follow from public sector competition, since certified hospitals would become free to sell all services provided by the NHS, while today, as we have seen, private provision is limited only to a portion of them.[25]

Finally, with public reimbursement of private expenditure and vouchers we could also have some privatization of financing. Such privatization is never clearly stated. The point is that, in case of public reimbursement, medical bills would have to be paid in advance and there could be a considerable delay in obtaining the refund. Furthermore, the sums reimbursed would be lower than the ones actually paid; otherwise, there would be no reason to choose this option instead of public sector competition which would leave consumers equally free.[26] As for vouchers, a privatization of financing could occur only if the amounts are insufficient to buy care. It is worth noting that the amount suggested at the time of the promulgation of the D.L. 502 were insufficient to buy insurance even for a young and healthy person.

For its supporters, in any case, there would be no conflict with equity. The NHS would continue to produce its services for those who do not choose to opt out and, in a richer society, most people would have the opportunity spend money on health care, and wait for public reimbursement of a portion of that spending, thereby diverting resources away from frivolous consumption (see, for example, Clerico 1994).

THE PRESENT CHALLENGE OF PRIVATIZATION: SOME CRITICAL REMARKS

A complete evaluation of the pros and cons of the different policies of privatization is beyond the scope of this article.[27] In this concluding section, I simply point to some of the shortcomings of these policies.

A number of problems are associated with these approaches and under-estimated by their proponets. Some problems are related to *the rates* themselves, for example:

- the risk of so-called 'DRG creep', that is, when episodes of illness linked to a lower priced DRG are charged as if they were linked to a higher priced one;

- the risks of both 'cream skimming' to the detriment of the more ill who often are also poorer and of quality deterioration due to the maximization of net revenues;

- the risks of under-providing indivisible and non-excludable services for which prices are not available, like prevention and health care education; and

- the increase in administrative costs and the risk of capture by producers present in all systems of administered prices.[28]

More general problems linked with the *working of competition*:

- some health care markets are natural monopolies that resist the introduction of competition even in the form of market contestability;

- furthermore, where competition can be pursued, the Italian situation is such that public hospitals would often find themselves in an uneven position *vis-à-vis* the private ones. For example, they would have higher labour costs any time private hospitals utilize public employees (for whom the public employer already pays most of the taxes) and, in any case, have to submit to more rigid regulation both in personnel policies and in access to capital markets.[29] To counter this, more privatization, again in the sense of the introduction of market-like rules, would have to be achieved within public organizations as well. In any case, certification procedures for private hospitals still have to be defined and, without them, private and public output could not be comparable;

- finally, if, as in Italy, there is a budgetary constraint, competition should produce a zero-sum game: while some hospitals would gain patients and resources, others would lose on both counts. This would then require planning on how to reconvert facilities and transfer manpower.

Some particular problems relate to the *specific competitive mechanisms selected*:

- the particular model to be adopted has to be better specified. Once this is done, if the contracting out option is chosen, price competition could not develop even when technically possible – for example, due to predatory pricing by incumbents or to collusion among potential competitors;

- if price competition does develop, besides the obvious restriction in consumers' choice, there would be an increased risk of quality deterioration (including increases in waiting times).[30] In case of public sector competition and the public reimbursement of private expenditure, this risk could be mitigated, given the incentive to attract consumers. The price would, however, be linked to a higher risk of increases in output and, therefore, of expenditure, the stimulus to increase output being a well-documented component of all systems of consumer-driven competition (see Dranove *et al.*1993).

- The capacity of consumers to increase quality (even in the non-technical, more observable aspects) should not be overvalued if average quality is low (in such a context, changing producers does not guarantee that the new producers will be better). If the model of public reimbursement of private expenditure is used, a two-tier system could also develop, where the lower quality public services are consumed mainly by those who cannot afford privately to await public reimbursement. In this sense, the optimistic assertion that in a richer society people should be able to divert consumption from frivolous destinations to health care should be better verified, since prices in the private sector (outside the NHS) are often so high that even many non-poor seem unable to afford them.

With respect to *vouchers for buying private insurance*, there are:

- the problems already indicated and related to the definition of the amount of the vouchers. If equity is to be ensured and if one believes that a substantial privatization of financing is incompatible with such an objective, then the amount of voucher should be high and differentiated enough to buy insurance for all, independent of the risk profiles of everyone. Such a course of action, however, would increase public expenditure, not only because it is costly to differentiate vouchers according to different risk profiles, but also because competition among private insurances is the most costly version of consumer-driven competition. Not only would the stimulus to increase output be strengthened – given the lack of sponsors otherwise present in the different schemes of managed competition – but there could also be increases in prices, both because greater fragmentation of care could imply higher administrative costs and because high prices, in imperfect markets such as those in health care, are often seen as a signal of high quality. Today, all health insurances in Italy face losses;[31]

- the problems, if vouchers are too low and insufficiently differentiated, linked to the development of a two-tier system. Favouring exit, in addition, may lead to the collapse of all voice mechanism (Sterpi 1993);

- the problems of inefficient distribution of risks, since the period of three years set for re-evaluating the choice to opt out is too short (for an optimal allocation of risk) both for the insurance companies and for the NHS that will remain the insurer of last resort for all the most expensive cases not covered by private insurance.[32]

I am perfectly aware that all institutions are in some way or other imperfect; that imperfections are especially pervasive in health care and that the NHS, in particular, is full of them. Thus, in pointing to these shortcomings, I do not implicitly assume that some perfect solution is available., I simply want to stress that precisely because all health care arrangements are imperfect, changes have to be examined carefully. The supporters of privatization, on the contrary, seem to overlook such requirements.

By so doing, they commit a fault that is very similar to the one they ascribe to the original design of the NHS. In exactly the same way, the attribution of the various objectives to the different actors is deemed sufficient for having those objectives satisfied. The introduction of incentives (and disincentives) is considered sufficient to guarantee an improvement. The final results risk, once again, falling very short of expectations. For after years of talking almost exclusively about health objectives, privatization policies tend instead to discard all reference to the substantive goals to be realized. This may be due to the typical economic assumptions in favour of the decentralization of decisions, often associated with privatization.[33] But it seems quite incoherent if health care continues to be delivered within a NHS context or even if it is simply publicly financed. Public health goals matter and have to be clearly articulated.

Furthermore, the changes envisaged continue to suffer many of the original faults of the Italian NHS. On the one hand, they continue to undervalue the complexities of incentive compatible mechanisms. They limit themselves to the setting of incentives (and disincentives) while paying little or no attention given to the development of monitoring and controlling systems, so necessary to the working of incentives themselves. On the other hand, they continue to undervalue the need to take into account the costs of the different mechanisms.[34]

Finally, exactly as in the original NHS design, no attention is paid to information requirements, when tackling such failure could lead to great improvements both in health and in economic terms. Since we are talking about imperfect markets, training appears to be particularly important, especially in the form of peer reviews and 'responsibility fora' in which individuals are urged to account for their actions as holders of public authority (see Phelps 1992). Similarly, the development of more information on the effectiveness of the health care services appears highly promising in view of the fact that only 30 per cent of services (at most) have been proven effective. In this context, policies aimed at reducing risks and redressing certain conditions linked to social stratification – that is, creating greater equality in living standards – are often found to be more effective in promoting health than health services and are therefore worth exploring (Marmot et al. 1994). The diffusion of health care information, in turn, could also moderate existing pressures on the part of the patients constantly to increase consumption.[35] Briefly, a poor administrative culture, similar to that in other southern European countries, continues to accompany the shift in favour of privatization. Careful evaluation of these different shortcomings, however, does not seem likely to occur. Years of unsatisfactory performance, coupled with the high visibility of the financial burden of health care, have drastically diminished citizens' confidence in the NHS, and simultaneously increased the desire for privatization *tout court*.

NOTES

1. Such a definition is provided by Sappington and Stiglitz (1987). On the ambiguity of the term 'privatization' see Kamerman and Kahn (1989).
2. This taxonomy is derived from both Bariletti (1993) and France (1994).
3. In case of freeze, the result could be described as 'privatization by default' (Estrin and Perotin 1988). On cost sharing and privatization of financing, see Birch (1986).
4. The reference is to all deregulation in addition to liberalization that could also represent a form of deregulation. For a definition of privatization as the reduction of any public activity, see Le Grand and Robinson (1984).
5. Remuneration schemes have to do both with monetary aspects and with the structuring of careers. For a detailed analysis of different remuneration schemes and their effects, see Milgrom (1992).
6. The difference between the two meanings is that, in this case, the innovation would only lie in the introduction of competitive rules. Obviously, when the public sector is already characterized by a public–private mix, the result could be some expansion of private production, but the result would not be intentional. In the preceding case, instead, we would have an intentional extension of private production (besides the introduction of competitive rules).
7. Quality is a complex characteristic having to do with both technical aspects – health services have to be produced in ways that are clinically appropriate and should be provided in ways coherent with different health conditions – and non-technical aspects such as the comfort of the different facilities, the reduction of waiting lists and the respect of patients' dignity. Obviously, the two objectives are interrelated in the sense that freedom of choice represents an important pressure for efficiency in production.
8. See, among others, Bovbjerg *et al.* (1987) and, more generally, the public choice perspective.
9. I use the term patients' satisfaction as shorthand for (and thus synonymous with) the non-technical aspects of quality.
10. See, for example, France (1994) and Istituto di Economia Sanitaria (1993). As for equity, it is true that inequalities in health status, in some parts of Italy, seem to be associated with 'super-equity' in access, in the sense that the poorer seem to consume more health care services than the rich (Mapelli 1994). A possible explanation lies in the ineffectiveness of many health services, that is to say, in the fact that there is not always a coincidence between providing more services and improving health.
11. The 1994 data are estimates. Data on public expenditure reported here and below in the text are taken from the *Relazione generale sulla situazione economica del paese* (1995).
12. In the case of the Italian NHS, one could also add that even the attention given to the objectives was insufficient, in the sense that there was little awareness of the economic constraints or of the need of rationing.

13. On the story of the National Health Plan, see Granaglia (1990).
14. More precisely, the state finances the different regions on the basis of a capitation fee adjusted to take into account both inter-regional mobility and the objective of making structural endowments more equal. The regions, in addition to the USLs, transfer resources to a particular class of hospitals, the highly specialized ones, through a mix of global budgets and fees per day of hospitalization, established at a regional level. The USLs spend the resources received to pay for their in-house activities, including those provided by the hospitals belonging to the USLs, and for the services carried out by University hospitals. The most common method, again, is global retrospective budgeting. Both highly specialized hospitals and University hospitals are public, but provide their services to the NHS through a *'convenzione'*. On the overall system of 'transfer' finance in the Italian NHS, see Cavazzuti and Giannini (1982).
15. Some important changes have occurred in recent years. For example, since 1991, there has been a clear separation between political and managerial responsibilities. USL and highly specialized hospitals are administered by a general director, appointed by the region with a private contract, and a sanitary and an administrative director both appointed by the general director, again, with a private contract. Also, personnel policies have changed in the sense that public employees contracts have become more similar to those in the private sector. Similarly, concerning transfer finance, local authorities have become more responsible in the use of the resources allocated to them. Still, the changes are inadequate and the legacy of the past is still alive.
16. For example, in 1992, the government proposed excluding from subsidized pharmaceutical and diagnostic care all citizens with a family taxable income above 40 million lire. The proposal for the balanced budget law of 1996 took into consideration the possibility of introducing a 'ticket' (i.e. a co-payment) on emergency care not followed by admission. Both proposals were soon abandoned. The remainder of financing is made up of the additional revenues of the autonomous regions.
17. However, the days of hospitalization sold amount to only 19 per cent of the total produced in the NHS. Wide inter-regional differences should also be mentioned: private hospitals play a much bigger role in the south, where there is a lack of public hospitals (see France 1994)
18. With respect to individual insurance, the premium cannot be deduced from taxable income, but medical expenses can be subtracted from the tax to be paid. Data on private expenditure come from ISTAT (1995).
19. Obviously, there are many other factors that could explain the unsatisfactory performance of the NHS. Among them is the fact that secretaries of health have often been representatives of the only party, the Liberal Party, that has always been against the NHS! In any case, the ones indicated are the main ones which have spurred growing support for privatization.
20. For good descriptions of this challenge, see Balassone and Franco (1995), France (1994) and Mapelli (1993, 1995).
21. In case of deficits, regions may increase social contributions, within given limits, and resort to local taxation. In the same perspective of increasing regional responsibility, can also be placed the many proposals under discussion according to which the NHS should, at least in part, be financed through local taxation. They are not discussed here, in so far as they represent an example of fiscal federalism rather than privatization. This new system should be fully realized by the beginning of 1998.
22. In Sweden, public competition is based on competition only among public producers. For a detailed discussion of public competition, see Saltman and von Otter (1992).
23. For example, in the mid-1980s, Mr Degan, a former Secretary of Health, proposed that, after paying a solidarity contribution equal to 50 per cent of the charged rate, citizens could opt out in favour of private assistance. The opting out could be selective: for all care or only for some services. Contributions to the NHS would vary accordingly. Even more drastic, was the proposal by the former Secretary of Treasury Goria, according to which only hospital care would remain truly universal, while all

other services would be limited to the poor.

24. I am not aware of any concrete proposals by the left or the trade unions. But positions taken in the public debate can be found in Mossetto (1993) and Ruffolo (1985). Other privatization proposals discussed in Italy advocate giving GPs the option of becoming fund holders, as in the reformed British NHS, and liberalizing the price of drugs.

25. Naturally, also in the contracting out version, there could be some extension of private supply, if private hospitals show a better capacity for charging lower prices, but it is less certain, given the prominent role played by public managers, who may feel pressured to continue to use public hospitals.

26. An exception would occur if tariffs were higher than the prices privately charged to consumers. Such a possibility, however, appears quite remote: private health providers, if unregulated, appear consistently to charge higher prices than public ones. If this were not the case, what would be done, in any case, with the financial surplus that would remain with consumers?

27. A detailed analysis, among other factors, .should consider the complementarity and substitution effects that could take place within the health care sector, including the effects of different remuneration schemes for GPs (see Nolan 1993). Furthermore, one should also distinguish in the analysis of incentives between the effects on administrators and those on doctors (see Frankford 1993). In analysing incentives, it would also be interesting to verify whether the effects vary according to different systems of property rights. It is, indeed, true that the incentives created by the new form of remuneration might mitigate the differences in behaviour between private and public hospitals; still some differences could remain and are worthwhile exploring. At the same time, the objective of equity may have very different meanings and evaluation would differ according to the one selected (see Granaglia 1994).

28. On administrative costs, see Bartlett (1991), Bariletti and France (1994) and France (1993), even though these authors develop their analyses within the specific context of the British version of contracting out. On DRG creep, cream-skimming and the effects on quality, see Propper (1992a, b) and on the effects on equity, see Le Grand (1991).

29. In the UK, in fact, the move towards contracting out has been accompanied by the transformation of public hospitals into trusts.

30. Obviously, this is true if competition is not hampered by either collusion among potential competitors or by predatory pricing by the incumbents.

31. On the general problems linked to the utilization of voucher schemes, see Luft (1984) and Le Grand (1991). On problems linked to non-price competition and administrative costs see Robinson (1988) and Himmelstein and Woolhandlers (1986). Not all forms of competition among private insurances are consumer-based. On the contrary, as exemplified by the use of HMOs (Health Management Organizations) in the United States, there could also be managed competition in the private sector. In this case, the negative effects in terms of increases in prices and in volume would be more under control. Again a detailed analysis here is impossible. The proposal debated in Italy, however, is based on the utilization more of traditional insurances rather than of HMOs.

32. It is interesting to contrast these shortcomings with the awareness of the problems shown by the Dekkar plan in the Netherlands. Although the Netherlands does not have an NHS and the Dekkar plan entails managed competition, this plan shares with this proposal the reliance on a voucher scheme to buy private insurance. In the Dekkar Plan, however, a great deal of attention is given to the differentiation of vouchers and the definition of the maximum amount of cost-sharing allowed.

33. Such a favour is due to centrality attributed to the sovereignty of individual preferences and to the corresponding belief that all interference with them should be seen as paternalistic.

34. More specifically, privatization proposals acknowledge the role of these costs. But, too simplistically, they tend to assume privatization as automatically capable of minimizing them.

35. The belief about the sovereignty of individual preferences could, again, be responsible

for such an underestimate. The underlying assumption, in this case, could be that even the provision of information about the means to reach given goals could be seen as interference. The consequence is that the only legitimate intervention is to alter the individual cost-benefit calculation as the privatization policies discussed here do. For a positive defence of the role of policies influencing preference formation, even in a liberal perspective, see Aaron *et al.* (1994).

REFERENCES

Aaron, J. *et al.* (1994): *Values and Public Policy*, Washington: Brookings Institution.

Balassone, F. and D. Franco (1995): 'La difficile riforma del welfare: il settore della sanità', *Stato e Mercato* 43 (April) pp.95–126.

Bariletti, A. (1993): 'Indirizzi di riforma economico-finanziaria dei sistemi sanitari: concorrenza amministrata e concorrenza pubblica', in G. France and E. Attanasio (eds.), *Economia sanitaria. Linee e tendenze di ricerca in Italia*, Milano: Giuffré, pp.1–18.

Bariletti, A. and G. France (1994): *Dispositivi pro-concorrenziali per il settore sanitario: un'analisi di economia dell'organizzazione*, Roma: Istituto di Studi sulle Regioni.

Bartlett, W. (1991): *Privatization and Quasi-Markets*, Bristol: Saus Publication.

Birch, S. (1986): 'Increasing Patient Charges in the National Health Service: a Method of Privatizing Primary Care', *Journal of Social Policy* 15/2, pp.163–83.

Bovbjerg, R. *et al.* (1987): 'Privatization and Bidding in the Health-Care Sector', *Journal of Policy Analysis and Management* 6/4, pp.648–66.

Cavazzuti, F. and S. Giannini (1982): *La riforma malata*, Bologna: Il Mulino.

Clerico, G. (1994): 'Istituzioni, Fallimento e Riforma del Ssn', *Economia, Società, Istituzioni* 3, pp.497–521.

Costa, G. *et al.* (1994): 'Introduzione. Equità nella salute: lo scenario italiano', in G. Costa and F. Faggiano (eds), *L'equità nella salute in Italia*, Milano: Angeli, pp.20–3.

De Alessi, L. (1989): 'The Effect of Institutions on the Choices of Consumers and Providers of Health Care', *Journal of Theoretical Politics* 1/4, pp.427–58.

Dirindin, N. (1993): 'Armonizzazione delle aliquote, regressività e fiscal drag nel sistema di finanziamento del Ssn', in G. France and E. Attanasio (eds), *Economia sanitaria. Linee e tendenze di ricerca in Italia*, Milano: Giuffré, pp.433–44.

Dirindin, N. (1995): 'La riforma del finanziamento del sistema sanitario', mimeo, Pavia, VII Riunione della Siep, 6–7 Oct.

Dranove, D. *et al.* (1993): 'Price and Concentration in Hospital Markets: The Switch From Patient-Driven to Payer Driven Competition', *Journal of Law and Economics* 36/1, pp.179–204.

Estrin, S. and V. Perotin (1988): 'Privatization by Default? Old Age Homes in Britain and in France', Research Note 11, London, The Welfare State Programme, Suntory-Toyota International Centre for Economics and Related Disciplines.

France, G. (1993): 'Mercati interni nel settore ospedaliero', in E. Granaglia (ed.) *Privatizzazioni e SSN. Alcune riflessioni sui mercati interni, Contributi per la discussione*, no.56, Milano: Bibliotechne, pp.35–80.

France, G. (1994): 'Modelli relazionali fra i servizi sanitari nazionali e i fornitori di prestazioni', in G. France (ed.), *Concorrenza e servizi sanitari*, Roma: Istituto di Studi sulle Regioni, pp.15–43.

Frankford, D. (1993): 'The Medicare DRGs: Efficiency and Organizational Rationality', *Yale Journal of Regulation* 10/2, pp.273–346.

Granaglia, E. (1990): 'La politica sanitaria', in B. Dente (ed.), *Le politiche pubbliche in Italia*, Bologna: Il Mulino, pp.367–82.

Granaglia, E. (1994): 'Concorrenza ed equità nella sanità', in G. France (ed.), *Concorrenza e servizi sanitari*, Roma: Istituto di Studi sulle Regioni, pp.133–51.

Himmelstein, D. and S. Woolhandler (1986): 'Cost Without Benefit: Administrative Waste in US Health Care', *New England Journal of Medicine* 314, pp.441–5.

ISTAT (1995): *Dati di contabilità nazionale*, Roma.

Istituto di Economia Sanitaria (1993): *La variabilità dei costi di erogazione dei servizi ospedalieri tra le regioni*, Milano, ricerca effettuata per la Commissione Tecnica per la Spesa Pubblica del Ministero del Tesoro.

Kamerman, S. and A. Kahn (eds) (1989): *Privatization and the Welfare State*, Princeton: PUP.

Le Grand, J. (1991): 'Quasi-markets and Social Policy', *Economic Journal* 101/408, pp.1256–68.

Le Grand, J. and R. Robinson (1984): *Privatization and the Welfare State*, London: Routledge.

Light, D. (1991): 'Effectiveness and Efficiency under Competition: the Cochrane Test', *British Medical Journal* 303/16 (Nov.) pp.1253–4.

Luft, H. (1984): 'On the Use of Vouchers for Medicare', *Milbank Quarterly* 62/2, pp.237–50.

Mapelli, V. (1993): 'La spesa sanitaria', in L.Bernardi (ed.), *La Finanza Pubblica Italiana. Rapporto 1993*, Milano: Angeli, pp.141–73.

Mapelli, V. (1994): 'Libertà di scelta ed equità nel sistema sanitario italiano: un'indagine campionaria', in G. Costa and F. Faggiano (eds), *L'equità nella salute in Italia*, Milano: Angeli, pp.253–72.

Mapelli, V. (1995): 'La sanità pubblica: la svolta delle tariffe prospettiche', in L. Bernardi (ed.), *La Finanza Pubblica Italiana. Rapporto 1995*, Bologna: Il Mulino, pp.307–36.

Marmot, M. *et al.* (1994): 'Spiegazioni per le diseguaglianze sociali nella salute', in G. Costa and F. Faggiano (eds), *L'equità nella salute in Italia*, Milano: Angeli, pp.273–328.

Milgrom, P. (1992): *Economics, Organization and Management*, Englewood Cliffs: Prentice Hall.

Mossetto, G. (1993): *Italiani senza rendite*, Bari: Laterza.

Nolan, B. (1993): 'Economic Incentives, Health Status and Health Services Utilization', *Journal of Health Economics* 12/2, pp.151–70.

Phelps, C. (1992): 'Diffusion of Information in Medical Care', *Journal of Economic Perspectives* 6/3, pp.23–42.

Propper, C. (1992a): *Quasi-Markets, Contracts and Quality*, Bristol: Saus Publication.

Propper, C. (1992b): *Is Further Regulation of Quasi-markets in Welfare Necessary?*, Bristol: Saus Publication.

Relazione Generale sulla Situazione Economica del Paese (1995): Roma: Poligrafico dello Stato.

Robinson, J. (1988): 'Hospital Quality Competition and the Economics of Imperfect Information', *Milbank Quarterly* 66/3, pp.465–81.

Ruffolo, G. (1985): *La qualità sociale*, Bari: Laterza.

Saltman, R. and C. von Otter (1992): *Planned Markets and Public Competition*, Buckingham: Open University Press.

Sappington, D. and J. Stiglitz (1987): 'Privatization, Information and Incentives', *Journal of Policy Analysis and Management* 6/4, pp.567–82.

Sterpi, S. (1993): '"Exit" e "Voice" nel Servizio Sanitario Nazionale italiano', in G. France and E. Attanasio (eds), *Economia sanitaria. Linee e tendenze di ricerca in Italia*, Milano: Giuffré, pp.327–44.

Policies for the Unemployed and Social Shock Absorbers: The Italian Experience

CARLO DELL'ARINGA and MANUELA SAMEK LODOVICI

This article analyses Italian policies for the unemployed, paying special attention to income support measures. After presenting the range of policies in this area, the analysis focuses on the effects of such policies on the labour market and presents the reform proposals currently under debate in Italy in the context of international experience and discussion.

Social shock absorbers are all those measures that reduce the negative social effects of unemployment. They include unemployment benefits, other social benefits (such as invalidity benefits, sickness benefits), early retirement schemes, training for the unemployed, temporary public work, etc. All these measures have positive and negative effects that should be attentively monitored, in order to design the mix which will have the least negative impact on the labour market. Traditionally, emphasis has been put on unemployment benefits, which represent the highest share in terms of expenditures and people involved. In recent years, unemployment benefits and other income support measures have been increasingly under debate. The economic literature has stressed the possible link between the benefit system, search activity of the unemployed and the duration of unemployment and this has shifted the attention of policy makers and analysts to the need to accompany unemployment benefits with 'active' policies that should increase the probability that unemployed workers will find a job. Increasing budget constraints have also underlined the need to look at the financing mechanisms of such benefits, to control public expenses on assistance measures and to monitor fraud. On the other hand, evaluations of active policies have shown the possible drawbacks of some of these measures (OECD 1993; Calmfors 1994).

The Italian experience in this field is interesting because Italy shows a peculiar mix of policies, with little weight given to general unemployment benefits and a tradition of employment protection policies. In addition, Italy is the only European country without assistance benefits for those who exhaust unemployment benefits, a lack that has led to the improper use of other welfare measures, such as disability pensions. In this article we analyse Italian policies for the unemployed, giving special attention to income support measures. Our purpose is to focus on the effects of such policies on the labour market and to present reform proposals currently under debate in Italy in the framework of international experience and discussion.

SOCIAL SHOCK ABSORBERS IN INTERNATIONAL CONTEXT

Unemployment Benefits

Unemployment benefits have two main roles: an insurance role, against the risk of income loss due to the loss of one's job; and an assistance role to protect the individual worker from poverty (and, hence, the collectivity from social conflict). In the 1970s, with the diffusion of welfare systems, the prevalent approach was to guarantee an income to the unemployed as a right against unfavourable circumstances. The state had an insurance role for such a risk because of equity reasons.[1] Besides this equity argument, public intervention in income support during unemployment was supported on efficiency grounds: while relieving the unemployed from immediate financial concerns, benefits also allow more efficient job search by the unemployed worker and more efficient job matching that may reduce the probability of people becoming unemployed in the future.

During the 1980s, a different approach prevailed: to the right to an income during unemployment was opposed the right to a job and to help in the search for a new job (that is, a shift to active from passive labour market policies). This new approach was stimulated by the increasing emphasis in the economic literature on the negative effects associated with high and long-term benefits and on the voluntary nature of unemployment in certain situations:

• unemployment benefits tend to increase the reservation wage and, in the absence of certain job search requirements, may reduce the incentive for effective job search and the willingness to accept existing job offers, at least as long as the benefit is available;

• in reducing the cost of unemployment to the single individual worker, unemployment benefits tend to increase the bargaining power of unions over wages and reduce incentives for firms to build a reputation as providers of secure employment;

- unemployment benefits also subsidize employers' seasonal demand for workers: in their absence such employers would have to offer higher wages in order to attract workers; and, finally,

- unemployment benefits may affect labour force participation, inducing the participation of those at higher risk of unemployment.

Some links have been established by the empirical literature between the level and duration of benefits and the level, duration and composition of unemployment. The effect estimated is, however, rather small. Only very large changes in benefit entitlements could achieve a significant reduction of unemployment in high-benefit countries. The effect on unemployment also differs according to labour force segment. The growth in unemployment benefits/entitlements has been shown to explain part of the rise in long-term unemployment and the disincentive effect on job search appears to be stronger for secondary workers (especially women with small children and older workers).

The difficulties in estimating the relationship between unemployment benefits and unemployment levels are related to the difficulties in measuring benefit entitlements and in taking into account all the institutional factors that influence such a relationship. The relation between the benefit replacement rate and unemployment may be of inverse causality: high unemployment countries may have introduced more generous income support measures. On the other hand, the relation may be indirect, with greater income support inducing higher wages and thus higher unemployment. Finally, it is extremely difficult to disentangle the effects of different elements in the functioning of the labour market and industrial relations on unemployment. Recent estimations based on aggregate pooled time series/cross country data that model unemployment rates as a lagged function of benefit entitlements show larger benefit-unemployment elasticities than single country estimates based on panel micro data (OECD 1994). This is probably due to the fact that cross-country data and long term relations incorporate the indirect effects of benefits on unemployment, that is, changes in wage bargaining and in employment patterns and the effectiveness of benefit administration.

The negative effects of unemployment benefits do not come from the existence of unemployment benefits *per se*, but to a large extent from their design: negative effects may arise if benefits are too high in comparison with current wage rates, if they last for too long and if they are not accompanied by job search requirements and measures to help the unemployed to find jobs. Any analysis of unemployment compensation effects on the labour market must consider all of their institutional features and their effects, not only on unemployment, but also on labour market participation. Analysis of the incentive/ disincentive effects of the benefit system should also consider the taxation of benefits and earnings, the means-tested nature of unemployment assistance benefits, child-care allowances, benefits for one parent families and benefits paid to those with low earnings (Atkinson and Micklewright 1991). The work-incentive/disincentive effects of benefits are very much linked to the taxation system: for if benefits are not taxable and income from work is, it is possible (as in the British example) that net income from unemployment benefits will be higher than income from low-wage, part-time jobs. In addition, other forms of income support to people that could work should be considered such as: sickness, disability and early retirement benefits. International institutions, such as the OECD and the EU, have recently been gathering information on all these forms of income support, in order to provide comparable data across different countries and better results on the relationship between benefits and unemployment (Eurostat 1994; OECD 1994; Centraal Planbureau 1995).

Early Retirement Pensions and other Social Benefits

In many countries unemployment benefits are only a small portion of total cash benefits paid to people of working age; often more relevant, both in terms of expenditure levels and number of beneficiaries, are non-employment benefits paid to provide people with a living income without working (invalidity benefits, sickness benefits, early retirement pensions, etc.). These benefits should insure people against other risks than unemployment and compensate for different needs; in practice, however, this distinction is rarely clear cut. Usually, such benefits have higher replacement rates than unemployment benefits and induce people to move out of the labour force. In the case of early retirement schemes this is an explicit objective. The possible effects of such benefits on the labour market have been studied only recently, together with links between these benefits and unemployment benefits.

Temporary Jobs in the Public Sector and Training Placements

These measures can help job search and skill acquisition by the unemployed, but they may also be used to detect abuse in the use of unemployment benefits and to operate a self selection mechanism so that only the really needy will take up such opportunities (Jackman 1995). For this reason, unemployment benefits are often made conditional on participation in such schemes after a certain period of unemployment. However, increasing public budget constraints and the risk of displacing regular workers in both private and public sectors are leading to a reduction in their use (Forslund and Krueger 1994). In addition, recent evaluation results show that workers involved in such schemes often develop a dependency pattern, with participation in temporary schemes followed by spells of unemployment.

In many OECD countries, new policy initiatives have been adopted to try to limit the negative and disincentive effects of social shock absorbers. The OECD Jobs Study (OECD 1994) summarizes the most important ones:

- reinforcing the insurance principle by reducing excessively easy entitlements to unemployment and related benefits;

- promoting job search by tightening control over search requirements and creating greater links between the administration of unemployment benefits and active policies. For example, limits on the duration of passive benefits have been matched by alternative income support provided through entitlement to places on active labour market schemes that require full-time attendance;

- cutting out-of-work benefits by reducing replacement rates and reducing benefit entitlements in line with the length of benefit duration;

- increasing the returns to being in work by avoiding poverty traps[2] (by increasing the value of child-care benefits for those in work, providing tax-cuts for low wage earners, extending payments of in-work benefits, using part of the benefit as a re-employment bonus);

- broadening the contribution base in order to reduce the burden on labour costs and thus reducing the adverse effects of the financing system on the employment rate of low wage earners. Systems to increase the financial contribution of the social partners are being discussed, with special attention to experience rating mechanisms.

International experience shows that various administrative provisions may contribute to these policy changes. For example, the decentralization of benefits and the administration of active policies to local governments should create incentives for implementing eligibility restrictions and for the introduction of job creation measures to reduce local unemployment rates. Also, the implementation of adequate information systems should allow a better matching of workers to job vacancies and facilitate the monitoring and evaluation of labour policies at the local level.

THE PECULIARITY OF ITALIAN POLICIES FOR THE UNEMPLOYED

In the area of policies for the unemployed, Italy may in many ways be considered a paradigm of the southern European model of welfare as depicted by Ferrera (1996). The fragmentation and disparities in the income support system for the unemployed, with extreme differences and gaps in the level of social protection given to core and marginal workers, are the result of a complex system guaranteeing full-time, stable jobs for core workers (traditionally males in middle age groups) through employment protection measures, income support to laid-off workers and a public monopoly in job placement. This system did not encourage the development of an efficient administration aimed at removing the causes of labour market exclusion.

In Italy, there is no comprehensive strategy of labour market intervention. Labour policies are fragmented into numerous legislative acts adopted *ad hoc* in response to particular problems. The main approach followed in labour market policies, at least up until the late 1980s, has been to avoid redundancies and layoffs – even in crisis and restructuring situations – through the use of collective action and public resources. This has favoured a large degree of discretionary power on the part of the Ministry of Labour and a lack of co-ordination with other areas of the welfare system: an example is the wide use of early retirement schemes to solve industrial crises during the 1980s, when the financial burden of the pension system was already becoming onerous and there was growing pressure to increase the retirement age.

The low level of expenditure on income support, its fragmentation into many different instruments and the improper use of some measures are other characteristics of the Italian labour market. This has created large disparities among workers in terms of employment protection, income support during unemployment spells and active policies to favour re-employment. Active policies are insufficient and ineffective, due also to the absence of a clear definition of roles for the different institutions involved in labour market policies.

Table 1 presents the structure of labour market expenditures in Italy compared to other OECD countries, according to OECD data. The OECD data set contains comparable statistics on the level of public expenditures in labour market programmes since 1985. Labour market expenditures are measured as a percentage of GDP in each country and are divided into seven areas of intervention. These data must be considered with caution, since they are based on information provided by national ministries of labour, which, at least in the Italian case, are not very accurate.[3] However the international comparison allows a first

TABLE 1
PUBLIC EXPENDITURE IN LABOUR MARKET PROGRAMMES IN SOME OECD COUNTRIES

	FRANCE 1993	GERMANY 1994	ITALY 1992	SPAIN 1994	UNITED KINGDOM 1993–94	UNITED STATES 1993–94	SWEDEN 1994–95
1. **Public employment services and administration**	**0.15**	**0.24**	**0.08**	**0.11**	**0.24**	**0.08**	**0.27**
2. **Labour Market Training**	**0.44**	**0.42**	**0.02**	**0.15**	**0.16**	**0.07**	**0.80**
Training for unemployed adults and those at risk	0.39	0.40	0.02	0.09	0.15	0.07	0.73
Training for employed adults	0.05	0.02	—	0.06	0.01	—	0.06
3. **Youth Measures**	**0.28**	**0.07**	**0.80**	**0.09**	**0.14**	**0.04**	**0.26**
Measures for unemployed and disadvantaged youth	0.10	0.06	0.27	0.09	—	0.04	0.26
Support for apprenticeship and related forms	0.18	0.01	0.53	—	0.14	—	—
4. **Subsidized employment**	**0.26**	**0.34**	—	**0.18**	**0.02**	**0.01**	**0.81**
Subsidies to regular employment in the private sector	0.10	0.06	—	0.09	—	—	0.19
Support to unemployed persons starting enterprises	0.02	0.01	—	0.04	0.02	—	0.08
Direct job creation (public or non-profit)	0.14	0.27	—	0.05	—	0.01	0.54
5. **Measures for the disabled**	**0.08**	**0.26**	—	**0.01**	**0.03**	**0.05**	**0.82**
Vocational rehabilitation	0.02	0.14	—	—	—	0.05	0.09
Work for the disabled	0.06	0.12	—	0.01	0.03	—	0.73
6. **Unemployment compensation**	**1.72**	**2.03**	**0.62**	**3.11**	**1.59**	**0.45**	**2.46**
7. **Early retirement for labour market reasons**	**0.38**	**0.49**	**0.26**	—	—	—	**0.02**
TOTAL	3.31	3.84	1.77	3.64	2.18	0.69	5.44
Total per 1% unemployment	0.28	0.56	0.17	0.15	0.22	0.11	0.68
ACTIVE MEASURES (1–5)	1.21	1.32	0.90	0.53	0.59	0.24	2.95
PASSIVE MEASURES (6–7)	2.1	2.52	0.87	3.11	1.59	0.45	2.48

Source: OECD 1995: 222–9, Table T

examination of the Italian situation: among European countries, Italy has the lowest level of expenditure for labour market programs (1.8 per cent of GDP, compared to a European average of 2.9 per cent in 1992).

Active measures have a weight only a little lower than that of other European countries (0.90 per cent of GDP, compared with an EU average of 1.08 per cent), but have a different composition, since they concentrate on the promotion of fixed-term training contracts and employment subsidies (through a reduction of social security contributions) for the young and those at risk of losing their jobs. Income support measures represent only 0.87 per cent of GDP, compared to an EU average of 1.85 per cent. This is due mainly to the fact that the level of ordinary unemployment benefit is very low and a relatively low percentage of the working population has the right to income support during unemployment (only 20 per cent of the unemployed, compared to an average of 40 per cent in the EU, according to Eurostat Labour Force data (Eurostat 1993).

Table 2 presents the main characteristics of the instruments available in Italy for income support in case of unemployment.

Some general observations may be derived from an analysis of the Italian system:

A Large Number of Benefits and a Differential Treatment of Workers[4]

Income support does not depend on the labour market position of unemployed workers, but on the characteristics of the job he or she has lost (sector, size of firm, type of employment relation) and on the modality of job loss (either collective or individual dismissal). Workers coming from medium or large-sized industrial and commercial firms,[5] dismissed temporarily or definitively due to restructuring or crisis, and building sector workers are the most favoured by the Italian system, while workers in small firms and in most service firms are eligible only for the much less generous ordinary unemployment benefits. Those with no employment experience and the self-employed are not eligible for any benefit at all. Moreover, Italian measures favour workers at risk of losing their jobs under different generous measures – *Cassa Integrazione Guadagni* (the Wage Supplementation Scheme), early retirement schemes, solidarity contracts – rather than all those who have lost their job.

There are no assistance measures for the long-term unemployed, once they have exhausted their unemployment insurance entitlements, and there are no special arrangements in terms of family benefits or housing benefits for the unemployed. Disability pensions have been used as

TABLE 2

INCOME SUPPORT MEASURES FOR THE UNEMPLOYED IN ITALY: NON AGRICULTURAL SECTOR

	Eligibility	Benefits	Max Duration	Contribution from firms and workers (in percentage of gross earnings)	No. workers in 1994	Expenses in 1994 (billions of lire)	Contribution /expenses (percentages)
TEMPORARY LAY OFFS							
Wage Supplementation Fund Ordinary (CIGO)	Workers temporarily laid off by industrial and construction firms	80% of last wage for first 6 months	12 months; 24 months in EU obj. 1 and obj. 2 areas	ordinary contribution: 2.20% for firms with more than 50 employees, 1.90% for smaller firms; additional contribution of 8% and 4% respectively in case of use. Construction firms: ordinary contribution 5.2%, additional 5%	69,267*	1,717	197
Special (CIGS)	Workers laid off by industrial firms with more than 15 workers and by commercial firms with more than 200 workers, due to restructuring, reorganization or crisis	80% of last wage; up to a maximum of Lit.1.5 million/mo. in 1995	24 months; renewable twice for 12 mo. in cases of restructuring or reorganization; once in cases of crisis	ordinary contribution: 0.6% from the firm, 0.3% from the worker. Additional contribution: 4.5% for firms with more than 50 employees and 3% for smaller firms. This contribution doubles after 24 mo. of CIGS	175,215*	2,332	50
Contratti solidarietà (Solidarity Contracts)	Workers in industrial firms and in some service firms with at least 50 employees till Dec. 1995. It must be used to prevent lay offs	75% of wage loss due to reduction of working time up to 1995. Then 50% in Northern Italy, 60% in the South	24 months, renewable for other 24 in the North and 36 in the South	none	50,220	323	0
Part-time and early retirement	older workers in firms that are eligible for CIGS	transformation of full time in part-time and retirement benefits to compensate	No time limits. Benefits end when worker goes back to full time or is dismissed	none	n.a.	n.a.	0
COLLECTIVE DISMISSALS							
Mobilità (Mobility benefits)	redundant workers either dismissed from industrial firms with more than 15 employees, or from commercial firms with more than 200 employees, or coming from CIGS. In 1993-95 mobility benefits were temporarily extended to other service sectors	80% of last wage up to a max. of lit.1.5 millions in the first 12 months. 80% of CIGS benefits from 13th month	12 mo. renewable once for workers over 40 years old twice for workers over 50 years old at a level 20% lower	Ordinary contribution: 0.3% of total wages. Additional contribution: 6 times the monthly benefit paid to each worker. In case of collective agreements this sum is halved. If no use of CIGS, it goes up to 9 monthly installments	260,469	3,278	37
Special benefits	workers dismissed by construction firms	80% of last wage max: 1.122,000 Lit.	from 3 to 18 months. Up to 27 months in the South	Ordinary contribution from firm: 0.8% of wages corresponding to insured workers	n.a.	included in the ordinary benefit figure	included in the ordinary benefit figure

TABLE 2 continued

	Eligibility	Benefits	Max Duration	Contribution from firms and workers (in percentage of gross earnings)	No. workers in 1994	Expenses° in 1994 (billions of lire)	Contribution /expenses (percentages)
Lavori socialmente utili (temporary jobs)	workers exhausting their CIG or mobility benefits, long-term unemployed	mobility or CIGS benefit + premium of at least 10% of benefit; if not eligible for CIGS or mobility benefit hourly wage of 7.500lit max 800.000 lit per mo.	12 months		75,221*	n.a.	0
INDIVIDUAL DISMISSALS Ordinary benefits	workers dismissed individually or collectively, but not eligible for mobility benefits. At least 2 years of contribution or 78 days for seasonal workers	30% of last wage; will go to 40% in 1996. Max amount: 1500000 liras in 1995	6 months. May be extended to12 months in the construction sector	Ordinary contribution from firms: non agricultural sectors: 1.61%, agricultural sector: 2.75%	408,00**	7,297	51
NON-EMPLOYMENT BENEFITS Early Retirement Schemes	workers at least 55 years old (men) and 50 years old (women) (50 and 47 respectively in steel work), employed in industrial enterprises receiving CIGS, with at least 15 years of social security contributions	5 to 10 years of contributions paid by the state			103,217	3,682	10

° 1994 estimates.
a. Expenses refer to direct erogations and indirect elements.
* Estimates of equivalent workers at zero hours.
^ projects approved by October 1995 with planned workers
** 1994 estimates based on equivalent full year people.

Sources: Demekas 1995; INPS 1995; Del Boca 1995; Confindustria 1995; Guerra 1994

assistance benefits in a biased way, thanks to their relatively lax eligibility requirements. Social benefits for the needy – usually the elderly – are provided by local authorities, with the benefit levels and duration varying widely across regions.

Given the low capacity of the Italian administration to monitor the use of income support measures, the possibility of moral hazard has been reduced by limiting the number of workers who have access to benefits to two groups: those employed in industrial firms and people over a certain age with poor employment opportunities in the agricultural sector and in the less developed areas of the country. This has helped limit expenditure on income support (Franco 1994). There are eight major types of income support for unemployment:

- The *Cassa Integrazione Guadagni* (CIG) (Wage Supplementation Fund) provides compensation for wage loss due to reductions in working hours. The 'ordinary fund' (CIGO) applies to temporary reductions in working time due to accidental or cyclical causes. The 'special fund' (CIGS), introduced in 1968, deals with industrial crisis or industrial restructuring and usually compensates for total working time lost for a period that can be very long (even years). The CIG, in fact, provides financial support for labour hoarding: workers are not laid off, but maintain their employment contract with the firm, even if they are out of work for many years. Until 1988, the CIGS was entirely financed by the state. During the 1980s, the CIGS became a *de facto* unemployment benefit for workers laid off permanently, even if they were formally still employed. In 1991 the CIG was reformed by L.233/1991, which reduced the benefit period and introduced a contribution from the firms and workers.

- *Early retirement measures* were introduced in the late 1960s to ease industrial restructuring problems by providing generous early retirement schemes to industrial workers employed in firms receiving CIGS benefits and having at least 15 years of social security contributions.

- *Solidarity contracts* were introduced in 1984 and were generously funded in 1993 and 1994. These schemes promote work sharing initiatives based on collective agreements in industrial and large-scale commercial firms. Solidarity contracts have been used mainly in order to prevent employment reductions in industrial firms.

- In Italy there are two main *insurance unemployment benefits*: the *'Trattamento ordinario di disoccupazione'* and the *'Indennità di mobilità'*. Both are granted to workers who have been dismissed or have resigned from their job.

- Since 1994, the *Trattamento ordinario* has been equal to 30 per cent of the worker's remuneration during the three months preceding unemployment[6] and can be obtained for a maximum of 180 days, including Sundays and holidays. To qualify for this benefit, a laid off worker must have been employed and have paid contributions for at least two years and must register with the state employment service.

- *Ordinary unemployment benefits* are also used to compensate seasonal workers who do not have a full year of employment. To qualify for the benefit, seasonal workers must have been working for at least 78 work days in the year preceding unemployment and the benefit is paid in proportion to the number of days worked, up to a ceiling of 151 days. This mechanism is in fact a means of subsidizing seasonal work and, in the absence of effective controls, encourages misuse (CNEL 1995).

- The *mobility benefit* is 80 per cent of gross remuneration during the first year of unemployment, but there is a maximum amount payable that makes it equivalent to about 65 per cent of the remuneration of the average worker. It lasts at least one year, up to a maximum of three years for older workers in southern regions. To qualify for the more generous mobility benefit, a worker must have an employment record of 12 months and be laid off within collective dismissals due to restructuring, re-organizing, the conversion of a company, a crisis situation in a region/sector/company, or to the bankruptcy of a company. In addition workers have to have been employed in industrial companies with more than 15 employees, or in commercial companies with more than 200 employees. During the 1993–94 recession, the possibility of access to the CIGS and the mobility benefit was extended to some other service sectors.

- *Disability pensions* have been frequently used as assistance benefits for workers with difficulties in finding a job. In fact, in the 1970s it was established that the degree of disability (and hence of the pension amount) should be determined in part on the basis of the person's socio-economic environment, and in particular on his/her employment potential.

Long Duration and High Replacement Rates for Some Benefits

In the case of the CIGS, mobility and early retirement, the length of the benefit period is increased by the possibility of using different benefits in sequence (CIGS, mobility, temporary jobs in the public sector, and/or early retirement). For example, older workers on mobility lists before

1993, who are five years short of early retirement age (55 years) and
have at least 15 years of contributions, may receive benefits until early
retirement; prime-age workers may combine the CIGS and mobility
benefits for a maximum of five to six years in southern Italy.

Few Retraining or Job Search Requirements

It is only since 1993 that the government has considered the use of
temporary job schemes (*Lavori socialmente utili*) as a screening device to
prevent moral hazard. According to these schemes, workers on the
CIGS, those on mobility lists and the long-term unemployed may be
employed for at most two years in social works by public
administrations, public enterprises or other institutions authorized by
the Ministry of Labour. Workers who refuse to participate without
justification should lose their benefits for the duration of the project. In
fact, up to now, these measures have been organized on a voluntary basis
and are not used to screen effective unemployment. It is not by chance
that these measures are a failure in northern Italy, where many workers
usually find an occupation in the black economy and wait for the end of
the subsidy before regularizing their position. On the other hand, in
southern Italy they are used as a way to extend income support for the
long-term unemployed and risk creating a pressure for permanent jobs in
the public sector.

The Predominant Role of State Transfers

It is only since 1988 that employers have been obliged to contribute to
these schemes.In 1991 contributions were increased and now almost
entirely cover CIG expenses. No contribution comes directly from
workers, except a small contribution (0.30 per cent of gross earnings) for
the CIGS, introduced in 1991.

Little Use of Active Policies

Job creation measures and employment services are particularly lacking
due to the ineffectiveness of public employment services and the legal
prohibition of private employment agencies. With the reform of the CIG
in 1991, some measures to help those on the CIGS and mobility lists
have been introduced, but are little used.[7]

   Table 3 presents estimates of the use of social shock absorbers in Italy
since the first oil shock. The lack of precise data on the use of the
different instruments (in terms of people involved) and their costs
requires the use of rather imprecise estimates, but they do give an idea
of the relative weight of each measure and of the main changes over
time.

TABLE 3
EVOLUTION IN THE USE OF SOCIAL SHOCK ABSORBERS SINCE FIRST OIL SHOCK IN ITALY

	1 oil shock (1974–76)	2 oil shock (1981–85)	Growth period (1986–90)	Recession period (1991–94)
SOCIAL MEASURES	CIG UB	CIG UB early retirement	CIG UB early retirements solidarity contracts	CIG mobility benefit UB early retirement solidarity contracts temporary jobs
BENEFICIARIES* (yearly average)	450,000	580,000	460,000	580,000
of which CIGS and early retirements	—	284,000	225,000	153,000
UNEMPLOYED WITH PREVIOUS JOB				
average stock per year in the period	231,000	356,400	512,000	911,000 (Jan. 95–Oct. 92)
absolute variation in the period	60,000	253,000	−33,000	325,000 (Jan. 95–Oct. 92)
WAGE AND SALARY EARNERS				
absolute variation in the period	331,000	−26,000	570,000	−715,000**
of which in the industrial sector	−97,000	−531,000	−1,000	−432,000**
TOTAL EXPENDITURES (BILLIONS LIT.)				
yearly average	2,070	7,800	10,904	16,262
in % of GDP	1.5	1.3	1	1.06

* CIG workers are estimates as equivalent at 0 hours, workers on unemployment benefits are estimated on the basis of the days of benefit entitlements.

** Due to changes in the labour force data series from Oct. 1992, absolute variations are estimated applying to dependent workers in 1990 the variations shown by labour units in National Accounts data.

Sources: INPS; ISTAT; Barbarulo and Guarna 1993; Guarna 1995; Del Boca 1995

Total public expenditures for income support as a percentage of GDP declined in the last recession relative to the previous one. This is due to an increase in contributions from the private sector (for CIGO and ordinary unemployment benefits) and a lower use of the most generous assistance measures. While in the 1980s CIG and early retirement schemes accounted for up to 70 per cent of total income support expenditure, since 1991 the incidence of insurance benefits has increased to 50 per cent and the differences in the level of income support guaranteed by different measures have been decreasing.

During the 1980s, CIGS and early retirement measures contributed to limiting the increase of explicit unemployment: a reduction of 532,000 units in industrial employment was translated into an increase of 'only' 253,000 unemployed with previous employment experience. On the other hand, the use of CIGS in that period was equivalent to about 220,000 workers at zero hours on average per year. Another 32,000 workers on average each year have been involved in early retirement schemes. With France, Italy is the country that has used this measure most. In contrast to other countries, in Italy early retirement schemes have been used to ease the social consequences of employment reduction in the industrial sector without increasing the number of unemployed. According to the State's General Accounting Office, in 1980–89 the number of persons officially recognized as disabled rose from 400,000 to 1 million. Recent surveys by the Ministry of Budget show that about one third of disability pensions go to non-eligible persons.

In the 1990s, the measures used to sustain income in the case of job loss have changed: there has been a reduction in the use of the CIGS and early retirement schemes, and an increase in the use of the CIGO (which is extended to white collars), mobility benefits, solidarity contracts (which were widely funded in 1993–94) and temporary work initiatives. In the 1991–94 period a yearly average of 'only' a little more than 150,000 full-time equivalent workers were involved in the CIGS or in early retirement schemes. On the other hand, the number of workers laid off with mobility procedures rose rapidly, reaching 294,000 workers by the end of 1994. Accordingly, the number of unemployed with previous employment increased dramatically (Figure 1).[8] At the same time, the attention given to active policies toward the unemployed has increased, especially at the local level. Regional employment agencies and local institutions have developed employment services for those on the CIG or on the mobility list and governments have promoted this trend with legislation that favours the creation of temporary jobs to provide a temporary placement to those whose benefit is expiring.

FIGURE 1
UNEMPLOYED WITH PREVIOUW JOB (DSS) AND EQUIVALENT WORKERS IN CIG
(CIGDISS) IN INDUSTRIAL FIRMS – 1970–1994
QUARTERLY MOVING AVERAGES

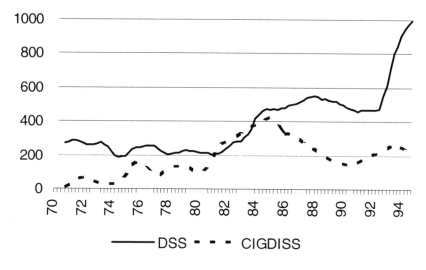

Source: Banca d'Italia

EFFECTS OF POLICIES ON LABOUR MARKET PERFORMANCE

The characteristics of social shock absorbers in Italy, together with the rigidity of hiring and firing regulations and constraints on employment contracts, have led to large distortions in the Italian labour market. The Italian literature (Neri 1990; Tronti 1991; Bertola 1993; Del Boca and Rota 1993; Boeri 1994; Liso 1994; Negri and Saraceno 1996) has largely discussed the effects of the unemployment compensation system on the Italian labour market.

On the *positive side* income support measures during unemployment have:

• reduced adjustment costs during recessions and the costs of industrial restructuring both for workers and firms. Firms are able to keep their labour force during downturns (labour hoarding) and have access to a high degree of working time flexibility, without bearing the full costs (either financial and/or social) associated with it. Until the mid-1980s, such costs were largely externalized by firms;

- greatly helped reduce industrial and social conflict, especially in southern Italy,[9] where income support may last for many years (sometimes more than ten), and during extensive industrial restructuring phases;

- encouraged the decentralization of collective bargaining to the firm level on more flexible working time and working conditions;

- reduced the costs for public finances (which have been lower than in other countries), due to the low extension of unemployment benefits coverage (it must be noted, however, that there is no clear measure of the total costs of this system); and

- transferred resources to profits. In this way the CIG and other income support schemes have financed industrial re-organization and helped to improve the long-term performance of the Italian industrial sector (Giavazzi and Spaventa 1989).

On the *negative side*, the main costs connected with the use of CIGS, mobility benefits and early retirement schemes have been:

- a 'freezing' of employment: 'Hirings as well as firings (...) have been frozen, so that turnover was drastically slowed down, and those employed could preserve their job' (Tronti 1991: 139). According to Tronti's estimates, a one percentage point increase in the number of hours covered by the CIG resulted, in 1972–88, in a 0.75 per cent slowdown in industrial hirings. This worsened the segmentation of the Italian labour market, discouraging labour mobility for protected workers and increasing the difficulties in finding 'secure jobs' for workers with little or no labour experience (those looking for their first job in particular). In addition, the lower risk of income loss has increased the power of insider workers in the unionized sectors by reducing competition from unemployed outsiders. In this way real wage rigidity has increased;

- an expansion of the black economy: workers on CIG or on mobility and early retirement schemes have no interest in giving up their generous benefits by finding a regular job: it is more convenient and rational both for the firm and the worker to work irregularly at least for the period during which there is a right to a benefit. This is also due to the inefficient system of control;

- an increase in workers' dependence on subsidies and long-term unemployment due to the long duration of CIG and mobility benefits;

- an adjustment of employment (in agreement with trade unions) via mass dismissals rather than small, individual adjustments due to the greater generosity of mobility benefits (linked to collective dismissals) compared with unemployment benefits (linked to individual dismissals). Individual dismissals are relatively more expensive and more risky than collective dismissals both for the firms (which have to pay an exit bonus directly to the worker and risk having to recall the worker in case of a decision of the court), and for the workers (who get a much lower and shorter unemployment benefit).

Tables 4 and 5 present some indicators of the level of 'sclerosis' and segmentation in the Italian labour market at the end of the 1980s. Table 4 shows the number of people who lost their jobs in the 1983–91 period in European countries, according to Eurostat labour force data. Involuntary separation rates in the manufacturing sector, and particularly dismissals, are lower in Italy than in other European countries and have a dynamic which does not follow the economic cycle, due to extensive use of the CIG. Table 5 presents the monthly inflows into and out of unemployment and long-term unemployment based on OECD estimates. Italy, together with Spain, has the lowest inflows and outflows of unemployment. Young people have much greater difficulty in gaining access to employment: inflows to unemployment are much higher for young people (51 per cent of total inflows compared with only 11 per cent of workers of at least 45 years old), and long-term unemployment is concentrated among the young.

RECENT TRENDS AND THE CURRENT DEBATE

Since the late 1980s labour market regulation has changed greatly in Italy:

- labour flexibility has increased with extensions in the possible uses of atypical contracts, the introduction of collective dismissals and the abolition of numerical hiring rules (lists) from public placement offices;

- differences in income support during unemployment have been reduced since 1991, by stricter regulations governing the use of the CIG, the gradual extension of CIG and mobility procedures to service sectors and an increase in the level of ordinary unemployment benefits;

- the increase in employers' contributions to the CIG fund has reduced public expenditure and produced a surplus of 2088 billion lire in 1994; and

TABLE 4

INVOLUNTARY OUTFLOWS FROM EMPLOYMENT WITHIN THE PREVIOUS
SIX MONTHS, DUE TO DISMISSALS AND END OF FIXED TERM CONTRACTS,
BY SECTOR, 1983–91

(relative incidence of involuntary outflows rate for type of separation and
sector divided by the national average)

	1983	1984	1985	1986	1987	1988	1989	1990	1991
GERMANY									
Manufacturing	n.d.	1.05	1.34	1.44	1.65	1.35	0.93	0.87	n.d.
other industries	n.d.	1.22	1.79	1.82	3.53	1.84	1.18	0.97	n.d.
personal services	n.d.	1.34	1.74	2.11	2.04	1.86	1.27	1.23	n.d.
other services	n.d.	0.64	0.93	0.96	0.96	1.12	0.78	0.63	n.d.
FRANCE									
Manufacturing	2.76	3.43	3.14	3.45	4.68	3.82	3.23	3.63	3.8
other industries	3.08	4.42	3.37	4.03	4.38	4.29	4.04	4.18	3.93
personal services	4.28	5.06	5.59	5.72	6.76	6.32	5.96	7.29	6.23
other services	1.22	1.44	1.49	1.65	1.83	1.85	1.9	2.25	1.75
ITALY									
Manufacturing	0.88	1.01	0.97	1.08	1.12	1.08	1.19	1.01	1.07
Other industries	1.09	1.85	1.42	2.03	1.87	1.74	2.11	1.47	1.56
Services	0.76	0.97	1.06	1.01	1.21	1.28	1.29	1.15	1.24
GREAT BRITAIN									
Manufacturing	3.71	3.12	2.84	3.01	2.81	2.33	1.99	2.39	4.46
other industries	3.99	3.47	3.29	4.45	3.73	2.9	2.28	2.2	4.86
personal services	3.26	2.96	3.38	3.32	2.64	2.23	1.96	2.2	3.04
other services	1.38	1.56	1.5	1.75	1.72	1.39	1.16	1.11	1.96

Source: Mosley and Kruppe 1993, Tab.4.8 p.80 on Eurostat, Labour Force Surveys data

TABLE 5

MONTHLY FLOWS INTO AND OUT OF UNEMPLOYMENT AND
LONG TERM UNEMPLOYMENT BY AGE

		Unemployment Inflows (in % of population)	outflows	Long-term unemployment (stock) (in % of total unemployment) 15–24	25–44	>45	men	women
Germany	1979	0.2					50	50
	1989	0.3	7.6	12	42	46	51	49
	1991	0.2	8.0	8	43	48	51	49
	1993							
France	1979	0.3	6.1	28	46	26	37	63
	1989	0.4	6.7	15	63	22	40	60
	1991	0.3	5.5	13	63	23	40	60
Italy	1979	0.3					50	50
	1989	0.2	2.8	59	37	5	40	60
	1991	0.2	3.6	52	43	5	39	61
United Kingdom	1979	0.6					75	25
	1989	0.6	13.7	22	39	39	71	29
	1991	0.6	13.4	18	43	39	74	26
Spain	1979	0.3	3.7	57	26	17	60	40
	1989	0.2	2.2	40	39	22	43	57
	1991	0.2	2.0	34	38	28	40	60
Japan	1979	0.3	19.5	9	52	39	70	30
	1989	0.4	22.0	11	32	57	71	29
	1991	0.3	23.6	13	42	46	75	25
United States	1979	2.1	47.4	28	39	33	60	40
	1989	2.0	48.2	16	55	29	70	30
	1991	2.1	37.3	14	53	33	68	32

Source: OECD 1993

- wage rigidities have been greatly reduced with the income agreements of 1992 and 1993.

Fewer improvements have been achieved in the area of active employment policies:

- employment services are still little under-developed;

- training and retraining activities suffer from a confusion, with no clear definition of roles and responsibilities among the different institutions involved;

- programmes mostly involve hiring subsidies and incentives to self-employment, are usually not well designed and are often widely dispersed (Gui 1994);

- the absence of monitoring and evaluation makes it difficult to specify those measures which are most effective and whose expanded use would correct the deficiencies of current policy.

There is wide agreement in the debate on unemployment benefits and income support on the need for a rapid reform of the Italian system. The income agreement of July 1993 included a provision on the need to raise the level of ordinary benefits to 40 per cent of previous earnings and to revise the entire income support system in order to extend insurance benefits to areas not covered (mainly the service sector and small firms). Since then, discussion has been stimulated by the expiry (mostly in December 1995) of the temporary measures introduced during the 1992–94 recession. In addition, the stricter regulation of the CIG and other welfare benefits since the early 1990s, in the context of reduced resources for the development of the southern regions,[10] is creating problems of social conflict in the less developed areas of the south. Finally, the privatization of public employment currently under way requires the extension of unemployment benefits and policies to public-sector workers.

The aim, as in other countries, is to design a system that adequately supports the unemployed, without, however, reducing the incentive to search actively for a new job and to accept existing employment opportunities. An additional element is the need to contain public expenditure. The debate is, however, in an early stage, and it is not at all clear how the system will be reformed, either through minor adjustments to existing measures, or by more radical reform. A major issue is, however, the capacity of the public administrative structure to become more effective and efficient in the management of labour policies. Existing proposals differ on the level, length and extension of proposed unemployment benefits, but all stress the necessity of the following:

Reducing the number of benefits now available and extending the insurance benefit to all those who have lost a job. At the international level, most countries are now converging on a system of income support based on three instruments:

- an unemployment benefit to insure against the risk of losing a job;

- a subsidy in case of reductions in working hours;

- an assistance benefit for low income groups.

Currently, two of these three basic measures are available in Italy: ordinary unemployment benefits (general unemployment insurance) and CIGO (insurance against working time reductions). These two measures may become the basis of the insurance system by eliminating all the other instruments currently available (such as mobility benefits, CIGS and early retirement schemes), improving their performance and, above all, increasing job search requirements. Ordinary benefits may thus be extended to all those who have lost their job, their level and duration may be increased to 50–70 per cent of previous wage, their duration may be extended (proposals range from 12 to 24 months) and eligibility requirements have to be linked to active job search, retraining activities and/or temporary work schemes.[11] Some proposals consider the possibility of linking the level and duration of benefit to the person's age, unemployment duration and years of contribution. Income support for seasonal workers should also be revised, finding new, transparent measures that avoid misuse.

With the increase in long-term unemployment, a new measure (assistance benefit) may be created for those whose insurance benefit has expired and are in difficult conditions. This should reduce the improper use of other instruments (invalidity pensions, maternity leaves, unemployment benefits in the agricultural sector, long-term mobility, etc.). These benefits may be differentiated according to personal and family conditions and be linked to all those active measures that increase the employment potential of the long-term unemployed. First job seekers should be supported by other measures, rather than by unemployment benefits. For example, their employment opportunities may be promoted by a combination of greater wage flexibility and active policies.

Introducing strong incentives for active job search and skills acquisition. The benefit level may be reduced as the duration of unemployment increases and it should be possible to add income from work up to a certain level so as to promote a gradual exit from unemployment. In addition, active measures must be integrated with unemployment benefits administration in order to monitor misuse and to increase the employment potential of those on benefits. Some measures are already available within mobility procedures to induce beneficiaries to accept existing jobs, but they have been used very little up to now, due to the difficult economic situation and the ineffectiveness of public administration.

Increasing the private sector contribution to the financing of unemployment benefits. Insurance benefits should be totally financed by contributions from firms and workers: higher expenditure during recession periods should be covered, in the medium term, by higher revenues during expansions. Assistance benefits and active measures should be financed from general taxation. Contributions may be proportional to gross earnings (as they are now) or be diversified by sectors/contracts (temporary work) in order to take into account differences in the risks of unemployment or working time reductions. Some proposals also consider the possibility of introducing an additional voluntary fund for those sectors/areas more prone to cyclical variations in production. This fund could be managed at the local level. In the case of CIGO, most proposals provide for an additional contribution when exceeding a predetermined amount of hours, so as to discourage misuse.

Improving the effectiveness of labour market intervention. A prerequisite for improving the effectiveness of labour market intervention is to have a more efficient administration and a transparent structure of intervention, with a clear distinction of roles and responsibilities among the different institutions involved, incentives for the co-ordination of passive and active measures, the diffusion of experience in the area of active policies and an improvement in monitoring and evaluation. The decentralization of labour policies at the local level, the integration of passive and active measures and the possibility of private and public co-ordination at the local level may promote greater responsibility and effectiveness in the use of available funds. This issue is particularly important in Italy and there are different reform proposals relating to the decentralization of labour policies at the regional level (Geroldi 1995):

- one is the revision of tax collection mechanisms: if local authorities (regions) have competence in the management of labour policies, they should also have a greater fiscal autonomy. Here the problem is how to define the areas of local competence and the distributive mechanisms necessary in order not to penalize less developed regions.

- a second relates to the procedures in defining local versus central responsibilities. According to one proposal, local authorities should directly assume all those competencies they consider best managed at the local level (bottom-up subsidiarity), while another proposal suggests that it is the central government (in this case the Ministry of Labour) that defines the functions which should be decentralized.

NOTES

1. Market failure may occur because those with a higher risk of unemployment would have to pay higher premiums. Usually low income workers have a higher risk of unemployment and longer unemployment duration, thus there is a case for public redistributive intervention.
2. The poverty trap relates to the fact that additional earnings lead to the withdrawal of benefits, higher tax and social security payments. People receiving benefit income are thus discouraged from accepting those jobs that do not offer a substantial rise in income (such as part-time jobs).
3. Recent estimates of total public expenditures for passive measures in Italy present a value of 1.3% of GDP in 1992, instead of the 0.87% reported by the OECD (Del Boca 1995). According to Del Boca, it is also possible that expenditure on active measures is underestimated.
4. For this reason, the Italian position in international comparisons depends largely on which benefit is considered. Average benefits indicators are also misleading due to the high differences in benefits levels and duration among different segments of the labour force.
5. Large commercial firms were included only in 1991. During the 1992–94 recession, benefits were temporarily extended to workers in some other service sectors and to commercial firms with at least 50 employees. A detailed description of income support measures in Italy, and their evolution in the 1980s may be found in Tronti (1991), De Luca and Bruni (1993) and Franco (1993).
6. The benefit was gradually increased since 1988 from a daily flat rate which was exceptionally low.
7. The benefit may be used as a 're-employment bonus' if the unemployed starts a new job before benefit expiry. In addition, the benefit may be used as a start-up sum by those choosing self-employment or as a subsidy, reducing labour costs, for firms that employ workers on mobility benefit. People on mobility benefits who accept part-time or fixed-term jobs are only temporarily suspended from cover.
8. There is a break in the Labour Force series in Oct. 1992, due to changes in definitions. Since 1992 unemployment is more strictly defined according to the Eurostat definition. Nonetheless, the number of unemployed with previous jobs increases dramatically.
9. There is a regional dualism in the effectiveness of labour market policies. While active labour market policies are more effective in most developed areas (the centre-north), passive measures are mostly used in less developed southern Italy. However, since the most generous schemes are related to past earnings, it is the north that receives the highest levels of average per capita assistance (De Luca and Bruni 1993). The less efficient functioning of local institutions in southern regions hinders the potential effectiveness of active policies. Work sharing programmes are relatively less used in the south because of the low levels of family incomes (CLES 1995).
10. Development policies for southern Italy were radically revised in the early 1990s due to tight budget constraints, EU directives on regional and industrial policies and changed attitudes towards special intervention in southern Italy.
11. An interesting proposal for a radical reform of the unemployment support system is that of Franco and Sestito (1995). The proposal is to create for each dependent worker an insurance fund on which to rely in case of unemployment. The fund would be financed by social contributions from the firm and the worker proportional to gross earnings so as to guarantee a financial equilibrium in the medium term. In order to reduce the potential incentive to a frequent and prolonged use of the insurance benefit, a financial constraint and a benefit duration constraint in the single unemployment spell are considered. The financial constraint would be linked to the level of the accrued capital. During each spell of unemployment, the benefit would be low at the beginning of the unemployment spell, then increase, and decrease toward the end of the benefit period, which should not last more than 12 months.

REFERENCES

Atkinson, A.B. and J. Micklewright (1991): 'Unemployment Compensation and Labor Market Transitions: A Critical Review', *Journal of Economic Literature* 24/4.

Barbarulo, G. and C. Guarna (1993): 'L'occupazione e gli interventi sociali in Italia agli inizi degli anni novanta', *Economia & Lavoro* 27/1.

Bertola, G. (1993): 'Vincoli istituzionali ai licenziamenti e domanda di lavoro in Italia', in F. Padoa-Schioppa Kostoris (ed.) *Squilibri e rigidità nel mercato del lavoro italiano: rilevanza quantitativa e proposte correttive*, Angeli: Milano.

Boeri, T. (1994): 'Indennità di disoccupazione', *Lavoro e Relazioni Industriali* 2.

Calmfors, L. (1994): 'Active Labour Market Policy and Unemployment. A Framework for the Analysis of Crucial Design Features', *OECD Economic Studies* 22 (Spring).

Centraal Planbureau (1995): *Replacements Rates: A Transatlantic View*, working Paper no.80, (Sept.), The Hague.

CLES (1995): *Analysis of Factors Favouring a More Effective Employment Policy in Italy*, mimeo, Rome.

CNEL (1995): 'Indennità di disoccupazione', *Documenti CNEL* no.61, Rome.

Confindustria (1995): *Il futuro degli ammortizzatori sociali* [The Future of Social Shock Absorbers], mimeo, Feb.

Del Boca, A. and P. Rota (1993): *Hiring and Firing Rules in Italy: What Practices Do Companies Follow?*, discussion paper no.9308, Università di Brescia, Dipartimento di Scienze Economiche.

Del Boca, A. (1995): 'Prospettive di riforma degli strumenti d'integrazione del reddito nell'ambito della spesa sociale', mimeo, *Commissione Tecnica della Spesa Pubblica* (Oct.).

De Luca, L. and M. Bruni (1993): *Unemployment and Labour Market Flexibility: Italy*, Geneva: ILO.

Demekas, D.G. (1995): 'Labour Market Institutions and Flexibility in Italy', *Labour* 1 (Spring).

Eurostat (1993): *Labour Force Survey Results 1991*, Luxembourg.

Eurostat (1994): *Social Protection Expenditure and Receipts: 1980–1992*, Luxembourg.

Ferrera, M. (1996): 'The "Southern Model" of Welfare in Social Europe', *Journal of European Social Policy* 6/1, pp.17–37.

Forslund, A. and A.B. Krueger (1994): *An Evaluation of the Swedish Active Labour Market Policy: New and Received Wisdom*, NBER working paper series, no.4802.

Franco, D. (1993): *L'espansione della spesa pubblica in Italia*, Bologna: Il Mulino.

Franco, D. (1994): 'L'indennità di disoccupazione', *Lavoro e Relazioni Industriali* 2.

Franco, D. and P. Sestito (1995): 'Il sistema di protezione sociale dei disoccupati: alcune riflessioni su una possibile riforma', *Politica Economica* 11/3, pp.389–413.

Geroldi, G. (1995): *Il finanziamento delle politiche del lavoro nell'ipotesi di un decentramento istituzionale delle competenze*, mimeo, Parma.

Giavazzi, F. and L. Spaventa (1989): 'Italia: gli effetti reali dell'inflazione e della disinflazione', *Rivista*.

Guarna, C. (1995): *I costi della disoccupazione*, mimeo, CNEL (Jan.).

Gui, B. (1994): 'I sussidi marginali all'occupazione. Un riesame delle potenzialità dello strumento e del suo utilizzo in Italia', *Lavoro e Relazioni Industriali* 1.

Jackman, R. (1995): *What can Active Labour Market Policy Do*, Centre for Economic Performance Discussion Paper no.226 (March), London School of Economics.

Liso, F. (1994): 'L' indennità di disoccupazione', *Lavoro e Relazioni Industriali* 2.

Mosley, H. and T. Kruppe (1993): *Employment Protection and Labour Force Adjustment. A Comparative Evaluation*, Wissenschaft Zentrum Berlin Discussion Paper FS I 92-9 (April).

Negri, N. and C. Saraceno (1996): *Le politiche contro la povertà in Italia*, Bologna: Il Mulino.

Neri, F. (ed.) (1990): *Le politiche del lavoro negli anni ottanta*, Milan: F. Angeli.

OECD (1993): *Employment Outlook*, Paris: OECD, July.

OECD (1994): 'Unemployment and Related Welfare Benefits', in *The OECD Jobs Study. Evidence and Explanations, Part II – The Adjustment Potential of the Labour Market,* Paris: OECD.

OECD (1995): *Employment Outlook,* Paris: OECD, July

Tronti, L. (1991): 'Employment Protection and Labour Market Segmentation: the Fifth Anniversary of the *Cassa Integrazione Quadogni', Labour* 1.

Welfare States and Anti-Poverty Regimes: The Case of Portugal

JOSÉ A. PEREIRINHA

This article addresses the issue of comparing welfare regimes with a particular focus on poverty policies. Some reflections are made on methodology and some data are presented in order to highlight the relevant differences among the northern and southern European countries. The main features of the Portuguese case are then presented and evaluated within the context of this broader analysis.

TOWARDS A COMPARISON OF WELFARE REGIMES WITH A FOCUS ON POVERTY

It is becoming widely recognised that most of the literature on comparing welfare regimes – especially that which proposes typologies of welfare states – ignores (or at least underestimates) the differences evident among countries in the area of poverty policies. At the same time, such approaches have traditionally failed satisfactorily to incorporate the southern European countries. Four approaches can be detected in the literature:

- studies which focus mainly on *inputs*, that is, the *demands* (or *needs*) for action either inside or outside the political system and the *resources* allocated to the policy. Many studies rely on resources allocated to welfare provision, justified either by the fact that this indicates the welfare effort of a country or because it is the easiest way of getting statistical data. But ranking the countries on the basis of the percentage of government expenditure on social protection in GDP provides a very rough indication of how actual social protection is implemented – its coverage, redistributive impact, entitlements/ rights, how welfare provision is delivered, and so on.
- comparative studies which focus on policy *outputs* (what the welfare system does) and/or policy *outcomes* (the consequences or impact of policy). Only recently has this became possible following the development of comparative data sets, namely the Luxembourg

Income Study (Smeeding *et al.* 1990), allowing an evaluation of the redistributive impact of social policies and, at the EU level, EUROPASS, which allows studies of the adequacy of social protection policies in alleviating poverty (Deleeck *et al.* 1992).

- studies of the *production process of welfare* which include the important contribution of Esping-Andersen (1990) which focuses on the degree of decommodification of rights and stratification in welfare organization and identifies three models of welfare capitalism: the liberal (UK), the conservative-corporatist (Italy, France, Germany and Belgium) and the social democratic (Denmark and Sweden). The southern European welfare states fit awkwardly, in part because of the focus on the decommodification of the rights of workers in the formal labour market (Taylor-Gooby 1991), leaving aside those in the informal labour market which plays an important role in the south. This categorization of welfare regimes also fails to incorporate explicitly the policy instruments used to combat poverty and social exclusion (Schulte 1993): those excluded from the labour market are often not covered by contributory regimes but rely instead on marginal means-tested benefits or the solidarity of civil society. Esping-Andersen is not directly concerned with redistributive issues but, instead, with the 'rights-conferring aspects of welfare provision … (and) is unwilling to concede the welfare-conferring potential of means-tested benefits in redistributive terms' (Castles and Mitchell 1990: 7).

- Castles and Mitchell (1990) develop a *welfare linkages* model as a method for identifying the relationship between the welfare effort of countries, the policy instruments used and the resulting policy outcomes in redistributive terms. This improves on Esping-Anderson's methodology by incorporating more explicitly distributional and outcome-equity issues. But poverty (and poverty policies) are not explicitly considered in their approach, and the case of the southern countries is still not adequately addressed.

Leibfried (1992) places poverty policy at the core of his discussion and pays greater attention to the special features of the southern countries in an attempt to improve on the Esping-Andersen model. The result is four 'worlds of welfare capitalism' rather than three, adding a 'Latin Rim' of southern countries (including France), characterized by a catholic social policy welfare regime alongside older traditions of welfare provision relying on church organisations, family welfare and private charity, with an important role played by the voluntary sector, with less developed general assistance schemes.

This analysis draws our attention to the institutional arrangement of social actors which plays such a crucial role in southern welfare regimes, especially in the area of poverty and social exclusion. Presently tendencies are emerging, although in ways which are not fully clear, which are changing institutions in the *welfare triangle* (state/market/civil society) of modern welfare regimes (Evers 1990; Wintersberger 1993). But in order to grasp these changes, especially in the case of the southern countries, a *welfare diamond* approach, which differentiates within civil society between the *household* and the *voluntary sector* may be more useful (Österle 1996), where the former refers either to the household or the extended family and friends/neighbours, and the latter refers to the rather heterogeneous non-profit sector, which is becoming more and more organized in formal terms in these societies.

In the following analysis we tackle two main tasks. In the first we use comparative data to illustrate the differences in the effectiveness of poverty policies in northern and southern Europe. Are there particular characteristics of a southern European policy regime? In the second we focus on the case of Portugal by considering the four basic elements of welfare provision: the inputs, the process, the outputs and the outcomes of policy.

POVERTY AND POVERTY RELIEF POLICIES: NORTH AND SOUTH IN FIGURES

This section focuses on the outputs and outcomes of the welfare system as crucial issues for evaluation of poverty policies which consist of monetary social transfers. Poverty policies go far beyond such policy instruments. Given the lack of statistical data, we have had to rely on two statistical sources which have been collected with a comparative purpose: the European Research on Poverty and Social Security programme – EUROPASS (Deleeck *et al.* 1992; Hausman 1993), and the European Community Household Panel project – ECHP (Cantillon *et al.* 1994). In both statistical sources, the southern countries are misrepresented, but they do allow a location of the southern countries in the EU context.

Table 1 presents some general statistics on income inequality and poverty in the EU using ECHP data. The fact that it was obtained from the first wave of the ECHP pilot survey (and is therefore based on a small sample) does not allow information to be presented for all countries, and the data has been aggregated into south (Italy, Spain, Portugal, Greece) and Ireland and north (the remaining EC 12 countries, with the exception of Germany and The Netherlands, due to unreliable or unavailable data on household disposable income). The statistical data for the two groups of countries are comparable but one should be careful about its provisional character. For computing poverty rates, by EC standard we mean a poverty line defined as 50 per cent of average equivalent household income.

In the south the average income is lower, with much higher income inequality and a higher poverty rate. About 15 per cent of households and 18 per cent of individuals are poor in the northern European countries and about 18 per cent of households and 21 per cent of individuals are poor in the south, according to their relative standards (Cantillon *et al.* 1994).

TABLE 1
INCOME DISTRIBUTION AND POVERTY IN THE EC, IN ECU (1993)

	EC	north	south
Average disposable income (mthly)			
– per household	1630	1712	1541
– per adult equivalent	1407	1519	1286
Theil inequality coefficient			
– total disposable household income	0.1870	0.1564	0.2222
– standardised household income	0.1596	0.1319	0.1882
% poor households, EC standard			
– standard for the EC	16.5	11.2	22.1
– standard for the north		15.4	
– standard for the south			18.4
% poor individuals, EC standard			
– standard for the EC	18.7	12.6	24.7
– standard for the north		18.1	
– standard for the south			21.1

Source: Cantillon *et al.* (1994), from ECHP

According to the same statistical source (Dirven *et al.* 1994), a higher proportion of households receive at least one benefit from social protection in the north (77 per cent) than in the south (60 per cent), but a much higher proportion of households live exclusively from such transfers in the south (20 per cent) than in the north (12.5 per cent). About 60 per cent of total households have income from other sources in the north, compared with 40 per cent in the south. Old age benefits are received by a larger number of households in the south (34 per cent) than in the north (23 per cent), while the reverse is the case for maternity/family benefits (39 per cent in the north and only 9 per cent in the south). The proportion of social protection benefits in household disposable income is higher in the southern countries (65 per cent of disposable income of recipient households and 40 per cent of total households) than in the northern countries (42 per cent of disposable income of recipient households and 31 per cent of total households), although this varies by income levels, as shown in Figure 1. About 60 per cent of total households have income from other sources in the north, compared with 40 per cent in the south. These indicators suggest that households in southern European countries are much more dependent on social protection transfers than in the north.

FIGURE 1

ANNUAL INCOME FROM SOCIAL PROTECTION AS PROPORTION OF ANNUAL
DISPOSABLE HOUSEHOLD INCOME BY INCOME DECILES (1993)

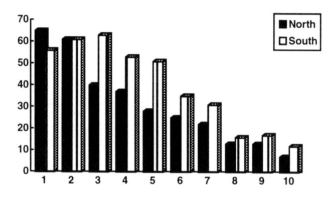

Source: Dirven, H.-J. et al. (1994), from ECHP

　　Using the same statistical source (ECHP), it is possible to evaluate the impact of social transfers on poverty relief, using as an indicator the proportion of households that become non-poor after the social transfers (Table 2). However, Table 2 refers only to those households that receive social protection transfers, and not to all households in the sample, so that the results should be interpreted accordingly.

　　Social protection transfers lift 40 per cent of households that receive them above the poverty threshold in the south, compared to 29 per cent in the north. Nevertheless, the proportion of poor households after transfers remains higher in the south. This means that although such transfers are more effective (in head-count terms) in the south for those households that receive social transfers, they only partially compensate for the high poverty rate. For those households that live exclusively on social transfers, no significant differences emerge between the north and the south as far as social transfer effectiveness is concerned.

TABLE 2
HEAD COUNT POVERTY RELIEF EFFECTIVENESS OF CASH TRANSFERS* IN THE EU
(1993) (%)

	All households receiving social protection			Households exclusively on social protection			Households with other income sources in addition to social protection		
	EU	north	south	EU	north	south	EU	north	south
Pre-transfer non-poor	46.8	54.5	40.3	0.0	0.0	0.0	62.2	66.0	61.2
Non-poor due to social protection	35.3	28.5	39.4	67.0	70.9	68.3	24.8	19.6	24.4
Post-transfer poor	17.9	17.0	20.3	33.0	29.1	31.7	12.9	14.5	14.4
Total – in group	100.0	100.0	100.0	24.8	17.4	34.2	75.2	82.6	65.8
Total – in sample	65.9	71.3	60.0	16.4	12.5	20.6	49.8	59.2	39.6

Source: B. Cantillon et al. (1994), from ECHP

* Proportion of households that become non-poor after the social transfers. Sample size: 1,272 households

Despite the importance of these results, the picture remains incomplete. The EUROPASS data provided by Hausman (1993) helps fill in some of the gaps.

In order to evaluate the adequacy of the social transfers in terms of their impact on poverty relief, one should consider either the effectiveness or the efficiency of such transfers. By *effectiveness* we mean the extent to which the social transfers succeed in reducing poverty, and two possible (but complementary) forms may be envisaged for such measure: one is to measure the poverty reduction in head-count terms (the proportion of households that become non-poor after such transfers); the other is to measure the proportional reduction of the poverty gap. By *efficiency* we mean the proportion of transfers that contribute to poverty relief. Both kind of indicators used in this article follow strictly the approach proposed by Beckerman (1979). Since a monetary poverty line is obtained, we can propose the derivation of five complementary indicators of the adequacy of transfers for poverty relief:

• The gross head count poverty relief effectiveness of social transfers (EH1) defined as the proportion of households that become non-poor after the transfers;

- The net head count poverty relief effectiveness of social transfers (EH2) defined as the proportion of those households whose income was below the poverty line who became non-poor after the transfers;

- The poverty gap effectiveness of social transfers (ET) defined as the proportion of the poverty gap that is reduced due to the transfers;

- The poverty gap net efficiency of social transfers (EC1) defined as the proportion of total transfers which reduce the poverty gap;

- The poverty gap gross efficiency of social transfers (EC2) defined as the proportion of social transfers paid to households whose income before transfers is below the poverty line, that lift a portion of such households out of poverty.

Table 3 presents some data relevant for this purpose. It should be noted, however, that Tables 2 and 3 are not fully comparable since, as mentioned above, Table 2 refers to the households that receive social protection transfers while Table 3 refers to all households, which may explain some discrepancies in the analysis.

Table 3 indicates a less effective impact of social transfers on gross head count poverty relief (indicator EH1) in the south than in Table 2. This may be due to the fact that a lower proportion of households in the south receive social transfers and that all households are included. The most evident trends to emerge are that, as the average social expenditure per head rises:

- the poverty gap net efficiency of social transfers (that is, the proportion of social transfers contributing to the elimination of the poverty gap, corresponding to our indicator EC1) decreases;

- the poverty gap effectiveness of social transfers (that is, the poverty rate reduction rate, corresponding to our indicator ET) rises; and

- the net head count poverty relief effectiveness of social transfers (that is, the proportion of pre-transfer poor households that become secure due to transfers, corresponding to our indicator EH2) rises.

It is also possible to obtain from this data three distinctive clusters of countries:

- Greece and Ireland – with low average social expenditure per head, relatively low poverty gap effectiveness of social transfers (ET), relatively low net head count poverty relief effectiveness of social transfers (EH2) and relatively high poverty gap net efficiency of social transfers (EC1);

TABLE 3

INDICATORS OF ADEQUACY OF SOCIAL TRANSFERS TO POVERTY RELIEF IN
SOME EU COUNTRIES (1984–1988)

	Inputs Needs/Demands		Resources	Outputs/outcomes Outputs			Outcomes
Country/ Region	Proportion of poor house-holds (hh)	Proportion of poor hh before transfers	Social expenditure per head as per cent of EU average	Effective-ness of social transfers (a) (ET indicator)	Efficiency of social transfers (b) (EC1 indicator)	per cent of pre-transfer poor hh that become secure (EH2 indicator)	per cent of hh secure due to social protection (EH1 indicator)
Catalonia	15.1	30.8	—	74.8	41.4	51.0	15.7
Greece	19.9	38.1	30.9	64.3	76.3	47.8	18.2
Italy	17.9	43.2	91.1	77.9	45.4	58.6	25.3
France	15.4	46.4	124.1	83.9	47.5	66.8	31.0
Ireland	17.2	46.2	60.1	83.0	53.7	62.8	29.0
UK	12.0	44.8	99.5	87.7	48.1	73.2	32.8
FRG	12.8	42.2	129.6	89.1	49.4	69.7	29.4
Belgium	5.7	41.4	117.8	95.9	42.7	86.2	35.7
Netherlands	7.2	39.8	133.2	90.9	42.3	82.0	32.6
Luxembourg	7.6	45.6	128.9	92.6	39.3	80.5	31.3

Source: Adapted and reinterpreted data presented in Hausman (1993) from EUROPASS

(a) Poverty gap reduction rate

(b) Proportion of social transfers contributing to the elimination of the poverty gap

• Italy and the United Kingdom – with average social expenditure per head, and with three measures – poverty gap effectiveness of social transfers (ET), net head count poverty relief effectiveness of social transfers (EH2) and poverty gap net efficiency of social transfers (EC1) – close to the EC average (of the nine countries covered);

• Belgium, France, Luxembourg, Netherlands and the former FRG – with high average social expenditure per head, relatively high poverty gap effectiveness of social transfers (ET) and net head count poverty relief effectiveness of social transfers (EH2), but a relatively low poverty gap net efficiency of social transfers (EC1).

It is interesting to compare these results with Esping-Andersen's (1990) typology which parallels this division of countries:

• Ireland is in the group of countries with a low decommodification score, a low degree of liberalism and socialism and a medium degree of conservatism;

- Italy and the United Kingdom are in the group of countries with low decommodification scores, a medium extent of liberalism, and a medium-low degree of socialism, although they are quite different in their degrees of conservatism (Italy high, UK low); and

- Belgium, France, the Netherlands and Germany are in the group of countries with a high-to-medium score of decommodification, a strong-to-medium degree of conservatism, a medium-to-low degree of liberalism, but quite different degrees of socialism.

This suggests that the relationship between Esping-Andersen's criteria and the effectiveness of poverty relief would be fruitful to explore.

MAIN FEATURES OF POVERTY IN PORTUGAL

Until the mid-1980s, poverty and social exclusion were neither openly referred to by politicians, nor a relevant subject of academic research in Portugal. Only since the early 1990s have they come onto the agenda of political parties and the social partners, and become a policy concern for government, in part because of external factors – EU debates on poverty and social exclusion, the Social Charter and the Council Resolution on social exclusion, and EU initiatives to combat poverty. The first known published study of the subject was based on the 1973–74 period, just prior to the 1974 revolution, and revealed a high rate of poverty (at 43.4 per cent of households and 43.2 per cent of persons) (Silva 1984). This study drew the attention of public opinion and social scientists to the major characteristics of poverty in Portugal, and raised some hypotheses as to its causes. The highest poverty rate was found among agriculture households, industrial workers and the retired population. Among the causal factors of poverty suggested were 'the model of economic development; the devaluation of the labour force (low wages) and agriculture (low wages and goods prices); and the weakness of social security schemes and, in general, of redistributive mechanisms...' (Costa et al. 1985: 36).

Since the mid-1980s several studies have been made on poverty in Portugal either by national researchers (Silva 1984; Costa et al. 1985; Ferreira 1993; Costa 1994) or in the context of international comparisons (O'Higgins and Jenkins 1989; ISSAS 1990; Ramprakash 1994). But such studies follow different methodologies and produce rather different results. Using very similar methodologies, the results of Silva (1984) and Costa et al. (1985) suggest that the poverty rate (in terms of the proportion of households considered as poor) has remained stable, or has slightly increased, in the period between 1973 and 1980, both relatively and absolutely, while between 1980 and 1990 there has been a slight reduction (Costa 1994; Ferreira 1993), although, in contrast to rural areas, in urban centres it increased. According to Costa (1994) (using an absolute approach to measurement), household poverty rates in rural areas and in urban centres converged by the end of the 1980s, on around 22 per cent of households, whereas, 'traditionally', poverty rates were much higher in rural areas. Measuring the poverty rate in terms of individual members of poor households, the trend is even more pronounced, with a decrease in rural areas from 27.9 per cent in 1980 to 20.6 per cent in 1990, and an increase from 18.1 per cent in 1980 to 22.3 per cent in 1990 in urban centres. Looking at the intensity of poverty assessed through estimates of relative poverty gaps as a percentage of the poverty line, and using an absolute approach for poverty measurement (Costa 1994: 108), the poverty gap has slightly increased in rural areas during 1980–90 (from 26.8 to 27.1 per cent) and has slightly fallen in urban areas (from 29.2 to 28.5 per cent). In brief, there has been a reduction in the incidence of poverty in the country as a whole, becoming relatively less of a rural phenomenon and more of an urban one, although its severity has increased for rural households. Nevertheless, Portugal still has the highest rate of poverty in the EU (ISSAS 1990; Ramprakash 1994).

But what of its incidence? According to Costa et al. (1985), against an overall poverty rate of 35 per cent in 1980, the incidence of poverty (using an absolute poverty approach) by social group was: 42.4 per cent for the aged and retired, 48–49 per cent for agriculture workers and farmers and 35.4 per cent for manual workers in manufacturing industries. By 1990, there were still major traits of traditional poverty (Table 4). According to Ferreira (1993), against an overall rate of 9.4 per cent (based upon a relative approach, that is, those with 50 per cent or less of the median adult-equivalent income), the highest poverty rates are found for those living alone (26.3 per cent of one-person household), which rise with the age of the head of the household (25 per cent for those above 75 years old), and decrease as the education level of the head of the household rises (22 per cent for those households whose head are illiterate). If we look at the situation of households whose heads are employers and self-employed in agriculture or agricultural workers we can conclude that important changes occurred for both socio-economic groups in the 1980s. There has been a significant decrease of their population share and the poverty incidence has risen for both socio-economic groups.

But rural areas are not homogeneous in terms either of socio-economic categories of households or their sources of income. These social groups are 'pluri-active',[1] and there is a trend for some manufacturing industries to locate in rural areas. In addition, a high percentage of the population in rural areas is old (with social security pensions as the main source of income). This may explain why the incidence of poverty has declined in rural areas since 1980, although it has risen for agricultural socio-economic groups, since the evolution of non-agricultural income sources has been relatively more favourable than agricultural incomes.

TABLE 4

SOME FEATURES OF POVERTY IN PORTUGAL (1980 AND 1990)

	Population share (%)		Adult-equivalent income (1)		Poverty rate (%)	
	1980	1990	1980	1990	1980	1990
Socio-economic category of the head of household						
Employer and self-employed Agriculture	15.0	7.1	95.2	86.3	11.0	11.3
Agriculture worker	6.2	3.5	75.8	74.3	18.3	23.0
Employer and self-employed Non-Agric.	10.5	12.9	116.2	117.8	5.7	3.9
Liberal professionals	0.5	0.6	241.5	203.0	0.0	2.7
Executive and technical workers	4.2	5.2	201.0	207.8	0.8	0.5
Industrial workers	24.8	24.4	93.2	92.3	8.1	3.9
Workers on trade and services	13.9	13.7	127.3	126.7	3.8	3.6
Retired	23.1	28.3	76.8	77.0	23.7	19.3
Others	1.9	4.4	155.5	117.3	3.2	7.7
TOTAL	100	100	100	100	11.5	9.4
Households' main income source						
Wages	57.0	55.7	108.9	110.9	7.1	4.7
Own account labour income	6.6	5.5	120.1	115.2	6.8	3.8
Capital income	1.3	1.7	144.9	158.1	12.0	1.57
Transfers	11.1	15.7	64.0	65.9	33.6	27.5
Other income sources	24.2	21.4	100.8	105.0	13.0	10.4
TOTAL	100	100	100	100	11.5	9.4

Source: Ferreira (1993)

(1) Ratio of average adult-equivalent income of the household group/average adult-equivalent income of all households (Total = 100)

The high poverty rates of groups living from agriculture are explained by the structural characteristics of this sector in Portugal, the vulnerable character of agriculture incomes and the low degree of monetarization of the activity of the poor land owners,[2] combined with the rather unbalanced impact of agriculture policy in recent years. Moreover, the characteristics of the poor agriculture population tend to be transmitted to successive generations.

The large amount of funds allocated to agriculture since 1986,[3] and public infrastructure support for agricultural activities, have had a significant impact on this sector. Such funds have, however, been allocated in a concentrated manner, producing a dualistic form of modernization in which most viable enterprises can survive and gain in competitiveness, while most of the agriculture population remains marginalized,[4] with negative effects on their incomes and contributing to the depopulation of rural areas (Avillez 1993). Since the accession of Portugal to the EC, prices have been subject to competition from foreign agriculture products and the relative prices of agricultural products have fallen. This has had different effects on agricultural enterprises, but the general trend has been to sustain, or even to deepen, existing disparities.[5] All of this suggests that the process of impoverishment may continue for some social groups in rural areas, despite the compensation provided by the implantation of some small and medium-size industries benefiting from the still abundant labour force and low wages.

The incidence of urban poverty has increased. In urban areas, low income is to a great extent associated with low skill levels, low wages, precarious jobs, long-term unemployment and, for the elderly, very low pensions. The functioning of the labour market and insufficient social protection largely explain these problems. Social exclusion in the labour market is basically the result of two effects:

- a *short-term effect* which results from the reduction in the rate of growth of GDP – bordering on recession – since the early 1990s, which is felt more acutely in some sectors and regions;

- a *structural effect* of an economy under pressure to change, combined with the characteristics of the labour force, which cannot accommodate demand for labour in the most modern and dynamic sectors and firms. In a segmented labour market, 'push-mechanisms' become dominant in relation to 'pull-mechanisms' for some segments, thus excluding certain categories of workers (the less skilled, those facing greater problems of sectoral, occupational and geographical mobility), given insufficient employment and vocational training policy, combined with inadequate social protection for the unemployed.

Despite rising unemployment since the early 1990s (4.1 per cent in 1992, 5.5 in 1993 and 6.8 in 1994), Portugal still has one of the lowest unemployment rates in the EU. The increase in unemployment was accompanied by a rise in the number searching for a new job (about 83 per cent of total unemployment) and in the share of the long-term unemployed (about 39 per cent of those out of work were searching for a job for longer than a year). Other factors are at work creating greater income insecurity for a significant number of workers, mainly those in sectors most vulnerable to foreign competition – short-term contracts (10.7 per cent of total workers in 1994), temporary jobs, the subcontracting involving the loss of social benefits, involuntary part-time jobs, work at home, low wages and delays in wage payments (involving, in 1993 about 24,000 persons, that is, 0.7 per cent of total workers).

The social seriousness of very long-term unemployment (VLTU) is widely recognized as a major symptom of social exclusion in the labour market, given very poor social protection and the considerable problems of finding jobs. Unemployment benefit is quite inadequate in Portugal and is available only for short periods. Thus, in 1991 only 12 per cent of the VLTU considered unemployment benefit as their main means of support, while most (more than 50 per cent) gave the 'family' as their main source of support, while 15 per cent took occasional jobs (Mendes and Castro Rego 1992). Social protection for the unemployed actually comprises two major benefits: unemployment benefit (an unemployment insurance scheme) and social unemployment benefit (social assistance). The unemployment insurance scheme was established in 1985[6] and was included in the general workers' social security regime. The amount and duration of benefit is related to the wages and contributory record of the unemployed and to his/her age.[7] The unemployed who have reached the end of the unemployment insurance benefit period, or do not fulfil the contributory requirements, are granted means-tested social assistance.[8]

Table 5 displays the number of beneficiaries of such benefits, the respective average amounts and benefit trends for 1985–93. Neither the share – of the total unemployed population – of those receiving insurance unemployment benefit nor of those receiving social assistance rose over this period. In 1993 only about 60 per cent of the unemployed received unemployment benefit, and only 25 per cent received social assistance. If the period of entitlement is short, the amount is also low. On average, the amount of insurance unemployment benefit is rising in relation to the minimum wage, being close to this level by 1993. But the average amount of social assistance benefit is little more than 60 per cent of the national minimum wage. This may help explain why the unemployed in Portugal may face serious situations of poverty.

Education is a crucial factor for good performance in the labour market, and differences in the educational attainment of the workers is an important factor of inequality and poverty in Portugal (Pereirinha 1988). Moreover, the intra- and inter-generational transmission of employment precariousness and low wages produce persisting social exclusion. The illiteracy rate is still very high in Portugal (11.2 per cent

TABLE 5

NUMBER OF RECIPIENTS (AND AMOUNTS) OF UNEMPLOYMENT BENEFIT AND
SOCIAL UNEMPLOYMENT BENEFIT

	1985	1986	1987	1988	1989	1990	1991	1992	1993
1. Number unemployed (a)	405.4	393.6	329.2	272.9	243.5	231.1	207.5	194.1	257.5
2. Rate of unemployment (%)	8.7	8.4	7.0	5.7	5.0	4.7	4.1	4.1	5.5
3. Unemployed receiving unemployment benefit (a)	13.6	24.7	28.7	24.7	29.7	41.9	57.3	83.6	113.0
4. (3)/(1)*100 (%)	3.4	6.3	8.7	9.0	12.2	18.1	27.6	43.0	43.9
5. Unemployed receiving social unemp. benefit (a)	57.8	48.7	40.2	37.5	31.9	27.4	36.6	48.6	63.0
6. (5)/(1)*100 (%)	14.2	12.4	12.2	13.8	13.1	11.8	17.6	25.1	24.5
7. Average unemp. benefit (b)	130.4	180.8	326.3	392.9	387.7	438.1	512.1	566.5	719.2
8. Ave. soc. unemp. benefit (b)	186.0	274.6	261.7	244.9	291.6	322.4	334.1	384.5	434.0
9. Minimum wage (c)	268.8	315.0	352.8	380.8	430.5	490.0	561.4	623.0	663.6
10. (7)/(9)*100 (%)	48.5	57.4	92.5	103.2	90.1	89.4	91.2	90.9	108.4
11. (8)/(9)*100 (%)	69.2	87.2	74.2	64.3	67.7	65.8	59.5	61.7	65.4

Source: Barreto (1996). Data from IN (Inquérito ao Emprego) and MESS (IGFSS)

(a) Thousands. Figures after 1992 are not comparable with those before this year; (b) average expense of unemployment benefit per unemployed receiving such benefit (thousand escudos/year), current prices; (c) Thousand escudos/year (estimated as monthly legal amount*14 months), current prices.

in 1991), and the education level of the Portuguese workers rather low, although there has been progress in recent years: in 1990, 68 per cent of workers had six or fewer years of education, down from 76.8 per cent in 1985. Over the same period, the percentage of young workers (under 25) with secondary education rose from 16 to 25 per cent (MPAT 1993). Mendes and Castro Rego (1992) found that most unemployed had been in non-permanent jobs and that the most important reasons for remaining unemployed were age, educational level and a lack of qualifications or skills. A significant number of the unemployed surveyed in that study considered professional training (either short-term or long-term) to be the best means of labour market re-entry.

As it functions at the moment, social security helps impoverish its beneficiaries. The low level of pensions paid is widely recognized as contributing to the poor living conditions of those households reliant on social security transfers as their main income source. Table 3 supports this conclusion: from 1980 to 1990, the number of people who were members of households headed by a retired person increased, with an average income 23 per cent below the average adult-equivalent income in the country and a poverty rate twice the national average. Households whose main source of income are transfers (mainly from social security) had a poverty rate three times the national average.

The present social security system in Portugal was established by the Social Security Act ('Lei de Bases da Segurança Social') in 1984, which rationalized previously existing schemes into two new ones:

- the general (contributory) regime, following Bismarckian principles of social insurance and aimed at persons in the labour market and their families, providing protection for old-age, invalidity, death, sickness, motherhood, labour accidents, unemployment, etc. This is a compulsory scheme, covering employees and the self-employed, and the amount of benefit depends upon the individual's contribution record. Active beneficiaries of the special agricultural social security regime were included in this regime in 1987;

- the non-contributory regime protects persons who are in socio-economic need and are not covered by the general regime, and covers old-age, invalidity, death, unemployment, etc., as well as compensating for extra family expenses. Benefits do not depend on any contribution record, but are means-tested and financed by state transfers. Social action complements the social security regimes by aiming to prevent and ameliorate situations of social need, dysfunction or poverty, ensuring protection for the most vulnerable groups in the society.

Table 6 presents the situation of pensioners. We estimated an absolute poverty line (separately for urban centres and rural areas) which allows an assessment of the real impact of social security pensions. Although all social security pensions have increased above the inflation rate in recent years, minimum pensions are well below our estimated poverty line, mainly in urban centres (about 35 per cent below the poverty threshold in 1995). The social pension is only 40 per cent of the estimated poverty line income. Pensioners in urban centres live, on average, very close to the estimated poverty line, explainable by the low wages generally earned by a significant proportion of the retired population when economically active and, in addition, by the very short contributory record of a large proportion of this group (in 1995, about 45 per cent of pensioners in the general regime had less than 10 years of contributions to the social security system).

TABLE 6

SOCIAL SECURITY BENEFITS AND THEIR COMPARISON WITH
AN ESTIMATED POVERTY LINE

	Unit	1992	1993	1994	1995
1. Poverty line urban centres (a)	'000 esc./month	37.9	39.0	40.9	42.5
2. Poverty line rural areas (b)	'000 esc./month	28.2	29.0	30.4	31.6
3. Minimum pension (gen. regime) (c)	'000 esc./month	22.8	24.7	26.2	27.6
4. Minimum pension (rural regime)	'000 esc./month	16.3	17.6	18.6	19.6
5. Social pension	'000 esc./month	14.6	15.7	16.6	17.5
6. Average pension (general regime) (c)	'000 esc./month	32.2	36.7	39.2	42.1
7. (3)/(1) * 100	per cent	60.2	63.3	64.1	64.9
8. (3)/(2) * 100	per cent	80.9	85.2	86.2	87.3
9. (4)/(2) * 100	per cent	57.8	60.7	61.2	62.0
10. (5)/(1) * 100	per cent	38.5	40.3	40.6	41.2
11. (5)/(2) * 100	per cent	51.8	54.1	54.6	55.4
12. (6)/(1) * 100	per cent	85.0	94.1	95.8	99.1
13. (6)/(2) * 100	per cent	114.2	126.6	128.9	133.2

Sources: Costa (1994), MSSS (1996), IN (data on price indices). Estimates by the author

(a) Estimated by Costa (1994) on the basis of the cost of a minimum food-basket in 1989, and an Engel co-efficient of 0.346, updated for 1990 onwards using the price index of food and the same value of the Engel co-efficient; the monthly value was obtained as the annual value/12.

(b) Estimated by Costa (1994) on the basis of the cost of a minimum food-basket in 1989, and an Engel co-efficient of 0.430, updated for 1990 onwards using the price index of food and the same value of the Engel co-efficient; the monthly value was obtained as the annual value/12.

(c) Old-age and invalidity pension.

RECENT SOCIAL POLICY TRENDS IN PORTUGAL AND THEIR POTENTIAL EFFECTS ON POVERTY AND SOCIAL EXCLUSION

Four major trends are evident in legislation and policy practice since the early 1990s:

• a broader and more active participation of the social actors in the design, implementation and monitoring of social policy;

• a greater decentralization and fragmentation of activities;

• a privatization of services, changing the traditional role of the state in services provision and financing;

• a better co-ordination of social policies to increase their effectiveness in combating social exclusion.

Health policy is one domain of state intervention where legislation in the 1990s may have had an adverse impact on poverty and social exclusion. The health care system in Portugal was transformed from a predominantly social insurance-based system into a tax-financed National Health Service in 1979, a change justified on the grounds of equity (either in terms of distribution of the burden of payments or in the provision of care). The policy orientations taken in the 1990s have sought to increase efficiency (with potentially negative effects for equity) and involve higher direct payments (a flat rate co-payment for health care), the creation of an alternative health insurance system (which benefits the better-off), and increasing public and private competition in services provision. The price will be increasing inequality in access to health care and social exclusion for the more vulnerable groups (Pereira and Pinto 1993).

As for employment and vocational training, following the Social Agreement on the Policy of Vocational Training in 1991, a more active participation on the part of the social partners and NGOs has been encouraged so as to improve the co-ordination of policies and institutions. Since 1990, vocational training policy has been an important component of social policy, addressed in particular to the initial training needs of young people and other groups experiencing most difficulty in finding employment. There is some evidence of a convergence between education policy and the objectives of vocational training policy. Since the reform of the educational system in 1986, policy has been concerned with combating social exclusion in education. The increase in the school-leaving age from nine to fifteen years was accompanied by a reform of the curriculum and new educational programmes which aim to prepare students for employment, including the creation of vocational training as a special education module.

As for social security policy, measures have been taken to improve the co-ordination of existing schemes and to provide incentives for alternative (private) social security protection. Despite annual above-inflation-rate increases in pensions in the recent years, their low level continues to creates serious economic difficulties for those reliant on them as their main source of income. Social action is available as a last resort for households in economic need, but financial constraints, and its discretionary character, reduces its effectiveness. In 1993, 230,000[9] people resorted to state social services, 28 per cent of these for the first time. 20 per cent of single people and 50 per cent of families seeking social assistance were in financial need: 62 per cent had a per capita income below 30 per cent of the national minimum wage.

As far as social services are concerned, the creation of a General

Directorate of Social Action (in 1991) revealed a political willingness to improve the co-ordination of public services with private institutions (NGOs[10]). A tendency for a greater decentralization of social services, through the creation of local services, corresponds to the need of increasing effectiveness in dealing with the problems of the most vulnerable groups at the local level.

However, there are still serious limits to the capacity of state institutions and policies to meet all social needs. An important step was taken in July 1996 with the decision to create a National Minimum Income. This is a means-tested benefit from the non-contributory social security scheme and includes a programme of social insertion, 'to assure resources to individuals and families that guarantee the satisfaction of the minimum vital needs and facilitate a progressive social and professional insertion' (art. 1). The per adult-equivalent threshold below which the entitlement is granted is the amount of social pension. Presently under a one-year experimental process of implementation, it is co-ordinated by a central Minimum Income Commission and various Local Commissions, involving the participation of municipalities, several government departments (social security, health, employment and social action), as well as NGOs in the design of social and professional integration measures.

Some (more effective) co-ordination is evident in the creation of programmes to address multiple disadvantages of the most vulnerable groups, such as the design and implementation of multidimensional programmes to combat poverty. Some of them have been launched by the EC in the context of the EC Poverty 3 Action Programme, and others – which are country-wide and financed by the state – are co-ordinated by two Regional Commissariats (one for the north and the other for the south), involving some 90 projects running for a period (on average) of from two to five years. Such projects involve as partners the central administration, municipalities, NGOs and other private bodies at the local level as a basic feature of their design and implementation. But, as the problem of poverty in Portugal is determined by structural factors which are rooted in the country's model of economic development (and which remain a powerful impediment to the eradication of poverty in the short term), these projects cannot provide a panacea.[11]

There are also institutional obstacles. The state still remains highly centralized in Portugal, and intermediate decision-making levels, between the central and local administrations (municipalities) are still absent, often creating difficulties of co-ordination with other social actors,[12] although the recent tendency to decentralize responsibilities to lower administrative levels of administration may help. But it is sometimes difficult to distinguish decentralization from the shedding of responsibility for social problems by the central government. The dependence of the NGOs on the state – especially for financial resources – also raises doubts about the actual effectiveness of the increased intervention they are called on to make in many areas of social policy. In recognizing the guarantee of minimum resources to households as a right of citizenship, the National Minimum Income is an important step towards poverty alleviation in Portugal. But, as a historically rooted phenomenon, poverty in Portugal is being aggravated by new mechanisms of impoverishment and combating it effectively requires greater political commitment, an improved co-ordination of social policies and innovation in economic policy.

NOTES

1. Presently 80 per cent of farmers work part-time, and 47.5 per cent allocate 50 per cent or less of their working time to agriculture (MPAT 1993).
2. In their survey of the poor, Costa et al. (1985) revealed that most land owners interviewed cultivated their own land, alone or with the participation of their relatives, and only 11 per cent rented part of their land (mostly aged people). But 35 per cent of land owners also cultivate land as tenant farmers, an indication that income from their own farms is insufficient for their needs. A large proportion (64 per cent) of production is for self-consumption.
3. According to Lopes (1996: 262), subsidies to agriculture rose from 6 per cent of agriculture value added in 1985 to 36 per cent in 1993, but, overall, agricultural value added declined by about 40 per cent.
4. The 'social type enterprise' still predominates and most Portuguese farms, north of the Tagus River, are of this type, being very small (representing about 75 per cent of total farms but only 13 per cent of total cultivated area), using very intensive and traditional methods of cultivation and suffering from low productivity (Avillez 1993). Poverty in the agriculture population corresponds mainly to this type of agriculture.
5. According to Avillez (1993), agricultural incomes declined in the period 1985–89: the cash value added per unit of labour at real prices declined by about 9 per cent and the cash income of family labour per family unit of labour/year at real prices declined by 16 per cent, although the decline was nearly three times greater in smaller farms than in larger ones. Lopes (1996: 261–2) estimates that agricultural prices fell in real terms by 40 per cent between 1985 and 1993.
6. Before this year, the Portuguese unemployment protection scheme, created in 1977, was not included in the social security regime, and was predominantly a social assistance scheme, since it was not related to the worker's income or his/her contributory record but was dependent on the economic situation of the unemployed.
7. The daily amount is determined as a percentage (65 per cent) of the unemployed average wage earned during the first 12 months of the previous period of 14 months (the minimum being the minimum wage and the maximum 3 times this minimum wage), and the duration is a function of the age of the unemployed (from a minimum of 10 months for those under 24, up to a maximum of 30 months for those over 55).
8. On condition that the per capita income of the unemployed's household is less than 80 per cent of the minimum wage, the amount is dependent on household size (a maximum of 100 per cent of the minimum wage for households with 4 persons or

more, and a minimum of 70 per cent for single people) and the duration is the same as the insurance unemployment benefit, or half if it is attributed continuously.
9. This corresponds to about 2 per cent of the Portuguese population. However, this figure should not be interpreted as the number of persons but rather the number of 'cases'.
10. By NGO we mean 'private non-profit institutions of social solidarity, created on the initiative of particular persons, with the aim of giving expression to the moral duty of solidarity and justice among the individuals, not under the administration of the state or any municipality, intending to pursue, among others, the provision of goods and services [to the population] (...)' (Dec.-Law 119/83), e.g. voluntary social solidarity associations, social action volunteer associations, mutual benefit associations, social solidarity foundations and 'irmandades da Misericórdia' (a traditional form of Christian charity dating from the end of the fifteenth century).
11. The experience of such projects may be of great relevance for the implementation of the National Minimum Income, since the successful design and implementation of programmes of social and professional integration very much depend on the forms of partnerships which can be arranged among the various local social actors.
12. Regionalization has only recently become a matter of political debate in Portugal, since it is backed by the present socialist government (in office since October 1995), but was opposed by its social-democratic predecessor.

REFERENCES

Avillez, F. (1993): 'Portuguese Agriculture and the Common Agricultural Policy', in J. Lopes (ed.), *Portugal and EC Membership Evaluated*, London: Pinter.
Barreto, A. (ed.) (1996): *A situação social em Portugal, 1960–1995*, Lisbon: ICS.
Beckerman, W. (1979): *Poverty and the Impact of Income Maintenance Programmes*, Geneva: ILO.
Cantillon, B. *et al.* (1994): 'European Community Household Panel. National Research Unit – Belgium', in R. Muffels *et al.* (eds), *A Pilot-Study for the Creation of a Monitoring System of European Social Policies*, Tilburg, Netherlands: TISSER.
Castles, F. and D. Mitchell (1990): 'Three Worlds of Welfare Capitalism or Four?', discussion paper No.21, Australian National University.
Costa, A. B., M. Silva, J. Pereirinha and M. Matos (1985): *A Pobreza em Portugal*, Caritas.
Costa, A.B. (1994): 'The Measurement of Poverty in Portugal', *Journal of European Social Policy* 4/2, pp.95–115.
Deleeck, H. *et al.* (1992): *Poverty and the Adequacy of Social Security in the EC*, Avebury.
Dirven, H.-J. *et al.* (1994): 'Social Security, Private Insurance and Pensions: Results from the First Pilot Wave of the European Community Household Panel', in R. Muffels *et al.* (eds), *A Pilot-Study for the Creation of a Monitoring System of European Social Policies*, Tilburg, Netherlands: TISSER.
Esping-Andersen, G. (1990): *The Three Worlds of Welfare Capitalism*, Cambridge: Polity.
Evers, A. (1990): 'Shifts in the Welfare Mix: Introducing a New Approach for the Study of Transformations in Welfare and Social Policy', in A. Evers and H. Wintersberger (eds), *Shifts in the Welfare Mix: The Impact on Work, Social Services and Welfare Policies*, Boulder, CO: Campus/Westview.
Ferreira, L.V. (1993): *Pobreza em Portugal – variação e decomposição de medidas de pobreza a partir de Orçamentos Familiares de 1980/81 e 1989/90*, CISEP.
Hausman, P. (1993): 'The Impact of Social Security in the European Community', in J. Berghman and B. Cantillon (eds), *The European Face of Social Security*, Avebury, pp.109–21.
ISSAS (1990): *La pauvreté en chiffres: l'Europe au debut des années 80*. Brussels: Eurostat.
Leibfried, S. (1992): 'Towards a European Welfare State? On Integrating Poverty Regimes into the European Community', in Z. Ferge and J. Kolberg (eds), *Social Policy in a*

Changing Europe, Boulder, CO: Campus/Westview.

Lopes, J.S. (1996): 'A economia portuguesa desde 1960', in A. Barreto (ed.), *A situação social em Portugal, 1960–1995*, Lisbon: ICS.

Mendes, A. and L. Castro Rego (1992): *Perfil do desemprego de longa duração em Portugal, 1991*, Lisbon: DSEEMT, IEFP.

MPAT (1993): *Preparar Portugal para o século XXI: Análise Económica e Social*, Ministério do Planeamento e Administração do Território.

MSSS (1996): *Segurança Social. Evolução recente: 1992 a 1995*, Ministérior da Solidariedade e Segurança Social.

O'Higgins, J. and S. Jenkins (1989): 'Poverty in Europe: Estimates for 1975, 1980 and 1985', paper presented at *Seminar on Poverty Statistics in the European Community*, Noordwijk, 4–6 Oct.

Österle, A. (1996): *Payment for Care and Equity*, Bath: CRESEP.

Pereira, J. and C.G. Pinto (1993): 'Equity in the Finance and Delivery of Health Care in Portugal', in E. Van Doorslaen, A. Wagstaff and F. Rutten (eds), *Equity in the Finance and Delivery of Health Care*, OUP.

Pereirinha, J. (1988): 'Inequalities, Household Income Distribution and Development In Portugal', Ph.D. dissertation, ISS, The Hague, Netherlands.

Ramprakash, D. (1994): 'Poverty in the Countries of the European Union: a Synthesis of EUROSTAT´s Statistical Research on Poverty', *Journal of European Social Policy* 4/2, pp.117–28.

Schulte, B. (1993): 'Minimum Income Policy in Europe', in J. Berghman and B. Cantillon (eds), *The European Face of Social Security*, Avebury, pp.311–20.

Silva, M. (1984): 'Uma estimativa da pobreza em Portugal, em Abril de 1974', *Revista de Ciências Sociais* 1 (June).

Smeeding, T.M., M. O'Higgins and L. Rainwater (eds) (1990): *Poverty, Inequality and Income Distribution in Comparative Perspective: The Luxembourg Income Study (LIS)*, NY: Harvester Wheatsheaf.

Taylor-Gooby, P. (1991): 'Welfare State Regimes and Welfare Citizenship', *Journal of European Social Policy* 1/2, pp.93–105.

Wintersberger, H. (1993): 'The Welfare Mix: Searching for a New Balance between the Public and the Private Sectors', proceedings of the workshop 'Decentralisation and Gearing the Various Policy Levels to the Private/Public Divide', Bordeaux, 8–10 Oct.

The Transformation of the Portuguese Social Security System

PIERRE GUIBENTIF

The series of ruptures which characterize the recent political history of Portugal has profoundly marked the development of social security in this country, both on the concrete level of administrative structures and benefit schemes, and on the level of the discourse describing and interpreting the existing system. This article summarizes these developments and assesses their consequences for contemporary social security policies.

Recent Portuguese history is notable for three major events: the revolution of 5 October 1910, which brought an end to the monarchy and, for the first time in the country's history, ushered in a republican regime; the *coup d'état* of 28 May 1926, which established a military dictatorship and was replaced, a few years later, by Salazar's '*Estado Novo*'; and the revolution of 25 April 1974, after which present-day political structures were drawn up. Like all other institutions in Portugal, social security has been profoundly marked by these events. Not only have they driven some of the main transformations that have taken place in what might broadly be termed 'social administration', but they have also made it more difficult to identify some of the changes and continuities that have not been affected by these important political developments.

For this reason it is not easy for a contemporary observer to understand how the Portuguese social security system is structured.[1] Yet such an understanding is needed, for two main reasons. First, because it is likely to foster favourable conditions for growing co-operation between Portugal and other states, mainly within the EU; and second, because the system is currently experiencing an administrative and financial crisis which demands a profound process of adjustment. The absence of systematic, pluralistic and publicly available information is one of the major problems to be overcome if such reforms are to be made. Priority has to be given to reconstructing the internal dynamics that underpin the current system. This is the purpose of the first section of this article which outlines the main stages of Portuguese social security's history, taking account not only of broad political transformations, but also of the less visible dynamics at work within the narrower field of social administration. At the same time, it is important to compare the evolution of the Portuguese system with the experience of other countries, thus making the Portuguese experience understandable to foreign observers and revealing the relationship between internal and external factors in conditioning Portuguese developments.

THE SIX PHASES OF PORTUGUESE SOCIAL SECURITY

The First Republic

When the Republic was proclaimed in 1910, the role of the Portuguese state in social affairs was a modest one. Establishments belonging to the state mainly consisted of orphanages and hospitals that had been set up during the nineteenth century (Fonseca 1965; Neto 1971).[2] The state also had the task of supervising the activities of private charitable and mutual organizations; these were either institutions belonging to the Catholic Church, which were mainly *misericórdias*, or mutual aid associations. The former came under the responsibility of the Directorate-General of Health and Public Charity and a Higher Council of Public Welfare (Fonseca 1965) and the latter under the Regional Mutuality Councils (Lima 1909:261ff.).

Reform of these structures in the years following the revolution was gradual. In 1911, the notion of 'public charity' (*beneficiência pública*) ceased to be used in the names of public bodies, and was replaced by that of 'public assistance' (*assistência pública*). The latter concept also figured in the new constitution, which was promulgated in the same year and 'recognized the right to public assistance' (Article 3, Section 29). This was the only reference in the constitution to social affairs, as there was no reference either to social insurance or to social welfare.[3] As for state structures, a new Directorate-General of Labour and Social Welfare was set up in 1912, and in 1916 Portugal had its first Ministry of Labour.

Attempts to introduce a major innovation were made in 1919. This consisted of a system of compulsory social insurance covering sickness, workplace accidents, and invalidity, old age and survivors' pensions (Decrees No. 5636–5640 of 10 May 1919). The task of implementing this system was given to a new Institute of Compulsory Social Insurance and General Social Welfare *(Instituto de Seguros Sociais Obrigatórios e de Previdência Geral – ISSOPG)*; the Institute was also made responsible for co-ordinating public bodies and overseeing private organizations working in the field of assistance.

There was an element of electioneering about the 1919 law as Augusto Dias da Silva, the socialist Minister of Labour who introduced the legislation, stood in the legislative elections immediately after he had presented the draft to the Council of Ministers. However, there were also other relevant factors. First, international factors: German and British legislation made a profound impression on Portuguese specialists and the reform appeared to have been based on an idea circulating in Portuguese government circles that the introduction of a social insurance system was a condition of Portugal's admittance to the League of Nations (Leal 1984: 67). On the domestic level, the legislation's intellectual genealogy was probably derived from José Francisco Grilo, who was the author of a work on agricultural mutuality. Grilo knew very well the literature available at this time on Portuguese and comparative law governing mutuality and social insurance, a literature which had recently been supplemented by the addition of a number of works inspired by Germany's 'armchair socialists' whose ideas were spread to Portugal particularly by Professor Marnoco e Sousa.[4]

Apart from government and academic agencies, it would appear that no significant role can be attributed to social actors, such as workers' and employers' organizations and mutual insurance companies, in drafting the 1919 laws (Cruz 1934:34 ff; Leal 1984: 67). It is likely that this weak social foundation largely explains why early implementation of the system was so limited, consisting mainly of setting up the above mentioned ISSOPG, which carried out an overseeing role and produced studies over a period of many years.[5]

The Estado Novo

The *Estado Novo* ('New State') was the product of a gradual evolution. The final years of the Republic were marked by growing political and social instability, and a military dictatorship was installed in 1926. In the 'situation' (to quote the phraseology used at the time) that was thus created, increasingly wide powers were handed over to António de Oliveira Salazar who benefited from both the prestige he enjoyed as Professor of Public Finance at the University of Coimbra and the support of conservative movements close to the Catholic Church, including *Centro Católico* and *Integralismo Lusitano* (Cruz 1980; 1982). Salazar was able to consolidate the regime in the longer term by ordering a plebiscite on a new constitution in March 1933.

Under the 1933 constitution, the 'right to public assistance' disappeared, and was replaced by two provisions: first, the state regulated the activity of 'corporations, associations and [workers] organizations', particularly those with objectives concerned with assistance and charity (Article 15); second, the state was to 'promote and support institutions of solidarity, welfare, co-operation and mutuality' (Article 41). The *Estado Novo*'s main principles in respect of social issues were articulated more clearly in September of the same year with the promulgation of a National Labour Statute that had been inspired by the Italian 'Labour Charter' (*Carta del lavoro*). According to Article 48 of the statute, 'The organization of labour shall include, to be progressively incorporated as circumstances allow, welfare funds and institutions that seek to protect workers in the event of sickness, invalidity and involuntary unemployment, and guarantee them retirement pensions'.

But the introduction of the *Estado Novo* had very little direct impact on the public assistance sector. Assistance had already been withdrawn from ISSOPG's field of competence in 1927, and handed over to a new Directorate-General of Assistance, which in turn came under the Ministry of the Interior. The *Estado Novo* retained the authoritarian characteristics of the military dictatorship, which had underpinned the closer relationship between providing assistance and maintaining social order. It was not in the field of assistance, but in that of work and *Previdência Social* (social welfare[6]) that the *Estado Novo* was distinctive from the military dictatorship, and, even more so with regard to the Republic. Significantly, this resulted from the setting up of an important *Sub-Secretariado de Estado das Corporações e Previdência Social*. It was important to stress the ineffectiveness of the measures that were attempted at the time of the Republic, and to contrast them with the virtues of the new social policy.

In this context, the *Estatuto do Trabalho Nacional* was supplemented by a series of decrees dealing with questions of *previdência social* (from then on the phrase 'social insurance' – *seguros sociais* – virtually disappeared from official parlance, where it did little more than describe in pejorative terms what was presented as one of the Republic's failures). As a result, ISSOPG was disbanded, and its competencies with regard to social benefits were transferred to a new National Institute of Labour and Social Welfare (*Instituto Nacional do Trabalho e da Previdência Social*), which took over many of the old ISSOPG's staff. The government also introduced the possibility of establishing *casas do povo* ('people's homes'), to be set up in rural communes to provide farm workers with modest social benefits.[7]

By the autumn of 1933, the regime's corporate and social character was largely dictated by considerations of political strategy. In the months immediately after becoming President of the Council of Ministers,

Salazar had to counter fierce pressure from the Portuguese National Syndicalist Movement, which formed part of the alliance of social forces which had brought him to power. This movement was directly inspired by fascism, and at the time enjoyed considerable appeal, particularly for young people. Promulgation of the National Labour Statute, which had clearly been copied from the Italian fascist Labour Charter, deprived the more radical National Syndicalists of one of their more powerful arguments and stirred up tensions that weakened this movement in the longer term (Pinto 1994: 234 ff).

Leaving strategic matters to one side, it is still important to acknowledge the importance that the 'social question' (Patriárca 1995) had for the newly elected regime. A comparison between its political programmes and earlier statements made by individuals identified with the Republican regime, before the *Estado Novo* was installed, is notable for the recurrence of one theme: the importance of the role that the state played between 'capital and labour' (See e.g. Grilo 1931: 13). At the time, the state–capital–labour triad seems to have been less an element of corporate ideology and more of a framework that transcended it and within which it was obliged to remain. In this respect, apart from its desire for social peace-making, the Portuguese political regime was more specifically characterized by its effective option in favour of 'capital'. This much was already clear from a comparative analysis of the National Labour Statute and the Italian *Carta del Lavoro* (Lucena 1976a: 179), and has been confirmed by detailed observation of the social measures adopted during the early years of the *Estado Novo* (Patriárca 1995: 647).

Later, the new National Assembly passed a Law on *Previdência Social* (Law No. 1884 of 16 March 1935). Under this legislation, the key measure was the creation of a series of *caixas sindicais de previdência* (trade union welfare funds); these were to be set up gradually as circumstances permitted, and were to be based on sectoral agreements between unions and employers' associations. Under this system, in contrast to the system of compulsory social insurance, the government demonstrated both its prudence (one should only set out to achieve what can be achieved) and its corporate preferences (the organic diversity of Portuguese society was thereby being taken into account).

The most important section of Law No. 1884 was a typology of social welfare institutions which was dominated by the legal category of *caixas sindicais de previdência social*, and also included the *casas do povo*, *casas dos pescadores* ('fishermen's homes'), so-called 'pension and welfare funds' (that is to say, company funds), mutual societies, and civil servants' protection institutions. This legal typology was to have long-lasting cognitive effects. Presented without critical comments – for obvious reasons, critical comments were rare in Salazar's time – it suggested the following: that the *caixas sindicais* (trade union funds) were the most important institutions; that all of the institutions set out in the typology would appear with Law No. 1884; and that they constituted a coherent whole. In practice, the *caixas sindicais* became important only many years after Law No. 1884 was passed, and the role of the unions was always limited. On the other hand, of the other institutions, mutual societies and company funds belonged to a tradition that went back to a time before Law No.1884, a tradition which is virtually unmentioned in literature published after 1935.[8] Moreover, Law No. 1884 did not result in any co-ordination between the various sectors that it sought to regulate – more specifically between the *previdência social* on the one hand and mutuality and social protection of civil servants on the other.

As for the institutions that already existed when Law No. 1884 came into force, there were some 30 retirement funds catering for approximately 75,000 individuals; there were also about 500 mutual aid associations with half a million members (Instituto Nacional de Estatística 1928 ff.). Given these figures, one may well ask why the *Estado Novo* did not use its position to make better use of the work of mutual societies. There would appear to be two reasons for this. First, mutuality had been required to play a role within the framework of the Republic's social insurance scheme; as we have seen, it was a matter of making a decisive break with this system. Second, from the outset, the *Estado Novo* endeavoured to minimize any kind of autonomous organization of action or discussion in civil society. It may not have been possible to envisage the total elimination of mutuality, but it certainly made sense not to contribute to its development and to limit its room for manoeuvre as far as possible. In fact, mutuality was going through a period of decline at this time (Guibentif 1985: 34) and, as far as Portugal was concerned, was forever reduced to playing a secondary role in the field of social protection.

A Discreet Renunciation of Corporatist Ideas

In the post-war period the structure of the *Previdência Social* underwent major reforms. These reforms went together with the adoption of a new framework legislation: Law No. 2115 of 18 June 1962. Just as Law No. 1884 stands somehow in the way of a satisfactory understanding of the origins of the Portuguese social state, so Law No. 2115 suggests a skewed view of later changes. Here again, this stems from the legislative method that had been adopted; it was, in fact, the same as that contained in Law No. 1884, in that it set out a typology of social welfare institutions.

The presentation of this typology, which was very close to that set out in the earlier legislation, aimed to reinforce the idea of continuity between the two laws. In a remarkable display of the priority given to the appearance of continuity, the term 'pension or welfare funds', which, when Law No. 1884 was in force, had been applied to funds that were not attached to corporate organization (that is to say, company funds), was maintained, but was now applied to funds designed to cover self-employed workers. Here, too, *caixas sindicais de previdência* appear to provide the system's main components, supporting the view that the scheme might continue to rely on the social partners. However, through a number of quite discreet provisions, Law No. 2115 legalized a major re-orientation that had in fact taken place years earlier. This change mainly involved the renunciation in practice of the corporate ideas that had originally underpinned the link established by law-makers between funds and trade unions. The Portuguese state was now intervening directly in the field of *previdência social*.

The change in the way the state intervened actually began during the Second World War. In 1940, in the absence of any initiative on the part of the social partners (Samouco 1993: 392), the government granted itself powers to set up new *caixas de previdência* (welfare funds) and, in 1943, further powers to extend the arena of existing *caixas de previdência* to new categories of beneficiaries. These changes produced numerous new funds, together with a steep rise in the number of members receiving benefits. For several decades, the *caixas* were the scheme's basic components. Owing to their multiplicity and diversity, the development of *previdência social* in Portugal during the years that followed is not easy to characterize. I will confine my remarks to a brief description.[9]

As mentioned above, there were already some 30 company funds in existence in 1935. They were based either in Lisbon or in Oporto, and mainly covered employees in banks, railway companies and government departments such as the dockyards, customs and the post office. Funds covering an entire professional sector were unusual, but there were a few, including those for doctors and the tobacco industry. After Law No. 1884 came into force, a number of sectoral *caixas sindicais* were set up, usually to cover no more than half of the country – the north or the south – according to whether they were based in Lisbon or in Oporto. It was in this context that two 'marketing and exporting of wine' funds were established in 1936, and two 'hotel industry staff' funds were set up, first in Lisbon (1938) and then in Oporto (1940). Two nation-wide sectoral funds were also founded in 1938 and 1939 covering employees in insurance and the rice industry. Lastly, seven company funds were created between 1938 and 1940, three of which had their head offices outside Lisbon and Oporto.

Most sectoral funds – about twenty altogether – were established between 1940 and 1948, and it was during this period that the two biggest funds (in terms of the number of beneficiaries – approximately 100,000 members each in 1950) came into being: the retail sector fund (1940) and the textile industry fund (1946). Most funds covered the whole country, although some were confined to a region; for example, Lisbon for the tailors' scheme, Madeira for the embroidery industry and Oporto for jewellers. At the same time, some twenty new company funds were started up, half of them based outside Lisbon. This development demonstrated a measure of interest on the part of employers in the company fund system (see Almeida 1993: 173). In 1947, for the first time funds were established covering whole districts, in Funchal (Madeira), Braga and Santarém.

Throughout this period when social benefit funds were undergoing considerable expansion, the government also decided to establish a series of family benefit funds. Some of them were based on existing benefit funds and were soon incorporated into them; the rest were set up in various districts as part of an initial effort to cover the whole country systematically.

This was, therefore, a heterogeneous scheme, consisting of sectoral funds (operating on a national or regional level), company funds, district funds and family benefit funds. An additional factor of complexity related to the range of benefits available; these varied from fund to fund, as each had different rules. Moreover, the scheme had a number of drawbacks. Here, I shall refer only to the unsatisfactory geographical distribution of funds, and serious problems relating to fund management; funds soon accumulated considerable sums of money because the 1935 legislation provided for a system of pure capitalization.

In the years that followed, the Portuguese administration concentrated its efforts on rationalization. Chronologically, one may distinguish five measures.

- In 1946 considerable efforts were made to centralize the performance of some of the funds' tasks. To ensure that the system's basic principles went unchallenged, this centralization took place not so much through the setting up of services of the central public administration, as through the establishment of 'social benefit fund federations'. These bodies were financed by the funds, which, to their own advantage, carried out certain tasks such as the provision of medical care, performed by a Health and Social Services Federation;

the construction of community housing and the printing of forms and information materials. At the same time, central state services were strengthened, a development which was marked in 1950 by the transformation of the Under-Secretary of State into a Ministry of Corporations and *Previdência Social*. This strengthening of central agencies continued for a number of years, and gave rise to the creation of a National Pensions Fund, an event that will be discussed below. Other innovations were a Central Social Security Fund for Migrant Workers (*Caixa Central de Segurança Social de Trabalhadores Migrantes*) and the National Workplace Sickness Insurance Fund (*Caixa Nacional de Seguros de Doenças Profissionais*), both of which were set up in 1965.

- In 1950, an attempt was made to harmonize fund rules. This initially took the form of drawing up model rules, whose influence was such that the schemes applied by the various funds were almost uniform throughout the 1950s (Leal 1966–67: 128). Law No. 2115 of 1962 allowed for the drafting of a regulation that was irrevocably applied to all institutions that agreed to be covered by the new legislation (Comissão de Reforma 1964; Correia 1968). This regulation was referred to as the *Regime Geral* (General Scheme), a phrase that was to become commonplace.

- In the early 1960s, the government achieved nation-wide cover by setting up district funds in those districts where they did not yet exist. For the most part, they were housed in premises that had previously been occupied by the district family benefit funds. Following a process that survived into the 1980s, these district funds took into membership most beneficiaries of *previdência social* – later *segurança social* (social security) – while the majority of the former sectoral and company funds were gradually run down. Article 13 of Law No. 2115 of 1962 ratified the district fund system, in a very circumspect manner, simply by turning the *caixas distritais* into a subcategory of the *caixas sindicais de previdência social*.

- The most important change took place in the context of Law No. 2115, and concerned the management of benefits. Until then, each fund had managed all the benefits that were available to members. The new *Regime Geral* was based on a division of labour between district funds, which were responsible for short-term benefits (sickness, maternity and family benefits), and a new National Pensions Fund, which had been set up in 1965 and dealt with long-term benefits (old age, and invalidity and survivors' pensions). This reform, which was accompanied by a change from a pure capitalization system to a mix of capitalization and pay-as-you-go system, was designed to facilitate fund management.

• Lastly, the link between the sector of the *previdência social* and the health and assistance sectors was increasingly perceived as a problem. It should be remembered that, even before the *Estado Novo* was established, the assistance sector had been transferred to the Ministry of the Interior. This system was abandoned in 1958 with the creation of a Ministry of Health and Assistance specifically charged with the task of overseeing hospitals and a number of institutes that had been set up in the 1940s and that were involved in assistance to groups such as families, minors and tuberculosis sufferers. Co-ordination was in need, especially in the field of health, because *caixas sindicais de previdência* were involved in this field, through their 'health and social services' (*serviços médico-sociais*), but also in other fields of social policy such as family policy. That was why Salazar's successor, Marcello Caetano, handed the two briefs (Corporations and *Previdência social*, and Health and Assistance) to one man, Baltazar Rebello de Sousa. Only a few months before the 1974 revolution, assistance was taken away from the ministry now known as the Ministry of Health and passed to a new Ministry of Corporations and Social Security.

These reforms – the establishment of district structures, the strengthening of central agencies, the generalization of uniform regulations and a link between the *previdência social*, assistance and health sectors – have remained unrevised to the present day. However, the long-term dynamic was seriously disrupted during the 1970s, first by measures adopted under Marcello Caetano, and subsequently by the changes associated with the revolution of April 1974.

Caetano's Estado Social

Both *previdência social* and health underwent major reforms between 1969 and 1973 throughout the period of Marcello Caetano's government. Caetano had hoped to save the political regime, now dangerously threatened by colonial wars and international isolation, by reassessing its social orientation.

With regard to *previdência social*, Caetano's reforms (Lucena 1976a, b) were less concerned with structures than with benefits. Various benefits in the *Regime Geral* were improved and made more accessible and new branches were introduced or brought on stream (survivors pensions; protection against professional diseases); protection for rural workers, which was administered by the *casas do povo*, was also slightly improved. Moreover, several new special schemes were set up, designed to protect people in certain jobs, such as servants (Carreira 1996: 74), news vendors and lottery ticket sellers; they were administered by institutions already involved with the *Regime Geral* (Guibentif 1995: 171 ff).

As for health and assistance, reforms in this period were mainly structural. The Ministry of Health and Assistance was re-organized (Leal 1985b: 929), the various assistance institutes were merged into a single Family and Social Action Institute comprising district-level delegations, and new health centres were set up in middle-sized towns (Castanheira 1984).

The Revolution of 1974 and the Consequences

The main cause of the 1974 revolution was the colonial war. The army officers who overturned the regime inherited from Salazar had one primary objective: to put an end to a military venture to which there was no solution. Their action initially received enthusiastic support from a large section of the population, partly because it opened the way to democratizing the country, and partly because the social situation had deteriorated during the years immediately preceding the revolution and many hoped that political change would mean an improvement in their material conditions. Therefore, in the expectation that a new constitution would be adopted, the provisional governments which ruled the country after the revolution had to introduce numerous measures in the field of social affairs, in order to guarantee their legitimacy (Mozzicafreddo 1992: 71). These measures included an assistance system for the unemployed, and a means-tested social pension, which was paid out by Family and Social Action Institute offices.[10] The organizational measures are also relevant to our subject. The two most important were:

• the dismantling of those administrative structures most closely identified with the fallen regime. In effect, this meant everything linked to corporate organization (Leal 1979). As a result, the Ministry of Corporations and Social Security disappeared and was replaced by a new Ministry of Labour. However, the new ministry did not include the social security brief. This was incorporated into a new Ministry of Social Affairs which also covered Health. Another body to be disbanded was the *Instituto Nacional do Trabalho e da Previdência social*, a key element in the corporate social benefit structure.

• the provision of medical care was a particularly sensitive issue at the time and, as I have already pointed out, shortly before the revolution it had led to the setting up of new health centres. The revolution was an opportunity to broaden an idea that had already been under discussion for some time: the creation of a National Health Service (*Serviço Nacional de Saúde*) that would bring together all health institutions and guarantee free care to the entire population. Two measures in particular were adopted: first, the 'social and health services' (*serviços médico-sociais*) of the *caixas de previdência* were separated from the funds themselves and were handed over to regional health administrations; and, second, hospitals belonging to the *misericórdias* were nationalized.

In addition to measures taken by provisional governments, the revolution naturally led to a major change in constitutional law in the field of social questions. The new constitution, which came into force in 1976, contained an important chapter devoted to 'Economic, social and cultural rights and duties'. The first two articles of this chapter are devoted to social security and health; they state that 'all are entitled to social security' (Article 63) and that 'all are entitled to health protection and have a duty to defend and promote it' (Article 64). In each case, the constitution indicates the organizational means for implementation – both charging the state with 'organizing, co-ordinating and subsidizing a unified and decentralized social security system', and providing for the setting up of a 'universal, free national health service'.

In 1977 the realization of a concept of 'unified and decentralized social security' led to a number of changes at the level of both districts and central agencies. The district structures were put to good use through the setting up of new regional social security centres, thereby bringing the old district funds and Family and Social Action Institute delegations together into one body. Central structures were also strengthened, mainly through the establishment of a new Directorate-General of Social Security, which supervised both the sector that had previously handled assistance and the sector responsible for *previdência social*, and by setting up an Institute for the Financial Management of Social Security. Various other bodies also underwent changes. For example, a new National Pensions Centre absorbed the National Pensions Fund, and the former *Caixa Central de Segurança Social dos Trabalhadores Migrantes* was replaced by a Department of International Relations and Social Security Agreements.[11]

These organizational reforms were supposed to mark a break between the old ideas of assistance and *previdência social* and a new integrated concept of social security. However, the official desire to highlight this change had two consequences. The first was that the continuity existing between many of the measures of the 1960s and those adopted in 1978 (strengthening district and central structures, linking *previdência social* and assistance) was ignored. The second was that this voluntarist reform led commentators to overlook elements that had not been integrated into the new system. These consisted of a series of sectoral and company funds, for which provision had already been made prior to the revolution for their integration into the *Regime Geral* and many of which survived into the 1980s.

As for health, the organization of the National Health Service was set out in Law No 56/79 of 21 July 1979. However, the implementation of this law fell far short of what had initially been intended. It is true that access to care was now better than when access to certain services – the social and health services run by funds and reimbursement for care provided by other services (hospitals) – was restricted to members of social benefit funds. However, the link between the various components of the 'system', in particular between hospitals and Regional Health Administrations, remained problematic. Over a period of time, as successive constitutional reforms took place, the principle of free health care was diluted into one of 'almost free health care'. The constitutional right to health care provided by the state remains a far cry from reality. In fact, to a considerable extent, the quantity and quality of service resources encourage users to turn to private medicine, which continues to develop in parallel with the public service, although treatment received in the private sector is reimbursed to only a very limited extent (Leal 1985: 940; Campos 1991).

Recent Developments

When the institutions of the Second Republic were established, what came to be known as social security corresponded at the time to certain rights that were duly recognized by the constitution, and to administrative structures that had been modernized in a number of ways. However, apart from some innovations – protection against unemployment, a non-contributory scheme, and generalized access for the whole population to medical care[12] – the reforms had a limited impact on the basic provisions. The *Regime Geral* remained the same. Numerous other schemes still existed, some of them administered by funds that had survived from the period before the *Regime Geral* was introduced, others administered by regional social security centres and the National Pensions Centre. Part of these 'special schemes' were dismantled during the 1980s and early 1990s and their beneficiaries integrated in the *Regime Geral*. A lot of them survived, conferring on the

Portuguese social security system the trait of fragmentation which has been considered a typical feature of southern European welfare states (e.g. Fererra 1996).[13] The social protection of civil servants continued to function according to quite different rules.[14]

The drafting of a new framework law was became necessary after the new constitution came into force in 1976. However, this new law was adopted by Parliament only eight years later (Law No. 28/84 of 14 August 1984), and its significance remained limited since no implementing regulation could be drawn up in the immediate aftermath of the vote. It was not until the late 1980s that the various branches of the *Regime Geral* were reviewed, and most of the regulations for applying Law No. 2115 of 1962 remained in force until then (Ferreira 1989; Neves 1993). As a result, the 1980s were a period of stabilization after the successive upheavals of the Caetano government and the revolution. We might even talk of a period of torpor compared with the dynamic process of reform that had characterized the 1960s. Three explanations may be advanced for this:

- the first is unquestionably financial. Portuguese social security had to deal with commitments inherited from the earlier period of great expansion, and this coincided with the government's attempts to put its public finances in order and the appearance of a more general fiscal crisis of welfare in western Europe;

- the second relates to Portugal's membership of the European Community, which commenced on 1 January 1986. Many post-revolutionary measures aimed to bring the Portuguese system closer to those of other European countries, at least from the point of view of technical development, even if the level of benefits was felt to be unsatisfactory (da Costa and Maia 1985; Cardigos and Pizarro 1994). Once this objective was attained, membership of the Community contributed to keeping the system as it was to a certain extent. In fact, one immediate consequence of membership consisted of important measures in a related field – that of vocational training – which now attracted considerable attention from both government and public opinion, and the means for putting innovative ideas into practice;

- the third involves political stability. From late 1985 to late 1995, the country was governed by the same centre-right party, the Social Democratic Party, and by the same prime minister. It is reasonable to suggest that the social security system, as it was when the Social Democrats won an absolute majority in Parliament, in many ways matched the line adopted by the government. Therefore, the government will only move carefully in making reforms and, it has to be said, will not encourage the dissemination of information that might stimulate the kind of discussion necessary for these reforms.[15]

But even during this recent period of stabilization, a number of reforms took place in both central and peripheral agencies. In Lisbon, the governmental structure has undergone significant changes in recent years. In 1983, the Ministry of Social Affairs disappeared; Health came under an independent ministry, while Social Security joined up with Labour in a ministry that was initially called the Ministry of Labour and Social Security and later the Ministry of Employment and Social Security. This system was almost identical to the one adopted towards the end of the Caetano government. Another less visible reform which might also be seen as a return to the pre-revolution system involved the division of the large Directorate-General of Social Security, which had been set up in the late 1970s, into two Directorates-General: 'Social Security Schemes' and 'Social Action'. In 1984 a Standing Council for Social Consultation (*Conselho Permanente de Concertação Social*) was established, but replaced by an Economic and Social Council after the second revision of the 1976 constitution in 1989. This had a considerable impact on the conditions in which social dialogue was conducted (Marques and Ferreira 1991). However, questions specifically relating to social security were not a priority in the Council's deliberations.

As for the peripheral agencies, it is important to note from the outset that it is only in the course of the last few years that beneficiaries of the old sectoral and company funds have been moved into the *Regime Geral* to any great extent. Similarly, in the late 1980s, administration of the agricultural workers' protection scheme was transferred from the *casas do povo* – in the main, these homes now organized cultural activities (Guibentif 1992: 41) – to regional social security centres.

Finally, the regional centres network was entirely re-organized in 1993, although curiously this did not give rise to any public debate. The eighteen regional social security centres that had been set up following the 1978 re-organization became subregional services, and came under five new regional social security centres, which corresponded to the five administrative areas into which Portugal is currently divided (Lisbon and the Tagus Valley, Centre, North, Alentejo, Algarve). In particular, this change involved the transfer of a number of tasks from district to regional level; the savings that this transfer promised to bring were said to be the main reason behind the change. Here, too, there was a wish to ensure 'terminological continuity': with the same name applied successively to two different things, discussion and careful consideration on the subject was unlikely to be promoted. It is also worth noting that, in a way, this reform implied a devaluation of the institutions that had provided a concrete link between Portuguese social security and recipients for about 30 years. The fact that it could happen without any significant reaction on the part of users perhaps confirms what is suggested by a number of other indicators, including the continuing use in everyday language of 'fund' and *previdência social* instead of the little-used 'social security': social security has a poor image among the Portuguese (Cabral 1995: 25ff), for it was a given fact, rather than something that had been achieved.

The Socialist Party's victory in the October 1995 elections has brought about significant changes in the field of social security. On the governmental level, the former ministry of employment and social security has been divided in two briefs: employment, on the one hand, and Solidarity and Social Security on the other. The latter ministry includes a Secretariat of State for Social Security and another for Social Integration.[16] Among the reforms which have been launched by the new government is the creation of a new minimal income benefit (*Rendimento mínimo garantido*) which has been, for the time being, implemented on an experimental basis, in some localities of the country. In order to prepare several structural reforms – including the development of a system of private pension funds – the government has set up a 'Committee for the White Paper on Social Security' which should present a global assessment of the existing system in the course of 1997, as a basis for a broad public debate.[17] The emergence of an effective discussion of social security matters certainly marks the beginning of a new stage in the history of the institution, but it is unclear exactly how this will evolve.

COMPARATIVE CONSIDERATIONS

The above discussion reveals strong affinities between the Portuguese social security system and the 'southern European model of welfare' (Ferrera 1996): fragmentation, poor effectiveness, and a universalistic National Health System mainly used by less privileged social groups, while the better off turn to the private health sector. A more detailed analysis of the outcome of the existing social security schemes, and particularly of the pensions schemes, would probably confirm that the 'dualism' referred to by Ferrera (a broad gap between a majority of poorly protected and a minority of highly protected persons) is also a trait of the Portuguese system. The strong role of the Church, an authoritative state, and a low level of industrialization all qualify Portugal for membership of the 'southern' club.

However, the Portuguese case is distinct in one particular respect: social security – as well as the earlier *previdência social* – has never been, until recently, an issue at the top of the political agenda, whereas, elsewhere in southern Europe, the Left in particular has played an important role. Since the 1930s, Portuguese governments have succeeded in running the system almost without any interference from civil society. The system could thus easily be exploited by clientelistic strategies.

Among the reasons for this is the existence of what Santos (1991) and Hespanha (1993) consider a strong 'welfare society' which has compensated for shortages of public social provision, thereby reducing the social pressure on the government. Another factor mentioned by Ferrera (1996) has certainly also had a strong impact: the weakness of bureaucratic and technical expertise in this field. As a social group, social policy professionals are not only needed for carrying out of policies, but also for supplying external social actors with relevant technical information, to support the formulation of political strategies – either directly, as participants in social movements, or indirectly, in providing analytical work accessible not just to insiders, but also to a broader audience (e.g., the role of a journal like *Droit social* in France). In Portugal, partly due to the dimensions of the country, partly to the development of its educational system, there have been very few specialists in social security matters. As long as some of them had some room for manoeuvre, the system indeed experienced significant reform (the late 1950s and 1960s). A paradox of the revolution of 1974 was that it deprived this group of specialists of their means for action, at a time when the reform of social protection had become a major issue.[18]

It is probably useful to add the following consideration to the explanation of the Portuguese case. The instrumentalization of *previdência social* and later social security was facilitated by the fact that these institutions were 'legal transplants', with the emulation of English and German models at the beginning of the century, the Italian model in the 1930s, the French model in the 1960s and the European model in the 1980s. Moreover, in Portugal the main actors involved in its inception – the unions and middle-sized and large enterprises – did not have the power to participate effectively in the management of the system, or in the definition of its future. This lack of input by the social partners in the past goes some way towards explaining the particular character within the southern group of countries of Portuguese social security.

236 SOUTHERN EUROPEAN WELFARE STATES

CONCLUSION

An analysis of Portugal's social security development reveals that information and discussion have been severely curtailed. If it is true that debate is urgently needed today, in order to define new priorities in resolving the crisis of the system, this debate must begin with an assessment of the current conditions of discussion, and a reflection on the ways of improving these conditions. At present it is questionable how far Portuguese social security specialists can contribute to the debate, or whether the social categories affected by policies have the means either of knowing or making known their needs and influencing the definition of policies.

NOTES

1. The article is focused specifically on the social security system. Apart from some comments on the health system, it is not my ambition to cover the Portuguese welfare state as a whole (see Mozzicafreddo 1992 or Santos 1991 for a broader approach). This is due to the scope of the research which provides the background of the article (Guibentif 1995), but also to the methodological assumption that the social security system, as a core element of the welfare state, has comparatively sharp borderlines, which provides a solid ground for the reconstruction of fields and actors, as well as constraints and strategies. Conclusions based on the observation of this domain may lead to useful hypotheses for considering other elements of the welfare state.
2. According to some authors, public assistance in Portugal begins with the creation of the *Casa Pia* in Lisbon in 1788. This establishment was designed for orphans and abandoned children. See Fonseca (1965).
3. Previous constitutions had guaranteed 'public aid' (*socorros públicos*).
4. For further information, see Guibentif (1986, n.13, 17, 27).
5. For details on the work of ISSOPG, see in particular the journal *Boletim de Previdência Social* (23 issues published between 1917 and 1933).
6. As a translation, *social welfare* is likely to embrace both a political aim and an administrative structure, more than concrete measures. This translation has, however, two flaws. First, it does not directly render the idea of 'foresight', which is explicit in *previdência* (as in the French *prévoyance* or German *Vorsorge*). Secondly, it could suggest a close relationship with the notion of *welfare state*. In fact, this association should be avoided, since the Salazarist Portuguese state did not correspond to what is usually designated as *welfare state*, and aimed to differentiate itself from the democratic *welfare states* existing elsewhere in Europe. Even the question of whether the contemporary Portuguese state may be qualified as a welfare state remains open, in the view of certain authors (e.g. Santos 1991: 33). Given these translation problems, I will use the Portuguese phrase.
7. Later on, as Fátima Patriarca (1995: 641) points out, the *casas do povo* were often inaccurately presented as an innovation of the *Estado Novo*. In fact, under a procedure also applied in other fields, the *Estado Novo* took advantage of a system that already existed, systematically erasing the antecedents. See also Barbosa (1930) and Guibentif (1985: 32) on the *casas do povo* prior to the *Estado Novo*.
8. For example, the report drawn up for the 1962 reform (*Reforma da Previdência* 1957) contains a chart of funds that existed in 1955, mentioning their year 'of constitution'. In many cases, as other sources make clear, this year does not correspond to the year

in which they were set up, but to the year in which statutes were ratified according to Law No. 1884 of 1935.
9. The following description is mainly based on a comparison between data supplied for the period under consideration by the Portugal Statistical Yearbook and those set out in *Reforma da Previdência* (1957). They were supplemented by an inventory of fund statutes deposited in the National Library of Portugal.
10. The *pensão social* was the first step towards a non-contributory scheme, which was introduced in 1979 (Guibentif 1995: 154).
11. These changes were carried out by the Government under Decree-Law No. 549/77 of 31 Dec. 1977, later amended by Parliament under a ratification procedure (Law No. 55/78 of 27 July 1978). See in particular Leal (1980), for critical comments on this reform, and Maia (1985), who played a relevant role in the drafting and implementation of Decree-Law No. 549/77.
12. Beyond protection against unemployment, a non-contributory scheme and generalized access for the whole population to medical care, which have been referred to above, it is worth mentioning attempts to implement a protection scheme designed for independent workers (Carreira 1996: 73).
13. For an overview of the existing schemes, see Guibentif (1995: 163 ff). According to figures recently discussed in Portugal, there are presently around 60 special schemes (statement presented at the last meeting of the *Forum Social*, a think-tank recently set up for promoting research and debate on matters of social protection) (*Público*, 10 Dec. 1996).
14. One attempt to harmonize the general scheme and the public servant scheme was the introduction of a common system of family benefits under Caetano (Leal 1983).
15. For example, there exists no academic journal on social security issues in Portugal, although the launching of such a publication was one of the objectives of the founding members of the Portuguese association of social security, created in 1985, a body which has worked in closely with the government since the late 1980s.
16. *Público*, 25 Oct. 1995, p.6.
17. There have been several public presentations of the new social security policy. See for instance interviews with the minister in *Já* (weekly newspaper), 16 May 1996, and *Diário de Notícias* (daily newspaper), 25 Nov. 1996, or his speech at the meeting 'Reformar a segurança social. Porquê e como', organized by the Committee for the White Paper on Social Security, 12 Sept. 1996.
18. See Leal (1979) for an analysis of this paradox from the inside.

REFERENCES

Almeida, Ana Nunes de (1993): *A Fábrica e a Família – Famílias Operárias no Barreiro*, Barreiro: Câmara Municipal.
Barbosa, Raul Tamagnini (1930): *Modalidades e Aspectos do Cooperativismo*, Porto: Imprensa Social – Secção da Casa do Povo Portuense.
Cabral, Manuel Villaverde (1995): 'Equidade social, "estado-providência" e sistema fiscal: atitudes e percepções da população portuguesa (1991–1994)', *Sociologia-Problemas e Práticas* 17, pp.9–34.
Campos, A. Correia de (1991): 'Estado-Providência. Perspectivas e financiamento. O caso da saúde', *Sociologia – Problemas e Práticas* 9, pp.9–26.
Cardigos, Sara, and Sebastião Nóbrega Pizarro (1994): *O sistema português de segurança social face às políticas de segurança social no quadro da comunidade europeia*, Lisbon: Ministério do Emprego e da Segurança Social.
Carreira, Henrique Medina (1996): *As Políticas Sociais em Portugal*, Lisbon: Gradiva.
Castanheira, José Luis (1984): 'Factores sócio-políticos determinantes do sistema de saúde português', *Desenvolvimento* 1, pp.67–85.
Comissão de Reforma da Previdência Social (1964): *Regulamento Geral das Caixas*

238			SOUTHERN EUROPEAN WELFARE STATES

Sindicais de Previdência – Memória justificativa e projecto, Lisbon: Serviços Mecanográficos – Federação de Caixas de Previdência.

Correia, Sérvulo (1968): *Teoria da relação jurídica de seguro social*, Lisbon: Centro de Estudos Sociais e Corporativos.

da Costa, Bruto, and Fernando Maia (1985): 'Segurança social em Portugal – Principais características e análise dos efeitos redistributivos', *Desenvolvimento 2*.

Cruz, Domingos da (1934): *A Mutualidade em Portugal*, Coimbra: Imprensa da Universidade.

Cruz, Manuel Braga da (1980): *As origens da democracia cristã e o salazarismo*, Lisbon: Presença.

Cruz, Manuel Braga da (1982): 'O Integralismo Lusitano nas Origens do Salazarismo', *Análise Social*, pp.137–82.

Ferreira, Coriolano (1989): 'A segurança social e a saúde na revisão constitucional', in (coll.), *Prática e revisão constitucional*, Lisbon: Instituto Dom João de Castro, pp.99–107.

Ferrera, Maurizio (1996): 'The "Southern Model" of Welfare in Social Europe', *Journal of European Social Policy* 6/1, pp.17–37.

Fonseca, Carlos Dinis da (1965): 'Assistência pública', in Henrique Martins Gomes and José Pedro Pereira Monteiro Fernandes (eds), *Dicionário Jurídico da Administração Pública*, Coimbra: Atlântida Editora, Vol.1, pp.553–7.

Grilo, José Francisco (1931): 'Legislação social em Portugal', *Boletim de Previdência Social* 21, pp.1–13.

Guibentif, Pierre (1985): 'Génese da Previdência Social. Elementos sobre as origens da Segurança Social portuguesa e as suas ligações com o corporativismo', *Ler História 5*, pp.27–58.

Guibentif, Pierre (1986): 'Avatars et dépassement du corporatisme – Le développement de la sécurité sociale au Portugal', in *Colloque sur l'histoire de la sécurité sociale*, Montpellier 1985, Paris: Association pour l'étude de l'histoire de la sécurité sociale, pp.207–33.

Guibentif, Pierre (1992): 'Die Entwicklung der sozialen Sicherheit in Portugal und der Beitritt zur EG – Verlauf und institutionelle Perspektiven', in Detlew Merten and Rainer Pitschas (eds), *Der Europäische Sozialstaat und seine Institutionen*, Berlin: Duncker und Humblot, pp.31–58.

Guibentif, Pierre (1995): *La pratique du droit international et communautaire de la sécurité sociale – étude de sociologie du droit à l'exemple du Portugal*, Genève (doctoral thesis).

Hespanha, Pedro (1993): *Vers une société-providence simultanément pré- et post-moderne*, Coimbra: Centro de Estudos Sociais.

Instituto Nacional de Estatística, *Anuário Estatístico Nacional*, Lisbon: Imprensa Nacional (annual issues).

Leal, António da Silva (1966-67): *Organização da Previdência*, Lisbon: Instituto de Ciências Sociais.

Leal, António da Silva (1979): 'Os grupos sociais e as organizações na Constituição de 1976 – A rotura com o corporativismo', in Jorge Miranda (ed.), *Estudos sobre a Constituição*, Vol. 3, Lisbon: Petrony, pp.195–353.

Leal, António da Silva (1980): 'Segurança Social', in *Verbo – Enciclopédia Luso-Brasileira de Cultura – Suplemento*, Lisbon: Verbo.

Leal, António da Silva (1983): 'Abono de família', in *Polis – Enciclopédia Verbo da Sociedade e do Estado*, Lisbon / São Paulo: Verbo, Vol.1, pp.1–13.

Leal, António da Silva (1984): *Temas de Segurança Social*, Vol. 1, Lisbon: Federação Portuguesa dos Centros de Cultura e Desporto da Saúde e Segurança Social.

Leal, António da Silva (1985): 'As políticas sociais no Portugal de hoje', *Análise Social* 87–89, pp.925–43.

Lima, José Lobo d'Avila (1909): *Socorros mutuos e seguros sociaes*, Coimbra: Imprensa da Universidade.

Lucena, Manuel de (1976a): *A Evolução do Sistema Corporativo Português – Vol. 1: O Salazarismo*, Lisbon: Perspectivas e Realidades.

Lucena, Manuel de (1976b): *A Evolução do Sistema Corporativo Português – Vol. 2: O Marcelismo*, Lisbon: Perspectivas e Realidades.

Maia, Fernando (1985): *Segurança Social em Portugal – Evolução e Tendências*, Lisbon: Instituto de Estudos para o Desenvolvimento.

Marques, Maria Manuel Leitão and António Casimiro Ferreira (1991): 'A concertação económica e social – A construção do diálogo social em Portugal', *Revista Crítica de Ciências Sociais* (Coimbra) 31, pp.11–41.

Mozzicafreddo, Juan (1992): 'O Estado-Providência em Portugal: Estratégias Contraditórias', *Sociologia -Problemas e Práticas* 12, pp.57–89.

Neto, Maria de Lourdes Akola Meira do Carmo (1971): 'Assistência Pública', in Joel Serrão (ed.), *Dicionário de História de Portugal*, Lisbon: Iniciativas Editoriais, Vol.1, pp.234–8.

Neves, Ilídio das (1993): *A Segurança Social Portuguesa. Problemas, Realidades e Perspectivas*, Lisbon: Instituto Superior Politécnico Internacional.

Patriárca, Fátima (1995): *A questão social no Salazarismo – 1930-1947*, Lisbon: Imprensa Nacional / Casa da Moeda, 2 Vols.

Pinto, António Costa (1994): *Os Camisas Azuis – Ideologia, Elites e Movimentos Fascistas em Portugal – 1914 – 1945*, Lisbon: Editorial Estampa.

Samouco, André (1993): 'O Estado-Providência e a sociedade rural. Revalorização de recuros e reordenamento de estratégias num novo contexto: a agricultura de pluriactividade', *Análise Social* 121, pp.391–408.

Santos, Boaventura de (1991): *State, Wage Relations and Social Welfare in the Semiperiphery: The Case of Portugal*, Coimbra: Centro de Estudos Sociais.

Reclaiming Welfare: The Politics of French Social Protection Reform

GIULIANO BONOLI and BRUNO PALIER

As the 1995 wave of strikes has powerfully shown, the French welfare state is currently the object of a political struggle between sections of the labour movement and the government. In this article, we look at the politics of the current transformation of the French social protection system. First, we describe the key features of welfare institutions; second, we look at the debate on the socio-economic problems that welfare is currently facing. Finally, we focus on how these issues appear in the political debate, through an analysis of interview data of influential political actors and a discussion of the 1995 Juppé plan, which provides the framework for future reforms. Our conclusion is that the current transformation process cannot be interpreted as simply a movement towards the restoration of financial equilibrium. Instead, it affects the very structure of the French model of welfare by promoting a shift from Bismarckian social insurance towards a non-employment based, state-controlled system.

Like most of its European counterparts, the French welfare state has undergone a phase of retrenchment and restructuring since the mid-1970s. This has largely been in response to a financial crisis which has taken the form of rising budget deficits produced by an increasing demand for welfare and declining rates of economic growth. While current debates on French social policy focus on this financial crisis, a crisis common to most advanced industrial countries, they equally reflect the view that the French model of social protection has become inadequate in the context of current changes in the labour market, particularly with regard to both youth and long-term unemployment. This thesis, which is widely supported in France (e.g. Rosanvallon 1995), argues that the contributory social insurance principle on which the

An earlier version of this article was presented at the British Social Policy Association Annual Conference in Sheffield, 18–21 July 1995, and benefited greatly from comments of conference participants. The interview data was collected for the project 'Squaring the Welfare Circle in Europe', directed by Vic George and Peter Taylor-Gooby, University of Kent, and financed by the ESRC.

French system is based has become outdated in the light of recent socio-economic change.

From a wider comparative perspective, the conservative-corporatist model, which can be found in most continental European countries, has also been criticized for its inability to create new jobs, since high levels of entitlement for workers and high levels of contributions have created a ring-fenced labour market to which 'the excluded' have little or no access. Because of its emphasis on contribution financing, contributory social insurance and high benefits for workers, the model is vigorously defended by those who are in employment or who are unwilling to trade some of their privileges to create more jobs for those excluded from the labour-market (Esping-Andersen 1990; 1996). In general, the fact that trade unions are powerful or at least have a significant mobilizing capacity is seen as an additional explanation for the 'frozen' status quo. The overall impression is that continental corporatist welfare states are finding it difficult to adapt to current socio-economic change.

This analysis is certainly convincing, in so far as it captures some general tendencies which are common to a number of continental welfare states. The French case, however, seems to be characterized by a larger potential for structural change (Taylor-Gooby 1996: 121). Both current debates and recent reforms indicate quite clearly that the changes in the French social protection system are not simply a matter of restoring the financial viability of the system, although this dimension does play a role. In fact, the most remarkable reforms adopted so far have sought to modify the institutional structure of the system. The overall direction of the change in France can be seen as a shift away from the Bismarckian corporatist model towards a generalized and uniform system of Beveridgean inspiration, especially in the field of health, family and 'insertion' policies.

Among the European welfare states, the southern ones have encountered the biggest structural changes during the last twenty years, changes which might ultimately mean that they transfer from one welfare regime to another, particularly in terms of the 'universalization' of health care (Ferrera 1996; MIRE 1997; Rico and Granaglia, this volume). While France is not usually considered part of southern Europe (Ferrera 1996), it seems to us that a comparison between France and the 'Latin rim' (Leibfried 1992) does help us to better understand French developments.

As in the southern countries, the structural reforms in France are a response to the perceived inadequacy of the French model given current socio-economic change. But they also have some important political implications regarding control over the social protection system. A more generalized and uniform system, which is tax-financed, also implies a bigger role for the state in the management and delivery of welfare. In 1945, French social reformers decided to devolve the management of social insurance to the 'social partners', but now the state wants it back. Naturally, profound transformations of this sort cannot be implemented without generating vast amounts of political controversy, as witnessed by the wave of strikes and demonstrations in November and December 1995.

The main focus of this article is on the political dimension of this transformation and particularly on the controversy between sections of the labour movement and the government. Politics is, of course, only part of the picture, in so far as other factors such as socio-economic and financial pressures – unemployment, social exclusion, the criteria for the EMU – are arguably affecting the current direction of reform. Nevertheless, the salience of the political debate and the importance of the political dimension justify, in our view, an analysis of the politics of the current transformation in France. Furthermore, it is in these political aspects that France most resembles southern European welfare states. It seems to us that the most instructive comparison can be drawn not so much between current institutional structures, but between the debate and reform dynamics of the different countries.

THE FRENCH MODEL: BETWEEN BISMARCK AND BEVERIDGE

In French literature on social policy, reference is often made to two distinctive models of social protection, usually referred to as the Bismarckian and Beveridgean models (Hirsch 1993; Chatagner 1993; Rosanvallon 1995; Castel 1995). This distinction encompasses a number of aspects of social policy, ranging from entitlements and benefits to financing. More specifically, a Bismarckian welfare state is one which typically grants earnings-related benefits, where entitlement is conditional upon a contribution record and financing is provided by employers' and employees' contributions. Conversely, in France, a Beveridgean system is seen as one in which benefits are directed at the whole population, are typically flat-rate and are financed through taxation. On a more abstract level, the criterion used to discriminate between schemes belonging to one or the other model is the underlying objective of any given scheme. In Beveridgean social policy, the main objective is poverty prevention, while the aim of Bismarckian social policy is income maintenance for employees. In France, this opposition between two models of welfare corresponds to the opposition of two models of 'solidarity' provided by the system: 'occupational solidarity' (*solidarité professionnelle*) versus 'national solidarity' (*solidarité nationale*).[1]

The main component of the French system is social insurance, and hence its allocation to the Bismarckian family of welfare states (Baldwin 1990), otherwise referred to as the 'corporatist conservative' regime (Esping-Andersen 1990) or the occupational welfare state (Ferrera 1993). Yet, in France, there is also a non-contributory component of the system, of Beveridgean inspiration, which caters for those who do not have access to insurance benefits and which, importantly, also provides some family benefits (Merrien 1995). This component was supposed to be residual but the most striking change of the last two decades is that it has grown considerably, creating a trend towards dualization in the system (Palier and Bonoli 1995). These changes invite us to revisit the main features of the French social protection system by considering certain unusual reference points, such as the 'common traits of the southern welfare state' (Ferrera 1996) in order to highlight some too often forgotten aspects of the French system.

The Bismarckian Component: Sécurité Sociale

The social insurance system (*Sécurité sociale*), established in 1945, is often presented as the final stage of an evolutionary process from social assistance to social insurance. Social assistance was seen as residual; the assumption was that through the expansion of social insurance, once the whole population was integrated into the social insurance system, social assistance would eventually become redundant. Social insurance's features correspond to those mentioned above: contributory, earnings-related benefits and financed through contributions. It is geared to employees (*les travailleurs*) and their families.[2] The system is divided into a number of different schemes covering different risks (health care, old age, family allowances) and different occupational groups.[3] As Maurizio Ferrera remarks, there are clear similarities in this respect with southern Europe: 'Italy and Greece probably constitute, together with France, the extreme examples of fragmented and corporatist welfare states – at least as regards income maintenance' (Ferrera 1996).

Indeed, in addition to the main scheme (*régime général*), which caters for employees in industry and trade, there are 122 separate schemes (*régimes spéciaux et particuliers*) covering occupational groups that were already covered by insurance arrangements before the introduction of *Sécurité sociale* in 1945 and declined to join the *régime général*. For instance, separate schemes exist for civil servants and employees of public utilities – electricity, the national railways (SNCF), the Parisian Underground (RATP), etc. Nearly 20 per cent of the population is covered by separate schemes. Moreover, there are also 19 autonomous schemes for self-employed (*travailleurs indépendants*), non-salaried, non-agricultural workers: that is, shopkeepers, employers, artisans, independent professions (*professions libérales*) (nearly 10 per cent of the population) who decide on the importance and the level of financial participation they desire in the social security system. Finally, the agricultural scheme covers people working in the agricultural sector (farmers and farm workers) and their families. Its institutional framework is the *Mutualité sociale agricole* (MSA), supervised by the Ministry of Agriculture.

The *régime général* can be viewed as the most important and complete scheme, as it covers two thirds of the working population, and provides insurance against the main social risks. It accounts for approximately 60 per cent of the benefits delivered by all the compulsory schemes. The other schemes cover only some social risks, with different levels of contributions and benefits. For some benefits (apart from sickness benefit) autonomous and agricultural schemes deliver less generous benefits, but require a lower level of contribution. The *régimes spéciaux et particuliers* (for public sector employees) are significantly more generous in the areas of health care and pensions.

The French social insurance system is supposed to be managed by representatives of employers and employees. Each scheme is divided into different funds (*Caisses*), which are headed by one of the trade unions involved in the management of the system. The initial intention was to set up a system which would be relatively independent of the state. The rationale behind this choice was that the insurance system should be managed by those who paid for it and had an interest in it (Kerschen 1995; Pollet and Renard 1995). Social insurance schemes, however, are subject to governmental supervision. The government is also responsible for setting the benefits and contributions level, which considerably reduces the effectiveness of the social partners' control over the system. What is important, however, is the fact that in France the social insurance system is not seen as a government policy but as a system which belongs to the realm of employment. The social insurance budget is considered separately from the general government budget (the former being higher than the latter). French social protection organizations cannot be characterized as 'an effective and strong state administration' (Ferrera 1996: n.4), since the social security funds (*caisses de Sécurité sociale*) are not part of the state.

The Beveridgean Component: Social Assistance and Family Policy

The second component of the French welfare state is the tax-financed residual system, which includes social assistance programmes,

programmes aimed at 're-insertion' – such as the RMI (*Revenu Minimum d'Insertion*) – benefits in kind and social minima. Policies falling into this category, which are also referred to as policies of 'national solidarity' (*solidarité nationale*), are run by the government and directed at the whole population, although in practice they cover only those who do not have access to the social insurance system.

The family benefits scheme is increasingly considered as part of this second component, though this has not always been the case (Borgetto and Lafore 1996). Family benefits were first introduced purely as a social insurance scheme. Financed through employers' contributions, they used to cover employees only, and were (and still are) managed jointly by representatives of employers and employees. However, the coverage of family benefits has been progressively extended to the whole population, becoming a 'truly universal scheme' in 1978 (Dupeyroux and Prétot 1993: 71). Any family living legally in France with one or more dependent children is entitled to family allowance. The benefits are delivered to households (as opposed to the mother or the father). The universal benefit (*Allocations familiales*) accounts for 47 per cent of total expenditure on family benefits. They are granted, without means-testing, for the second child and all subsequent children. Their amount varies according to the number and the age of the children. In addition, the scheme now grants a number of means-tested benefits, which are not seen as consistent with the principles of social insurance. Finally, as a result of the introduction of the CSG, family benefits are now financed partly through taxation. In relation to the distinction between social insurance and government tax-financed provision (*solidarité nationale*), the family benefits scheme represents a hybrid, blending elements of both systems. Evolution in family benefits can thus be characterized as 'a departure from institutional corporatism' (Ferrera 1996) towards a programme based on universalistic principles, a movement which could be compared with developments in health care in southern countries. The dual character of southern European welfare states, which are characterized by a dichotomy between a Bismarckian pension system and a Beveridgean health care system (Italy, Spain) can be found in France as well, with the difference that, in the latter, family benefits provide the Beveridgean component.

A Dual Welfare System

The balance between the two systems is strongly tilted in favour of social insurance. The French social protection system is thus mainly directed at income maintenance for employees rather than at prevention of poverty. It is important to note that the two systems are seen as two different, non-integrated ways of providing welfare. A powerful justification for this is the fact that while social insurance is in theory managed by the social partners, tax-financed provision is supposed to be the government's responsibility. The perception that the two systems must operate independently is widespread among French policy-makers and experts, and it has a strong normative dimension. Pierre Rosanvallon, while adopting a critical view of it, points out the significance of such a perception in the French debate:

> 'Social insurance should be distinguished from government tax-financed provision': this cry is becoming one of the most widespread platitudes of the end of this century. Everything – from administrative constraints to philosophical uncertainties – is pulling in that direction (1995: 82).

The normative dimension is particularly relevant in relation to financing. The use of funds collected through taxation in order to finance the social insurance system is not seen as legitimate. Conversely, money collected through contributions cannot be used to finance assistance (or *solidarité nationale*) that is, to benefit people who have not contributed to the social insurance system. The distinction between the two systems relates to two different (though partly overlapping) collectivities: the social insurance system is designed to cover employees only, while the tax-financed system functions as a last resort safety net for the whole population.

Beyond the traditional characterization of the French model of welfare as part of the continental corporatist family, the comparison with southern welfare states allows us to underline some French specificities: the strong degree of occupational fragmentation, the dual dimension of the system, the importance and specificity of family policies, the non-state apparatus dimension of social insurance organizations. The parallels between France and southern Europe are perhaps even more striking when it comes to current debates and reforms. Indeed, when analysing the main critiques of the French system articulated in the political debate, notions like 'polarization of the protection offered', 'particularistic welfare' or 'low degree of penetration of the state within the welfare sphere' seem to be characteristic of the arguments presented.

FACING THE CRISES IN THE FRENCH WELFARE STATE

The current crisis of the French social protection system is multidimensional:

- there is a financial dimension: since the 1970s, the balancing of the social insurance budgets has become an increasingly difficult exercise;

- the negative impact of work-related contributions on job-creation has been recognized as a major issue;

- the effectiveness of a system based predominantly on contributory social insurance is being undermined by the emergence of social exclusion;

- there is also a political dimension which reflects the struggle for control of the social insurance system which is currently being fought out between the government and some trade unions.

The Financial Crisis: Balancing Budgets

The deficit of the *régime général* budget was 2.8 per cent of total social expenditure in 1974 and 1975, 4 per cent in 1978, around 2 per cent from 1981 to 1987, between 0.9 per cent to 1.8 per cent from 1988 to 1992, and has been around 5 per cent since 1993. In 1995, the deficit of the social insurance system was 67.3 bn FF (around 2 per cent of total social expenditure, and less than 1 per cent of GDP). The cumulated debt of the various social insurance schemes was estimated at around 250 bn FF by Alain Juppé in summer 1995, an estimate which included the expected deficit for 1996 (Annual Report of the *Commission des Comptes de la Sécurité Sociale*, various years).

Over the years, numerous measures have been taken to deal with this situation. On average, every 18 months since the 1970s, a new *plan de sauvetage de la Sécurité sociale*[4] (programme for rescuing the social insurance system) has been adopted. Typically these plans consist of increases in contributions paid by employees and economizing measures. Measures adopted in this context have included retrenching provision, such as increases in user charges in health care, reductions in the level of reimbursement of medical expenses, reductions in the generosity of pensions (higher contribution record for lower benefits, reform in 1993), in unemployment benefits (creation of the *Allocation unique dégressive* in 1992) and in family benefits (which were frozen for 1996 and therefore declined in real terms). Governments have also adopted other measures aimed at increasing revenues, such as the creation of different taxes (taxes on alcohol and tobacco and the creation of the *Contribution sociale généralisée* (CSG) in 1989 – see below).

The Economic Crisis: Contribution Financing and Employment

Beyond the current deficit crisis facing the French social welfare system, the very structure of financing is problematic. As mentioned above, schemes geared towards employees are financed solely through employers' and employees' contributions, without government subsidies. As a result, contribution financing plays a bigger role in France than in all other EU countries: 80 per cent of social protection is financed through employment-related contributions (Eurostat 1995: 164). This issue is central to the French debate, since the high level of contributions is seen as having an overall negative impact on the country's economic competitiveness and as being responsible for the high rate of unemployment. The argument is that social insurance contributions inhibit job creation, since they have a direct impact on the cost of labour. This claim is supported by international comparisons, which highlight the poor performance of the French economy in terms of job creation. Between 1983 and 1991, total employment increased on average by 0.5 per cent in France, whereas it grew by 1.7 per cent in the EU as a whole, by 1.3 per cent in Japan and by 1.9 per cent in the US (OECD 1994: 5).

The overall cost of labour is not significantly higher in France than it is in other similar countries (Euzéby 1994). However, it is argued that the negative impact of insurance contributions on employment is strongest in the case of low wages. In fact, because of the existence of a ceiling on contributions to the old age pension scheme, the proportion of gross salary paid in contributions is actually higher for low wages than for high ones. For instance, total contributions paid on a minimum wage (SMIC) amount to 48 per cent, while the same figure for a salary three times as high is only 41.6 per cent (Join-Lambert 1994: 334). As a result of this, and because of the existence of a minimum wage, the cost of low-wage labour is artificially inflated.

The minimum wage, currently set at around 6,000 FF per month, is strongly supported by French public opinion (Rosanvallon 1995: 80), and it would be suicidal for any government to try to reduce it substantially.[5] Indeed, it was raised by 4 per cent in 1995. This reflects French scepticism towards the Anglo-American approach to job-creation (Esping-Andersen 1996: 13–15), which, though perhaps more successful in numerical terms, creates other problems such as poverty traps and the 'working-poor' (Albert 1991). As a result, the only viable option left to policy makers in order to deal with the high cost of low-wage labour is to reduce contributions. This view is shared by the majority of French commentators (Join-Lambert 1994: 331; Hirsch 1993: 43; see Euzéby 1994 for the opposite view).

Indeed, some steps in this direction have already been taken, the most notable of which is the creation of an ear-marked tax (CSG).[6] The new tax, although it plays a relatively minor role in the overall financing of social protection (its rate is currently set at 2.4 per cent of all incomes), provides a basis for the future expansion of tax-financing. In addition, since the late 1970s, governments of different political orientations have adopted contribution-exemptions in order to encourage job creation. These measures usually target socially disadvantaged groups, such as the long-term and young unemployed, or small companies, which are considered to be the most affected by the relatively high cost of unskilled labour. The mini-budget presented by the Juppé government in June 1995 includes a number of contribution-exemptions, topped up with government subsidies, in particular for the young and long-term unemployed and for small and medium-sized companies (*Le Monde* 24 June 1995).

It has been argued that this series of measures, aimed either at reducing the impact of contributions or at replacing them (CSG), *de facto* amounts to a partial shift away from contribution financing towards tax-financing (Pellet 1995). Like southern European countries, France is attempting to shift from contributions to taxes. However, as in the southern countries, while a partial shift has taken place, it is still a relatively small part of the overall picture. In fact, while there is strong and widespread support for moving further in the direction of more tax-financing, there is also a substantial amount of resistance to such moves, which, as we shall see below, comes mainly from the trade unions.

The Social Crisis: Protecting the 'Socially Excluded'

The process of shifting financing from contributions to taxation is related also to the second main shortcoming of a predominantly contributory social insurance system: its inability to deal with those who do not have access to the system – the long-term or the young unemployed who have never been involved in the labour market. The size of these groups has grown constantly in recent years, and they represent the most pressing social issue in France. For them, the social insurance system, which is the main provider of social welfare, is of little use. The result is a two-tiered system which exacerbates social divisions and inequality between two groups: employees with full entitlement to generous social insurance protection and those who, with little or no connection to the labour market, rely on minimum income or social assistance programmes (Hantrais 1996).

In France, some sections of the population (especially employees of public firms) are accused of enjoying a privileged or 'hyper-protected' status, comparable to that of southern Europe where such 'peaks of generosity' in income maintenance are denounced (Ferrera 1996). Thus, the discrepancy between the generosity of social insurances and the residuality of *solidarité nationale* appears more pronounced. As the number of people excluded from the generous social insurance system increases, the notion of polarization of the protection offered (used to characterize southern welfare) becomes more relevant to the French situation.

Problems of this nature have developed significantly since the late 1970s, as a result of the economic crisis. In France, such problems were seen as radically new, first because of their scale (number of unemployed people, number of long-term unemployed people, seriousness of the recession); and second, because the economic changes behind the new social problems, such as economic globalization, more flexibility in the labour market and job insecurity, were also unprecedented.

In this context, the inadequacy of a welfare state based on contributory social insurance became increasingly evident. As a result, pressure to develop new policies built up. Since the early 1980s 're-insertion' policies have been introduced. These policies are seen in contrast to the traditional features of social insurance, underlining the inadequacy of the former system. While the social insurance system is geared towards employees, the new policies target the most disadvantaged, or socially 'excluded'. Rather than treating all sorts of situations with the same instruments, social re-insertion policies are geared towards specific groups and are designed according to local needs. That is why re-insertion policies are characterized by a high degree of devolution, namely to local authorities. In addition, unlike the social insurance system which treats social risks separately (old age, sickness, unemployment), re-insertion policies address a whole range of relevant social problems in an integrated manner, so that housing and vocational training are now included in the realm of social policy.

These features are typical of the new policies developed since the mid-1980s aimed at vocational training and at integrating the young or long-term unemployed. In this context, the creation of the RMI (*Revenu Minimum d'Insertion*) is certainly the most significant achievement. As it became evident that the social insurance system did not cover the whole population and that a new safety net was needed, former president Mitterrand, during the presidential campaign of 1988, proposed the creation of a guaranteed minimum income to cover those who '... have nothing, can do nothing, are nothing. It is the pre-condition to their social re-insertion' (1988).

The law establishing the RMI was accepted by a unanimous vote of the French parliament at the end of 1988. Its main feature is the guarantee of a minimum level of resources for each individual, which takes the form of a means-tested differential benefit, and a re-insertion dimension, in the form of a contract between the recipient and 'society'.

People resident in France and over 25 years old are eligible for the RMI (subject to a means-test). The recipient must commit himself or herself to taking part in re-insertion programmes, as stated in the contract, which is signed by the recipient and a social worker. Such programmes can involve job-seeking, vocational training or activities designed to enhance the recipient's social autonomy.

Thus, the RMI must be seen in the context of an ongoing adaptation process of the French welfare state, which follows the recognition of the inadequacy of a system predominantly based on social insurance. The RMI, being tax-financed, belongs to the realm of government provision (as opposed to social insurance) and is an example of the recent orientation of the French welfare state. In view of the current political debate on social protection, as well as the recent reforms, it seems that structural changes are now affecting the very heart of the social insurance system.

From Social Insurance to State Welfare: The Political Dimension

The current political debate on the future of social protection is characterized by the opposition of two different and fairly incompatible conceptions of what the French social protection system should look like. On the one hand, governmental, political and administrative actors support a shift from the original structure, characterized by a dual welfare state where the social insurance system is dissociated from the state tax-financed residual system, towards a system in which the state plays a much larger role. On the other hand, a vociferous section of the labour movement[7] is strongly attached to the original structure of French welfare and is calling for an even stricter distinction between the two systems (mainly the Confédération générale du travail and Force Ouvrière). In their view, the social insurance system should continue to cover employees only, be financed through contributions and be managed by representatives of trade unions and employers. Conversely, the state tax-financed sector should continue to fulfil its function of last resort safety net for those who do not have access to the social insurance system.[8]

Restoring Coherence Between Coverage and Financing

The contrast between the two conceptions is more pronounced in areas such as health care and family benefits than in those relating to pensions and unemployment insurance. The reason behind this difference is that neither family benefits nor health insurance can easily be classified as belonging to one or the other of the two components of the French dual welfare state. While they were initially set up as insurance schemes, catering for employees only, their coverage has been expanded to cover the whole population. According to the government, universal coverage requires that these two schemes be moved from the realm of social insurance to that of state tax-financed provision.

Health care is perhaps the area where conflict between the two conceptions of social policy is strongest. The government seems particularly keen on transforming the current insurance-based scheme into a universal, state-managed and tax-financed one, a transformation which took place in southern countries during the 1980s. There are two main reasons for this:

• the desire to reduce contributions and, as a result, the cost of labour, is high on the government's priority list;

• an expansion of tax-financing in health insurance would justify a more substantial involvement of the government in the management of the health care system, which would make cost containment more feasible. The idea of empowering the state in the management of health care is strongly supported by the government. As an RPR (government party) MP put it:

> In France, the parliament has very little power in the area of social protection, since the social protection budget is not voted in the *Assemblée Nationale* ... We still don't have a parliamentary vote on a ceiling for expenditure. I believe that if we could impose a ceiling, we would then be able to stop the rise in health expenditure (interview, RPR, 26 May 1994).

In contrast, *Force Ouvrière* (FO), the union which headed the Health Insurance Fund till July 1996 takes the view that:

> The health insurance scheme for employees tends to be considered by the government as a universal scheme. As a result, the government imposes on the health insurance scheme the financial and political burden of covering that part of the population which is unemployed, lives in poverty, etc. .... what we would like to see is clarification of the obligations of the state and the obligations of the health insurance scheme (interview, FO, 25 May 1994).

The contrast between the unions and the government is striking. While the latter would like to move from an insurance scheme towards a government run, tax-financed, health care system, the unions have in mind exactly the opposite: going back to the initial conception of pure social insurance for employees, and to transfer financial obligations concerning the non-employed onto the state budget. Such a move, it is argued, would offset the financial imbalance of the health insurance scheme, solving at least the most pressing problem related to health expenditure.

RECLAIMING STATE CONTROL OVER SOCIAL PROTECTION

These differences of approach are clearly linked to a question of power. The current debate on health insurance reflects the general changes occurring in French social policy today. The shift towards more tax-financing is a response to socio-economic pressures, but it is also being used by the government as a justification to reclaim control over the system. The devolution of the management of social insurance to the 'social partners' is now seen as problematic: the government is accusing the 'social partners' of having hijacked the social security funds, of abusing their position within the system at the expense of the general good. Some trade unions are suspected of using welfare institutions in a 'particularistic' manner (Oudin 1992). This debate parallels developments in southern Europe. The fact that the state is trying to reclaim control over a social insurance system which is managed by representatives of employees mirrors a trend which can also be observed, for example, in Italy – the difference being that in the latter case the social insurance system became an instrument of 'clientelistic politics' in the hands of political parties. Both trends, however, can be viewed as an attempt by the state to reclaim control over welfare.

In France, it is generally accepted that if government money, collected through taxation, is to finance a substantial part of the social insurance system, it will become more difficult for the social partners to justify their managerial role. Interestingly, this view is shared by both camps. The unions 'oppose the tendency towards shifting financing from contributions to taxation as it implies the transfer of decision-making power' (interview, FO, 25 May 1994). Conversely, according to a senior civil servant:

> The financing system based on contributions has created a system of discussion among people who *believe* that they are the representatives of employees and employers. Such a system has resulted in much abuse. The CSG [ear-marked tax] can remove the legitimacy, or pseudo-legitimacy, of the trade unions, which have not done much for the welfare state, and will thus allow parliament to examine the social insurance budget (interview, Ministry of Social Affairs, 1994).

Thus, the importance of the debate on financing cannot be fully appreciated without taking into account its implications in terms of the management of the social insurance system. In France, trade unions are weak and divided, with a rate of unionization among the lowest in the OECD. The proportion of unionized employees is not known exactly, but it is estimated variously at between 10 per cent and 15 per cent (Join-Lambert 1994: 110). French trade unions thus have a relatively limited degree of influence on government policy, except in the area of social protection (Jobert 1991). Their managerial role in social insurance is a source of legitimacy in the eyes of public opinion (Rosanvallon 1995: 81). In particular, the unions are often regarded as the 'defenders' of the social protection system, who oppose the government's attempts to retrench provision. In this context, it is easy to understand the strong attachment of the unions to the current system of joint-management by labour and capital organizations. It is their most visible sphere of activity and, social protection being highly valued in French public opinion, involvement in its management is a major source of popular legitimacy. To some extent, the moral status acquired by the unions through their involvement in social insurance mitigates the lack of legitimacy due to the low rate of unionization.

In this context, we may better understand both the content of the Juppé plan, and the reactions of trade unions.

THE JUPPÉ PLAN OF 1995[9]

The tendencies observed in interview data collected in 1994 have been confirmed by subsequent developments. In particular, the 1995 Juppé plan and the reaction of certain trade unions reflect much of the political debate a year earlier. The discussion of the 1995 Juppé plan provides some insights into the likely direction of future developments, since the plan is supposed to provide a framework for welfare reform in coming years. Juppé's intentions were disclosed to parliament in November 1995. The plan was generally regarded as highly ambitious, as it tried to achieve both substantial savings and changes in the social protection system.

In the light of the above discussion, the main measures included in the plan can be divided into three categories, according to their objectives.

- Some elements are aimed at restoring the financial viability of the system. They consist mainly of increases in revenues and in savings on the expenditure side, partly in order to comply with the Maastricht criteria for monetary union.

- The plan aims at the complete transformation of family benefits and health insurance schemes from social insurance to universal tax-financed schemes.

• It contains clear signs of the government's determination to reclaim control over the system by reducing the influence of the unions on management.

With regard to financing, a new tax has been created to pay off the accumulated debt of the social insurance system, estimated at 250 billion FF. This tax, called RDS (*Remboursement de la Dette Sociale*), will be levied on all sorts of income at a rate of 0.5 per cent for the next 13 years. The creation of this new tax reinforces the fiscalization process we have already observed. Revenues have been further boosted by increases from 1.4 per cent up to 3.4 per cent in the rates of health insurance contributions payable by pensioners and unemployed people. A ceiling of 2.1 per cent on the rate of growth in health expenditure has also been imposed, although it is difficult to see how this measure can be implemented in practice. Finally, family benefits have not been upgraded in 1996.

Additional savings and equity improvement were expected to come from a reform of the separate pension schemes (*régimes spéciaux*) that exist for particular occupational groups. The government's intention was to erode some 'peaks of generosity' in harmonizing benefit formulas and entitlement conditions between private sector employees covered by the *régime général* and separate schemes, mainly in the public sector. It was this measure that triggered the massive wave of strikes of November 1995. One week after the announcement of the Juppé plan, strikes occurred in the SNCF and RATP and spread across the public sector. The intensity of the movement, which peaked on 12 December 1995 – when some 2 million people were reported to have taken to the streets in various French cities – forced Juppé to make some concessions. As a result, it was decided to drop pension harmonization from the reform package. While reductions in public sector pension rights were certainly what triggered the reaction of the strikers, it seems clear that some trade union federations (CGT and FO), were deeply concerned with other elements of the package relating to the control of the social insurance system.

This takes us to the second objective of the Juppé plan concerning structural change in the areas of health care and family benefits. The proposals include plans to shift from contribution-based financing to CSG in the area of health insurance. These changes are supposed to make the system more compatible with economic requirements and more equitable, as they extend the financing basis of the scheme from wages to all sorts of revenue. Changes in health care financing are complemented by changes in the coverage of health insurance. The government intends to introduce a universal health insurance scheme, where everyone would receive the same benefits in kind, and where contributions would be harmonized. This project is still being debated, with a first series of measures to be adopted in autumn 1996. With regard to family benefits, the plan intends first to make them taxable, and subsequently to make them means-tested. This would firmly break with the social insurance principle, thereby completing the transformation of a scheme which was initially introduced as a pure insurance-based programme.

These changes can also be interpreted as a means of increasing the state's control over social protection, identified above as the third objective of Juppé's proposals. The plan, in fact, takes these trends even further, proposing a new 'architecture' for the entire system, a new 'chain of responsibilities'. Changes reflecting this new direction were implemented in February 1996 when the French constitution was amended so as to allow Parliament to decide on the general orientations and political objectives of the social security system, particularly with reference to expenditure. Each social insurance fund will be given a spending target fixed by Parliament. On the basis of these spending targets, the government will then negotiate with the different funds a series of 'agreements on objectives and management' (*conventions d'objectifs et de gestion*). In other words, the 'social partners' remain responsible for the management of the social insurance funds, but within a framework which has to be negotiated with the government.

The organization of the management structure of the system is also being transformed. The composition of the governing boards of the insurance funds is being changed. Employers and employees will be represented in equal number (previously employees were the majority). More importantly, there will be four new members appointed by the government, and one or two more representatives of mutual and family associations. The director of each fund, even the regional and local ones, will be appointed by the government. These changes are intended to increase the role of the state within the social insurance system. During the summer of 1996, the presidency of the main health insurance fund changed: FO was replaced by CFDT, a trade union which supports the structural transformation of the French social protection system.

Both actual and planned changes put forward in the Juppé plan seem to confirm that the current transformation of the French welfare state has three dimensions:

- it is a matter of balancing budgets and, in this respect, France is no different from the rest of western Europe;

- structural features of the system are changing: the importance of social insurance principles has decreased in favour of universality and uniformity;

- the state is expanding its control over the social protection system and in delivering welfare.

These tendencies towards universalization, a uniformity of benefits and the empowerment of the state have more in common with developments in southern European welfare states than with their northern continental counterparts. But further comparative studies of the social protection systems of France and southern Europe are needed if we are to ascertain whether the structural changes are related to France's exposure to the warm climate of the south, making her less 'frozen' than other continental countries.

NOTES

1. While 'Solidarité nationale' might appear a rather vague concept, in the French context it has a very precise meaning and refers to all social policies that, in contrast to social insurance, are directed at the whole population, managed by the government, and are tax-financed.
2. As the first article of the law establishing the social security system says: 'Il est institué une organisation de la Sécurité sociale destinée à garantir les travailleurs et leurs familles contre les risques de toute nature susceptibles de réduire leur capacité de gain, à couvrir les charges de maternité et les charges de famille qu'ils supportent' (ordonnance du 4 oct. 1945). For a complete presentation of the French social protection system, see for example Join-Lambert 1994 and Dupeyroux and Prétot 1993.
3. Unemployment benefits are also insurance-based in France, but they are not delivered through the Sécurité sociale system.
4. Plan Durafour (Dec. 1975), plan Barre (Sept. 1976), plan Veil (April 1977 and Dec. 1978), plan Barrot (July 1979), plan Questiaux (Nov. 1981, plan Bérégovoy (Nov. 1982 and March 1983), plan Dufoix (June 1985), plan Séguin (July 1986, Dec. 1986 and May 1987), plan Evin (Sept. 1988 and Dec. 1990), plan Bianco (June 1991), plan Veil (Aug. 1993) and plan Juppé (Nov. 1995).
5. In 1994, the Balladur government attempted to introduce a scheme involving exemptions from the minimum wage, allowing companies to employ first-time young employees at 80 per cent of the minimum wage. The government, however, had to renounce this measure following a massive protest movement led by the trade unions.
6. The CSG (Contribution Sociale Généralisée) is a totally new form of tax in France. Unlike insurance contributions, it is levied on all kind of incomes (not only salaries), including capital revenues and welfare benefits. Unlike income tax, it is proportional, it is ear-marked for non-contributory welfare programmes and it is also levied on low incomes. Despite the use of the term 'contribution', the CSG is treated as a tax, rather than a social insurance contribution (the French equivalent of contribution is 'cotisation').

7. The French labour movement is highly fragmented. There are five main confederations of trade unions with different ideological orientations: CGT (*Confédération Générale du Travail*, Communist orientation); FO (*Force Ouvrière*, Socialist and Trotskyist orientation); CFDT (*Confédération Française Démocratique du Travail*, Socialist orientation): CFTC (*Confédération Française des Travailleurs Chrétiens*, Catholic) and *Confédération Générale des Cadres* (white collar union).

8. The debate on the relative merits of social insurance and state-financed universal provision is not confined to France, though it is certainly more topical there than elsewhere (Bonoli, George and Taylor-Gooby 1996). For instance, in Germany, the trade unions are also calling for the restoration of the insurance principle in social insurance schemes (Clasen 1996).

9. For a more comprehensive presentation of the contents of the Juppé plan, see Bouget 1996 (in English), or *Droit Social* 1996 (in French).

REFERENCES

Albert, M. (1991): *Capitalisme contre capitalisme*, Paris: Seuil.

Baldwin, P. (1990): *The Politics of Social Solidarity: Class Bases of the European Welfare State 1875–1975*, CUP.

Bonoli, G., George, V. and Taylor-Gooby, P. (1996): 'Politics against Convergence: Current Trends in European Social Policy', *Swiss Political Science Review*.

Borgetto, M. and R. Lafore (1996): *Droit de l'aide et de l'action sociales*, Paris: Montchrestien.

Bouget, D. (1996):'The French Social Welfare System and the Juppé Plan', *Working paper series 3*, Center for Welfare State Research, Copenhagen.

Castel, R. (1995): 'Élargir l'assiette', *Projet* 242, pp.9–16.

Chatagner, F. (1993): *La protection sociale*, Paris: Éditions Le Monde.

Clasen, J. (1996): *Social Insurance in Germany*, paper presented at the study day on 'Social Insurance in Europe, Sheffield, 15 July.

Dupeyroux, J. and X. Prétot (1993): *Droit de la sécurité sociale*, Paris, Dalloz.

Droit social (1996): special issues on the *Plan Juppé*, 3 (March) and 9–10 (Sept–Oct.), Paris.

Esping-Andersen, G. (1990): *The Three Worlds of Welfare Capitalism*, Cambridge: Polity.

Esping-Andersen, G. (1996): 'Welfare States without Work: the Impasse of Labour Shedding and Familialism in Continental European Social Policy', in G. Esping-Andersen (ed), *Welfare States in Transition*, London: Sage.

Eurostat (1995): *Basic Statistics of the European Communities 1994*, Brussels.

Euzéby, A. (1994): 'Chères charges sociales', *Le Monde* 1/2/94, p.vii.

Ferrera, M. (1993): *Modelli di solidarietà*, Bologna: Il Mulino.

Ferrera, M. (1996): 'The "Southern Model" of Welfare in Social Europe', *Journal of European Social Policy* 6/1, pp.17–37.

Hantrais, L. (1996): 'France: Squaring the Welfare Triangle', in V. George and P. Taylor-Gooby (eds), *European Welfare Policy – Squaring the Welfare Circle*, London: Macmillan.

Hirsch, M. (1993): *Les enjeux de la protection sociale*, Paris: Montchrestien.

Jobert, B. (1991): 'Democracy and Social Policies: The Example of France', in J. Ambler (ed.) *The French Welfare State*, New York: NYUP, pp.232–58.

Join-Lambert, M.-T. (1994): *Politiques Sociales*, Paris: Dalloz.

Kerschen, N. (1995): 'The Influence of the Beveridge Report on the French Social Security Plan of 1945', in MIRE, *Comparing Social Welfare System in Europe – Volume I – Oxford Conference*, Paris: MIRE.

Leibfried, S. (1992): 'Towards a European Welfare State?', in Z. Ferge and J.E. Kolberg (eds), *Social Policy in a Changing Europe*, Boulder, CO: Westview, pp.245–79.

Merrien, F.-X. (1995): 'The French Welfare-State and its Crisis', paper presented at the conference, *La fin du modèle suèdois?*, Paris, Jan.

Mitterrand, F. (1988): *Lettre à tous les français.*

MIRE (1997): *Comparing Social Welfare Systems in Southern Europe*, Paris.

OECD (1994): *Employment Outlook*, Paris: OECD.

Oudin, J. (1992): 'Rapport d'information sur les aspects financiers de la protection sociale, Rapport d'inorfamtion du Sénat, n°31, annexe au procès verbal dela séance du 28 octobre.

Palier, B. and G. Bonoli (1995): 'Entre Bismarck et Beveridge, "Crises"de la Sécurité sociale et politique(s)', *Revue française de science politique* 45/4.

Pellet, R. (1995): 'Etatisation, fiscalisation et budgetisation de la Sécurité sociale', *Droit social* 3 (March) pp.296–305.

Pollet, G. and D. Renard (1995): 'Genèses et usages de l'idée paritaire dans le système de protection sociale français', *Revue française de science politique* 45/4.

Rosanvallon, P. (1995): *La nouvelle question sociale. Repenser l'État-providence*, Paris: Seuil.

Taylor-Gooby, P. (1996): 'Eurosclerosis in European Welfare States. Regime Theory and the Dynamics of Change', *Policy and Politics* 24/2, pp.109–23.

Dimensions of Social Policy in Greece

DIMITRIOS N. VENIERIS

This article argues that social policy has been implemented in an *ad hoc* fashion in Greece and has rarely been based on the concepts of solidarity and citizenship. Policy formation has always lacked determination and planning, and has instead been dominated by political opportunism and dilettantism. This unbalanced and fragmented approach has focused on social security measures, mostly in favour of particular socio-professional groups, exacerbating inequalities and preventing the construction of even a minimum degree of consensus in favour of structural social policy reform. A re-orientation towards a comprehensive social policy would require political will and public support. Neither currently exist.

Social policy in modern Greece largely reflects the adverse historical legacy of four centuries of disastrous Ottoman rule and the idiosyncrasies of a political system which, as a result, lags behind western Europe in its ability to cope with economic development and social change and build strong representative institutions (Legg 1969). The social context also lags behind in its assimilation of notions such as solidarity and citizenship. The traditional bonds between the state and society – party political affiliations and clientelistic relationships – have tainted social policy developments.

The distribution of cash benefits – mostly pensions – plays a predominant role in the 'Bismarckian' welfare system of this country. Income maintenance is based on occupational status and relies on a fragmented corporatist system. The social security infrastructure incorporates influential occupational contributory schemes and weak social assistance organizations. The coercive institutionalization of 'deserving' and 'undeserving' citizens – mainly defined not upon need or contributions, but upon political criteria – has shaped the evolution of the social security system.

The late Professor Brian Abel-Smith made valuable comments on early drafts of this paper, for which I am indebted.

THE FOUNDATIONS OF UNIVERSAL SOCIAL POLICIES

The first ever compulsory social insurance law was passed in Parliament a few weeks before the Smyrna catastrophe in 1922, which marked the bitter end of the Greek presence in Asia after 2,500 years of expansion and civilization. Embracing many of Bismarck's basic principles, this law inaugurated the Greek social welfare system. However, it was never implemented – mainly due to the socio-political upheaval of this period. On the contrary, a raft of social assistance measures was established in an effort to cope with the resettlement of one and a half million refugees, following the Asia Minor disaster. In 1932, a radical and comprehensive social insurance bill introduced by the Venizelos' government was also not implemented. The new conservative government presented, after a year, another bill introducing insurance coverage for all white and blue collar workers in urban areas, but with critical amendments and structural differences compared with the postponed law: important adjustments, for example, were made in favour of powerful groups – the employers and occupational lobbies (Tsalikis 1967). The bill was passed by parliament after long debates and became law in 1934. Covering more than a third of the working population, this law provided the cornerstone of universal social insurance in Greece.[1] The new Social Insurance Organization (IKA) provided low earnings-related pensions for old-age and disability, and introduced health insurance following a combination of principles derived from Bismarck and Beveridge.

The law of 1934 – enforced in late 1937 due to the prevailing political turbulence – remained the framework for social insurance for almost twenty years, but it failed to resolve the anarchy in the system.[2] The main insurance gaps in the law were the exclusion of the massive agricultural population and the absence of unemployment benefits. Greece developed a social policy in which the priorities were defined not by need, but by socio-political impact. Political objectives contributed to the establishment of privileges on a small, average and large scale. This original legislation was to a considerable extent a balanced framework for the establishment of a uniform social insurance scheme. But, as is the tradition in Greece, it was widely violated from all sides. The IKA was established to function as a social insurance organization but it was gradually forced to operate as a social policy instrument. For example, many insured were entitled – following state intervention – to receive IKA's benefits, and especially pensions, earlier than normal. The 1930s therefore left a legacy of irrational social policy provision.

Greece experienced a tragic period between 1940 and 1949. The bitter civil war that followed the end of the Second World War left the nation once again deeply divided and wounded. Valuable time and resources were lost, the morale of the Greek people collapsed and the country was paralysed.[3] This was the outcome of the abdication of responsibility by the leaders of the country who failed to prevent the conflict and the unorthodox role played by foreign allies. Social policy at this time was by and large reduced to social assistance services – mainly providing curative and preventive medical care and benefits in kind – relying heavily on international aid.

THE 1950s–1960s RECONSTRUCTION

The social insurance legislation of 1951 attempted to correct the deficiencies of the 1934 law. This included a re-orientation, according to recent European developments and influenced by the Beveridge Report, towards a more universal form of coverage. The insurance sectors covered were old-age, disability, death, sickness, maternity and unemployment. A decisive step towards a concept of uniform coverage was made by granting eligibility to several neglected minor categories of working people. The establishment of further insurance funds was – once more – prohibited, since the relevant adjustment of the preceding legislation had, in fact, never been implemented. The creation of supplementary funds, however, was still allowed.

It is interesting to note that the philosophy of the law was to a large extent based on the Beveridge Report's conclusions. Emphasis was given to health insurance – public health was at an unacceptably poor level – and the creation of free, universal state provision along the lines of the British model was discussed. This was a significant step towards a wider social policy – a minimum level of provision and a form of health insurance were introduced – against a background of extreme social polarization. A large segment of the population sharing progressive ideas – the losers of the civil war – were treated as second class citizens, and any debate on the welfare state was absent (Katrougalos 1996). The IKA was to remain the main social policy tool, but state subsidies – although adopted in the law – were not provided for the next thirty years (Venieris 1994).

In 1960, following a serious deterioration in the IKA's financial situation, the conservative government was forced to intervene by restricting contributory conditions. The move towards universalism was taken without any relative financial adjustments. Moreover, the IKA became a contributor to social injustice and insurance inequalities, providing low pensions to the long contributing majority, while – forced by the state – allocating pensions in favour of minor groups of people having worked for a minimum period. But of course, governments were mainly concerned with their extremely short run political ambitions and not with long-run social benefits, reflecting much of the individualistic character of their voters.

The introduction of agricultural social insurance in 1961 marks the establishment of a wider welfare coverage extended to more than half of the Greek population. Until then, such universal social policies were missing – mainly because of the lack of any socio-political consensus. Finally, the Karamanlis government introduced the Agricultural Law which provided for the establishment of the Agricultural Insurance Organization (OGA). Although the detail of the law was widely criticized, its principle was supported by all political parties (Venieris 1994). The new scheme covered every person living from agricultural activities and was eventually financed by the state. It provided old-age and widows' pensions at the age of 65, health care coverage and the insurance of agricultural produce.

The social assistance level of provisions and the lack of actual contributions clearly indicates that the OGA – basically a pension scheme – was more of a social policy tool than a social insurance agency. The scheme failed to alleviate the massive migration problem from rural areas to big cities, especially Athens; internal migration proved to be a short-run solution but a long-run disaster. What was achieved was a scheme financed by the state which could function with very modest benefits and administrative costs. The level of cash benefits was not index-linked but open to political discretion. Those living in the rural areas – still the dispersed majority of the Greek population/electorate – were provided with a uniform social security scheme which to some extent improved their standards of living and alleviated poverty. In terms of social insurance the OGA granted less than adequate protection. It was a typical non-contributory scheme providing flat-rate benefits aiming to secure minimum standards, according to Beveridgean principles. It made minor progress towards solving a major problem.

THE CRISIS OF THE SO-CALLED 'WELFARE STATE'

Governments intervened increasingly in socio-economic developments in the post-war period in Greece. Unfortunately, this intervention lacked continuity, planning and co-ordination and resulted in centralized decision-making driven by short-term political expediency. The large geographical inequalities in the provision of services, the incredible discrepancies of coverage and finance among the insurance funds, the gaps in the provision of services – especially in rural areas – the problems in hospital care, the absence, in fact, of social assistance services, and the lack of co-ordination among all ministries and involved organizations, all pointed to a social policy infrastructure in serious need of reform.

While rising social welfare spending in most northern and central EC countries in the 1950s and 1960s gave way to policies of retrenchment after the mid-1970s – due not just to the oil crisis, but also to the need to contain the costs associated with demographic change and escalating unemployment – spending continued to rise in the lower-spending Mediterranean countries. The outcome is a tendency towards convergence in levels of spending, with the highest levels in the north (the Netherlands, Denmark and France) and rather lower rates in the south (Greece, Portugal and Spain) (Taylor-Gooby 1996). However, the Mediterranean countries retain their particular characteristics, which are explainable by a number of common factors: the historical weakness of the state apparatus; the predominant role of political parties as the main actors for interest articulation and aggregation; ideological polarization and, particularly, the development of a maximalist and divided political Left (Ferrera 1996).

Greece is a case in point. The nature of social policies pursued in Greece in the 1970s and the 1980s exacerbated the existing malfunctions and in some cases enhanced the privileges of the influential groups. The social transformation of the 1970s brought the Greek Socialist Party (PASOK) to power for the first time, which prioritized the establishment of a Greek welfare state – a dream which many had voted for. 1982 is probably the year in which the most impressive welfare cash benefit increases were ever made in Greece. Social insurance expenditure escalated and other social policies – such as that for the care of the elderly (KAPI) – were developed with relative success.

The policies implemented before the mid-1980s upgraded the lowest pensions considerably and extended social insurance coverage in both the rural and urban sectors. These developments were accompanied, however, by unfavourable demographic changes and a legacy which allowed the drawing of benefits below the statutory age, reducing the ratio of employees to pensioners from 2.8:1 in 1979 to 2:1 in 1989 (Petmesidou 1991). Other important steps were also taken. It was only in 1982 that the state agreed to subsidize the IKA. Until then, the scheme was forced to borrow under unfavourable conditions while, scandalously, the state invested the IKA's savings profitably, paying interest far below normal bank rates. In 1983, the socialist government made a considerable step towards a non-contributory universal scheme, by establishing the Greek National Health Service (ESY). However, this was not matched with the necessary increases in public health expenditure or with a stable consensus among all the interested parties. Nor, despite the fact that its creation represented a remarkable social policy landmark, was the Greek NHS able to define priorities or introduce effective planning and financing. Consequently, it failed to fulfil its broad objectives.

The implementation of expansionary social policies soon became a hopeless task. This was due to the structural deficiencies of the social security system, including its chaotic functioning, the lack of effective public management and control, the inefficient and irrational allocation of resources and most of all the dreadful background economic scenario. As expected, the rapid growth of the public sector and of the resources distributed by the state in the early 1980s far exceeded the capacity of the Greek economy. Moreover, although social expenditure as a percentage of GDP increased rapidly from the early 1980s (it was just half of the OECD average in the 1970s), Greece was still far behind the OECD average in terms of public expenditure on pensions, health, education and unemployment.

After 1985, the socialist government was forced to introduce a 'stabilization programme' for the economy. Meanwhile, the 'black economy' was flourishing. The expansionary social policies of the early 1980s – though needed and welcomed – enlarged dangerously the deficits of the social security sector. The IKA was almost bankrupted and the state was compelled to subsidize it after 1982. Fragmented political decisions made with little foresight and spread over many decades, had driven not just the IKA but the whole social policy system to the verge of collapse.

THE 1990s: POLICIES OF RETRENCHMENT

One of the main priorities of the conservative government, elected in April 1990, was the re-organization and financial restructuring of the social security system. At the end of 1990, the social insurance deficits were expected to reach half of the overall public deficit.[4] In July 1990, the leaders of the three major political parties – the conservative, the socialist and the left alliance party – agreed on a minimum consensus in order to attempt to tackle the serious problems of the system. Behind this manoeuvre were the pressures coming from the EC Council of Ministers for a solution, since one of the main prerequisites for the huge EC loan to Greece earlier that year had been the radical reform of the country's embarrassing social insurance system.

The announcement of the new reform proposals provoked an immediate and vociferous reaction from the trade unions. The week commencing 10 September remains one of general socio-political upheaval in the memory of the Greek people. The strike-wave which hit the country created nation-wide chaos. The prime minister was forced to announce his government's intention to re-examine the reconstruction of special funds and to postpone any decision for the second phase of the long-term social insurance reform programme. The governmental U-turn suspended the most painful (and efficient) reforms, in order to pacify the striking work force. The government set out first to meet the major demands of the most sensitive and militant part of the protesting employees, and second to divide them.

The general objectives of the 1990 social insurance bill were to be achieved by intervention in almost all sectors and pension adjustments were made for public servants, introducing stricter contributory conditions and abolishing the most generous provisions. The reform failed to achieve its principal objective for two essential reasons: the short period of preparatory elaboration and analysis, which was not based on thorough studies, and the failure to alleviate the existing large disparities at all levels. A feeling of injustice prevailed among the insured, particularly in the low income classes. As usual, criticisms arose and spread under the veil of political prejudice. Rarely have the press or experts – not to mention politicians – so excelled in politicizing their explanations of the essence of such measures to working people and failing to spell out the necessary radical rectifications needed to rescue the social security system.

Consequently, the minimum consensus and collective spirit vital for social policy reform were lost in a morass of party political infighting and the selfishness of the privileged socio-professional groups. The measures introduced for the IKA – which were reasonable in most instances – should have been followed by a vigorous reform in the other schemes, which had been favoured by adjustments in the past. The mass of IKA's insured members, most of whom – more than 60 per cent – were of the lowest income classes, were made the victims of the 1990 reform. The others simply lost some of their privileges. But of course, social justice and political feasibility are two different things. Moreover, the new policy failed to fulfil even its short-run accounting objectives since the radical measures were withdrawn. The economies achieved never reached expectations and most of them were lost due to the cost of the long strikes.

The 1990 intervention came too late and achieved too little. Soon after, an EC Committee asked for another reform. Aiming to rectify the miscalculations and inefficiencies of the new policy, two further legislative adjustments were launched by the same government in the following two years. The main concern of the 1991 legislation was the restriction on pension conditions and the curtailment of abuses. A second, and more far-reaching, law was introduced in 1992. It retained a collective accounting character but it also endeavoured to find a way gradually to merge the numerous fragmented insurance funds in one unified insurance institution. This intervention was a step in the right direction. Nevertheless, it failed to create an effective new system since the long-term adjustments introduced were designed to pay dividends only after two to three decades. It failed to establish cost containment and control policies. Even so, it set up the national record of insured persons – a measure expected to have numerous positive effects. The long-run policy intention is to provide a positive basis for the harmonization of the social security system and to secure the reliable functioning of the scheme (Venieris 1995).

The policies of retrenchment pursued after 1990 – under, of course, the vast pressure of overwhelming deficits – contributed to the amelioration of the large-scale insurance inequalities. Nonetheless, the hyper-active social security legislation of the 1990s – three laws within three years – sustained almost all the chronic diseases of its predecessors, preventing the establishment of a comprehensive social policy infrastructure. In this context, these policies largely remained fragmented and improvised recipes struggling to correct one another. Characterized by a pure accounting philosophy to cut deficits, and a lack of unified strategy and direction, they provoked further socio-political unrest and a further diminution of social protection.

Within the boundaries of the EU, the southern European welfare states are currently confronted by similar developmental challenges of both an external and internal nature (Ferrera 1996). The external challenges derive from the painful process of European economic and monetary union. The internal ones stem from an economic recession that has produced rising levels of unemployment with serious socio-economic repercussions. The structural crisis of southern European welfare protection appears to be chronic and unmanageable. Policies aimed at a more equitable redistribution of benefits and an organizational and financial restructuring of health care are very difficult to implement. Sadly, rational and radical policies of this kind are not the norm in this area – especially in Greece.

CONCLUSION

The pursuit of politicized and particularistic social policies in Greece produced a fragmented welfare state and encouraged an exacerbation of inequalities in favour of influential groups. Social policy legislation has been mainly focused on fragmented and corporatist social security measures which have absorbed a huge part of social expenditure. Health, income, tax, housing, educational and other social policies have remained rather marginal. This was partly because these areas failed to attract either political attention or public support.

Entitlement to social insurance benefits has not always been dependent upon the fact of the contribution alone. It has also been based on political criteria. Entitlement to social assistance benefits reflected a division between the 'deserving' and 'undeserving' citizens – that is, those who were 'political friends' and those who were not. Once the link between contributions and the accrual of rights disappears, so too does the notion of social insurance. Of course, the social insurance system failed, in addition, to respond to the structural social and economic developments. But most importantly, once the link between need – income level, family size and other circumstances – and the rational allocation of scarce 'means-tested' benefits is severed, the notion of social assistance fades away.

The highly politicized process of decision-making and a poor administrative infrastructure has never produced a planned, comprehensive social policy, defining viable aims and sound priorities. Welfare benefits have almost exclusively been a subject for political bargaining. This failure reflected, in turn, the low impact of societal demands for, and ideas of, solidarity and citizenship. The lack of a social vision and politics has been given the overwhelming share of responsibility for the misinterpretation of social policy . In fact, social policy in Greece is *intended* to be subordinate to 'social politics'. The inherent individualism of the society and the absence of political commitment prevent the formation of even a minimum consensus on priorities in this area. Unfortunately, no effective social policy reform can be achieved without one.

NOTES

1. In 1931 the existing occupational pension funds covered only a low 6.5 per cent of the overall working population.
2. The number of insurance funds – main and subsidiary – increased from 93 in 1934 to 150 in 1940. Additionally, there were overwhelming dissimilarities between IKA and the other privileged funds.
3. According to the Ministry of Social Assistance (1946) 10 per cent of the population was killed during the two wars, and 25 per cent of children were left orphans. The battles forced more than ten per cent of the population to leave their homes and to overcrowd the 'security centres' in urban areas, to be safer.
4. This was 9.3 per cent of GNP. The respective percentage was 6.6 in 1985. According

to OECD statistics, total pension revenues rose from 12.7 per cent of GNP in 1985, to 15.1 per cent in 1989, which is 70 per cent higher than the average of OECD countries – though most of them have a larger percentage of older people.

REFERENCES

Ferrera, M. (1996): 'The "Southern Model" of Welfare in Social Europe', *Journal of European Social Policy* 6/1, pp.17–37.

Katrougalos, G. (1996): 'The South European Welfare Model: The Greek Welfare State, in Search of an Identity', *Journal of European Social Policy* 6/1, pp.39–60.

Legg, K.R. (1969): *Politics in Modern Greece*, California: Stanford UP.

Ministry of Social Assistance (1946): *Destroyed Cities and Villages During the 1940–4 War*, Athens.

Petmesidou, M. (1991): 'Statism, Social Policy and the Middle Classes in Greece', *Journal of European Social Policy* 1/1, pp.31–48.

Taylor-Gooby, P. (1996): 'Paying for Welfare: The View from Europe', *The Political Quarterly* 67/2.

Tsalikis, G. (1967): *The Development of Social Insurance in Greece to 1940*, Ph.D. thesis, University of London.

Venieris, D.N. (1994): *The Development of Social Security in Greece, 1920–1990: Postponed Decisions*, Ph. D. thesis, University of London/LSE.

Venieris, D.N. (1995): 'The Social Insurance System in Greece: An Exploration', *Social Insurance Law Review (EDKA)* (Greek) 10/442 (Oct.).

Biographical Notes

Manuel Aguilar and **Miguel Laparra** are Lecturers in Social Policy and Social Services at the Universidad Pública de Navarra. They have worked on the design and evaluation of several regional minimum income programmes in Spain. Their recent and current research has focused on the socially excluded and labour market integration strategies. They are co-authors of *La caña y el pez* (FOESSA 1995), *El salario social sudado* (Popular 1989) as well as several books on the development of the minimum income programme in the Madrid region.

Giuliano Bonoli is an assistant at the *Institut des Sciences Sociales et Pédagogiques* at the University of Lausanne. He previously worked as a research fellow at the University of Kent. His recent publications include 'Entre Bismarck and Beveridge: crises de la sécurité sociale et politique(s)', *Revue française de sciences politiques* 1995 (with Bruno Palier); and *European Welfare Futures* (Cambridge: Polity 1997) (written jointly with Vic George and Peter Taylor-Gooby).

Carlo Dell'Aringa is Professor of Economics and Director of the Institute Industrial and Labour Economics at the Università Cattolica of Milan. He is a member of the editorial board of the journal *Labour* and a member of the Employment, Labour and Social Affairs Committee of the OECD, Paris. He has recently been appointed President of the Italian National Agency for Collective Bargaining in the Public Sector. His main areas of research include migration, collective bargaining and wage determination, industrial relations and economic performance. His recent publications include 'Collective Bargaining and Relative Earnings in Italy', *European Journal of Political Economy* 10 (1994); 'Wage Dispersion and Unionism: Do Unions Protect Low Pay?', *International Journal of Manpower* 2/3 (1994) (both with C. Lucifora) and 'Industrial Relations and Labour Policies in European Countries', (with M. Samek Lodovici) in J.R. Niland, R.D. Lansbury and C. Verevis, *The Future of Industrial Relations* (London: Sage 1994).

Valeria Fargion is Senior Lecturer at the Faculty of Political Sciences, University of Florence, and teaches Public Policy. She received her Doctorate at the European University Institute of Florence and has worked for several years at the University of Bologna. Her main research interests are in the comparative study of the welfare state with particular reference to social assistance programmes. She is currently working on the pattern of distribution of social expenditure across the Italian regions. Her publications include: 'Stato e Previdenza in Italia', in G. Freddi (ed.), *Scienza dell'Amministrazione e Politiche Pubbliche* (Rome: NIS 1990), 'Aspetti politici e istituzionali del caso italiano', in *FORMEZ'La distribuzione regionale della spesa pubblica* (Naples 1992), and *Geografia della cittadinanza sociale in Italia* (Bologna: Il Mulino forthcoming).

Pierre Guibentif is Professor at the *Instituto Superior de Ciências do Trabalho* (ISCTE – Lisbon) and at the *Universidade Autónoma de Lisboa* (UAL – Lisbon). He holds degrees in law and sociology, as well as a doctorate in law from Geneva University, Switzerland. His main field of teaching and research is sociology of law. A selection of his recent publications includes 'Approaching the Production of Law through Habermas's Concept of Communicative Action', *Philosophy and Social Criticism* 20/4 (1994) pp.45–70; with Marta Tavares de Almeida and João Caupers, 'Efeitos de algumas normas do código do procedimento administrativo – Estudo de caso em avaliação legislativa', *Legislação* (INA-Oeiras) 12 (1995) pp.5–49; *La pratique du droit international et communautaire de la sécurité sociale-Étude de sociologie du droit à l'exemple du Portugal* (doctoral thesis), Geneva/Lisbon, 1995.

Elena Granaglia is researcher in Public Finance at the University of Rome, La Sapienza, Law School, and Professor of Public Finance at the University of Teramo, Law School. Among her recent publications are 'Etica e politiche pubbliche', in G. Capano and M. Giuliani (eds), *Dizionario delle politiche pubbliche* (Firenze: NIS 1996); 'Politiche sociali e dimensioni dell'eguaglianza distributiva', *Qualità ed Equità* 1 (1996) and 'Etica, economia e valutazione delle politiche pubbliche', in S. Maffettone and S. Veca (eds), *Filosofia, Politica, Società* (Roma: Donzelli 1995).

Teresa Jurado Guerrero is a sociologist and graduate of the University of Mannheim, Germany. From 1996 she has been a doctoral student at the European University Institute in Florence. She is writing a doctoral thesis on 'The Institutionalisation of Family Solidarity Patterns and the Development of the Welfare State: Spain, Italy and France in Comparative Perspective'.

Manuela Samek Lodovici is Senior researcher at the Istituto per la Ricerca Sociale of Milan, Professor of Labour Economics at the Università Cattolica in Milano and of Macroeconomics at LIUC, Castellanza. Her main areas of research include the evaluation of labour policies, industrial relations and economic performance and local labour markets. Her recent publications (both with C. Dell'Aringa) include 'Industrial Relations and Economic Performance', in T. Treu (ed.), *Participation in Public Policy Making. The Role of Trade Unions and Employers Associations* (de Gruyter 1993) and 'Industrial Relations and Labour Policies in European Countries', in J.R. Niland, R.D. Lansbury and C. Verevis, *The Future of Industrial Relations* (London: Sage 1994).

Claude Martin (Chargé de recherche at the CNRS, Centre de Recherches Administratives et Politiques, Institut d'Études Politiques, Rennes) is a sociologist and Director of the 'Laboratoire d'analyse des politiques sociales et sanitaires' (LAPSS) in the National School of Public Health and Associate Professor at the University of Montreal. His main areas of research are family and social policies, links between social and family solidarities, caring for the elderly, single-parent and reconstituted families, and comparisons of welfare states in Europe. He is co-editor with F. Lesemann of the journal *Lien social et Politiques*, published in Rennes and Montreal. His recent publications include *L'après-divorce. Lien familial et vulnérabilité* (Rennes: Presses universitaires de Rennes 1996) and 'Father, Mother and the Welfare-State: Family and Social Transfers after Marital Breakdown', *Journal of European Social Policy* 5/1 (1995) pp.43–63.

Manuela Naldini is a political scientist and graduate of the University of Torino, Italy. Since 1995 she has been writing her doctoral dissertation on 'The Evolution of Social Policy and Family Models: the Italian and Spanish Cases in Historical and Comparative Perspective' at the European University Institute in Florence.

Bruno Palier is a temporary lecturer in political science at the University of Paris I (Sorbonne). He also works for the MIRE (*Mission Interministerielle Recherche et Experimentation*), in the French Ministry of Social Affairs. He has published (with Giuliano Bonoli) 'Entre Bismarck and Beveridge: crises de la sécurité sociale et politique(s)', *Revue Française de Sciences Politiques* 1995.

José António Correia Pereirinha is Professor of Macroeconomics and Social Policy, and scientific co-ordinator of the Master Course in

Social Policy at the School of Economics and Business Administration (Technical University of Lisbon) (ISEG–UTL). He is also Researcher at the CISEP – Research Centre on the Portuguese Economy (ISEG–UTL) – in the areas of social policy, inequalities and poverty. He is the author of several publications in the areas of income inequality and poverty analysis. His publications include *Inequalities, Household Income Distribution and Development in Portugal*, PhD, ISS, The Hague, Netherlands 1988, *Social Exclusion in Portugal: Situations, Processes and Policies* (Lisbon: CISEP 1994) and *Spatial Location of Social Exclusion in Portugal* (Lisbon: CISEP 1994).

Martin Rhodes is a Senior Research Fellow in the Robert Schuman Centre at the European University Institute, Florence and co-editor of *South European Society & Politics*. His main areas of research are comparative social and labour market policy in Europe, European social policy making, regional economic development, political corruption and Italian politics. His recent publications include a number of edited volumes, including *A New Social Contract?: Charting the Future of European Welfare* (Macmillan 1997) (with Yves Mény), *Developments in West European Politics* (Macmillan 1997) (with Paul Heywood and Vincent Wright), *Crisis and Transition in Italian Politics* (Frank Cass 1997) (with Martin Bull), *The Regions and the New Europe: Patterns in Core and Periphery Development* (Manchester University Press 1995) and numerous articles on European social policy and welfare states.

Ana Rico is Associate Professor of Economics of Organization in the Carlos III University of Madrid and currently writing a PhD on health care decentralization in Spain, under the supervision of Prof. J.M. Maravall. Her current research interests are in comparative social policy, outcome measurement and the consequences of health care reforms on equity. Her most recent publications include 'Outcome Measurement in Schools', in P. Smith (ed.) *The Measurement of Outcome in the British Public Sector* (London: Taylor and Francis 1996); 'Aspectos redistributivos de la financiación sanitaria regional', in *Igualdad y redistribución de la renta y la riqueza* (Madrid: Editorial Visor y Fundación Argentaria 1996); 'Descentralización y mercados internos en Gran Bretaña: enseñanzas prácticas de las primeras experiencias de implementación de la', in *Mercados internos y reforma sanitaria* (Barcelona: Asociación de Economía de la Salud, 1997); and (with A. Guillén and A. Fonseca) 'Recent Reforms and Trends: Spain', in European Comission (ed.), *Social Protection in Europe* (Luxembourg 1995).

Haris Symeonidou is Head of Research (since 1974) at the National Centre of Social Research of Greece, involved with demographic surveys, research on women and family policy. Recent publications include *Fertility and Employment of Women in the Greater Athens Area* (Athens: The National Centre of Social Research) (in Greek); *Socio-economic Factors Affecting Fertility in Greece, Vol. A, Analysis for the Greater Athens Area* (Athens: the National Centre of Social Research 1992) (in Greek); and *Socio-economic Factors Affecting Fertility in Greece, Vol. B, A Comparative Analysis between Areas* (Athens: The National Centre of Social Research) (in Greek).

Dimitrios N. Venieris studied Business Administration at the University of Piraeus and Social Policy and Planning (MSc) at the London School of Economics. He completed his PhD thesis on social security in Greece – under the supervision of the late Professor Brian Abel-Smith – at the London School of Economics in 1994. Currently, he teaches Social Policy at the Department of Social Administration, Democritus University of Thrace.

Index